SURVIVING ON THE STREETS
How to Go DOWN
Without Going OUT

SURVIVING ON THE STREETS
How to Go DOWN Without Going OUT

by Ace Backwords

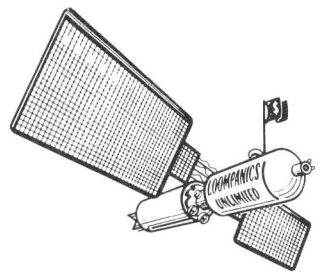

Loompanics Unlimited
Port Townsend, Washington

This book is sold for informational purposes only. Neither the author nor the publisher will be held accountable for the use or misuse of the information contained in this book.

Surviving On The Streets
How to Go DOWN Without Going OUT

© 2001 by Ace Backwords

All rights reserved. No part of this book may be reproduced or stored in any form whatsoever without the prior written consent of the publisher. Reviews may quote brief passages without the written consent of the publisher as long as proper credit is given.

Published by:
Loompanics Unlimited
PO Box 1197
Port Townsend, WA 98368
360-385-2203
fax: 360-385-7785
e-mail: service@loompanics.com

Photographs by Ace Backwords, B.N. Duncan, Elizabeth Thursday, and Larry Wolfley

Interior cartoon strips by Ace Backwords

ISBN 1-55910-201-0
Library of Congress Card Catalog 2001093748

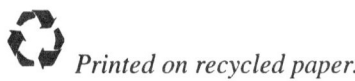
Printed on recycled paper.

Contents

Part One

Introduction 3
Prologue 5
Chapter One
    Problems, Problems, Problems: Things You Will Have to Deal With 7
Chapter Two
    Your Stuff 15
Chapter Three
    Where to Sleep 21
Chapter Four
    Your Homeless Home, Be it Ever So Humble 27
Chapter Five
    How to Deal With the Cold and Rain 37
Chapter Six
    Still Dealing With the Goddam Cold and Rain 39
Chapter Seven
    The Rain as a Metaphor for a Bunch of Philosophical Shit 49
Chapter Eight
    Wild Critters 53

Part Two

Chapter Nine
    Dealing With the Cops (and Being DEALT WITH by the Cops) 61
Chapter Ten
    Street People vs. The Merchants 69
Chapter Eleven
    The Homeless Activist 75
Chapter Twelve
    Food: Eating Low Off The Hog 81
Chapter Thirteen
    Money or... Get a Job You Bum! 93
Chapter Fourteen
    Washing Up 103
Chapter Fifteen
    Stashing Your Stuff and Other Complications 105

Part Three

Chapter Sixteen
The People 109

Chapter Seventeen
Drugs and Alcohol 127

Chapter Eighteen
Violence 139

Chapter Nineteen
Why Homeless? Why Now? 153

Chapter Twenty
Mass Immigration 155

Chapter Twenty One
Counterculture Casualties 161

Part Four

Chapter Twenty Two
Four Street People: Profiles in Weirdness 167

Chapter Twenty Three
Getting Off The Streets 173

Chapter Twenty Four
Psychological Skid Rows 181

Chapter Twenty Five
Surviving on The Streets 187

Epilogue 193

Dedication

Dedicated to all the homeless men and women — and their pets — who have survived a cold, wet winter sleeping outside. And especially to those who are out there right now. And also to all the people who helped them to make it through the night. And to my guru, Swami Muktananda.

Part One

TWISTED IMAGE by Ace Backwords ©1988

Introduction

Homeless. I'm sure many of you have seen the street people huddled around the city streets and wondered to yourself what their lives are really like.

I'm sure to some of you, it's your worst nightmare: to end up on Skid Row, to lose your home, the four walls that buffer you against the outer world. To lose all your treasured possessions. To lose your job, your security. To lose everything that you cling to. To become a loser. A bum. A lost soul in a twilight world with nothing.

To others it might be a cherished fantasy. To quit your job and hit the road like Kerouac. Like a rolling stone with no direction home. No responsibilities. Nothing to tie you down. Total freedom. A permanent vacation on the open road to adventure.

Between these two poles lies the reality of life on the streets.

It's a reality that may surprise you. Because it's a reality you can't begin to understand unless you've experienced it first-hand. In truth, most people thrown out on the streets are totally unprepared for the situations that they will be dealing with. Most of the lessons you learn, you will learn the same way I have, *the hard way*. That said, there's an inherent limitation to any book that professes to teach you how to survive on the streets, and how to survive the countless turbulent and unpredictable pitfalls that await you.

Nonetheless, I envision this book as something I might have benefited from reading back in the summer of 1974, when I was 17 years old and put my thumb out for the first time on that off-ramp at the beginning of Route 80 in New Jersey, and headed out into the big, ol' world, headed towards Godknowswhat.

Prologue

Prologue

    I woke up, wiped the sleep out of my eyes, laid there in my damp sleeping bag for a while, easing myself into another strange day. I had been sleeping in the Berkeley hills in the woods for several years now. In many ways it was a beautiful way to live. But the cold, rainy, winter nights could be rough.

    My sleeping bag was protected from the rain by a long plastic tarp wrapped around me like a burrito. It was a surreal way to wake up, to lie there in my plastic cocoon, and see the morning sun creeping out from behind the dark clouds, the sunlight refracting between several layers of semi-transparent plastic inches above my face.

    I laid inside my plastic burrito for awhile, taking hits from the bottle of day-old, cold coffee in my backpack. When you have nowhere to go and nothing to do, each moment takes on its own resonance. My sides were stiff from where I had slept on a rocky part of the ground. Finally, I had to get up and piss. So I pulled myself from my sleeping bag and carefully unpeeled myself from the layers of plastic, being careful not to spill onto my sleeping bag any of the excess pools of rainwater that had accumulated on the top of my tarp during the night.

    After pissing in the bushes I took out some day-old bread and rice from my backpack and threw it across the creek for my flock of blue jays who were already cawing to be fed. I sat on a dry piece of plastic for a while, and watched the blue jays swooping and squawking and doing their pecking order thing over the food while I finished off my bottle of cold coffee.

Surviving On The Streets

I packed up all my gear into a big plastic bag and stashed it in my secret stash spot in an enclosed hollow within the shrubbery. I brushed some leaves and dirt off my blue ski knit hat, and ran my hands through my matted, scraggly hair and tried to pat it into place as best I could. Then I trudged down the dirt path and out of the woods to the road that led back down into town and into so-called civilization.

I'm sure I was quite a sight. The side of my jacket was caked with mud, my backpack was bursting open at the seams, and one of the soles of my boots was coming off, giving me a *ka-PLONK, ka-PLONK* cadence as I walked down the road.

At the end of the long road a construction crew was busy jack-hammering away on the concrete at deafening volume. One of the workers was standing in the middle of the road wearing an orange city-worker vest and holding up a small STOP sign to divert the traffic. As he looked at me approaching him, I could tell exactly what he was thinking:

"Man, this job might suck, but at least I'm not sleeping in the dirt like THAT poor slob!"

And as I passed him, I thought:

"Man, sleeping in the dirt might suck, but at least I'm not standing in the middle of the street, holding up a stop sign, and listening to jack-hammers all day long like THAT poor slob!"

And it was great. Because we both made each other feel better about facing the day.

Chapter One
Problems, Problems, Problems:
Things You Will Have to Deal With

GUTTER RAT

Chapter One
Problems, Problems, Problems: Things You Will Have to Deal With

Okay. Let's assume, for reasons known only to you (and probably not even *entirely* to you), that you've just ended up homeless. And now, there you stand — with sleeping bag in trembling hand — on the verge, on the very precipice, of entering that mysterious, baffling, and frightening world known as *"the streets."*

Let's take a quick overview, shall we, of some of the problems that you, as a homeless street person, will face. Number one, first and foremost among your problems is:

1. It's Against the Law!!!!!!!!!!!!!!

This is the brutal, unavoidable reality of homelessness. It will dog you everywhere you go. It will color virtually every facet of your street existence. And the sooner you face this sad fact, the better.

Very likely, everywhere you lay down your weary sleeping bag, **somebody** is going to tell you: **"NOT HERE, BUDDY!"** and the entire weight of society will be with them and not with you. That's just the way it is.

You can make all the righteous speeches you want about how **"Sleeping is *not* a crime, man!"** You can wax poetic about those noble American Indians — those *Indigenous People* — who had no concept

Surviving On The Streets

of land ownership, who roamed across this great land sharing the land equally with one and all. Get it all out of your system. Good. Now let's deal with reality.

Just about every square foot of space that you plop your ass down onto is owned by **somebody.** And the public spaces that **aren't** — such as parks and sidewalks — have been set aside specifically **NOT** to be lived on. Okay?

To try and live in these spaces is against the law. It's called "trespassing." This poses a major problem for you, because, of course, you have to live *somewhere*. But, fortunately for you, there's a wide range of legal interpretations and degrees of punishment regarding this "crime" of homelessness, and you'd be well advised to spend a bit of time examining this wide spectrum, rather than looking at it as a black-or-white situation.

You must face the fact that virtually every facet of your existence is either illegal, quasi-illegal, immoral, or highly annoying to somebody. Especially to some poor slob who's spent all day clawing away at some shit job that he hates, to pay for his tiny little bit of personal turf, only to find you and your street pals camped out in front of his doorway, complaining loudly about the raw deal in life you got, while you get stoned and drunk and party all night right outside his window.

Some street people never quite get the hang of this sad fact: **You're breaking the law**. They come up to me with dreary regularity; "Ace, I just got busted for sleeping in public! Fucking pigs!" They end up getting one trespassing ticket after another, at $125 a pop, which can add up quick. Then they actually miss their court date, or they don't pay the fine, and end up with a warrant for their arrest, and they end up getting thrown in jail and getting enmeshed in the whole penal machine, and into an endless series of bureaucratic hassles that can go on for months and even years. It's a horrible, annoying, infuriating loop to get stuck in.

Now I'm a firm believer in standing up for yourself, of not being pushed around, by cops or anybody, of finding out where that line is drawn and pushing it to its limit. In fact, that's one of the main premises of this book. It's, in fact, the only way you're going to carve out any space for yourself on the streets.

What I'm against is waging wars that you're going to lose. As an embattled street person, you're already waging too many battles on too many fronts. You cannot allow yourself to be caught in the webs of endless bullshit, most of which you can very easily avoid if you just use a little common sense.

Now some street people feel they've been pushed and pushed and pushed. Everywhere they go they're told to go somewhere else. Finally they reach the point where they feel they have to take a stand or else they'll be pushed all the way into the Pacific Ocean. They start getting real defiant. Now if you want to prove that you're a heroic martyr and that society is fascist and evil for grinding your face into the dirt, you will have ample opportunities to demonstrate this premise. But all you'll prove is that you're a dunce.

Take it as a given that everywhere you go, the answer will be "no." The trick is to learn to distinguish "no" from **"NO!!!"** This can be a subtle distinction, especially amidst the ever-shifting sands of street life. But be advised not to be ham-fisted about this.

How you distinguish that fine line between "no" and **"NO!!!"** will determine whether you get away with skating through the urban landscape basically doing whatever the fuck you please, or end up being persecuted and hassled by cops, merchants, and residents everywhere you go.

Consider the classic line from the *Baboon Dooley* comic strip; **"Baboon, the world isn't out to get you — it's out to ignore you, if only you'd let it."**

Make this your mantra. I know it isn't as glorious of an attitude as the *rebel/outlaw-who's-an-incredible-threat-to-the-system-man* pose. But in the long run, it will save you endless hassles with The Man. Or, to quote a hoary old platitude from Dylan: "…to live outside the law, you must be honest."

*Chapter One
Problems, Problems, Problems:
Things You Will Have to Deal With*

2. You're Out of Synch With the Rest of Society

Face it: You are the veritable square peg in the round hole. Everyone else is neatly coifed and rushing off to work, or has somewhere to go. You, on the other hand, are staggering around with a grungy backpack as if embarking on an expedition to nowhere (which, in a sense, you are). You are *Tarzan of the Jungle*, suddenly plopped down into the middle of Manhattan; looking for a warm tree to sit next to, or perhaps an alligator to wrestle with for your lunch. You are totally out-of-synch with the world of Versetellers, credit cards, and the day-to-day concerns of virtually every person around you. It's quite possible you don't even have a clue as to NBC's new fall line-up of must-see TV shows. Could anyone be more out of touch than that?

As a homeless person, one moment you could find yourself in the dark woods locked into a brutal struggle for survival with the very Forces of Nature itself, being battered by gale force winds, rainstorms, freezing cold, and critters of the forest (I'm not exaggerating here — it can be a bitch). And the next moment you're sitting in a spotless restaurant under harsh fluorescent lights and central air-conditioning, while an immaculately groomed waitress takes your order of coffee while she looks at you out of the corner of her eye like you're the *Creature From the Black Lagoon*. ("And is it *dangerous?*" she wonders to herself.)

You experience this jarring juxtaposition constantly. Because you are living in two worlds simultaneously. You are like a cowboy in a Western movie who suddenly rides his horse right into the set of a futuristic Sci-Fi movie. The set constantly shifts under your feet as if you're an actor in the wrong movie, which, in a sense, you are. There are very few decent scripts written for *The Homeless Person* in the urban movie that you're forced to play out.

This highlights the serious problem for the average street person, because he usually ends up homeless in the first place precisely because he ALREADY felt alienated from society at large. There's a very real danger that an extended period of homelessness could push you over the edge of alienation and disconnection from society, to the point where you end up inhabiting a twilight-zone netherworld existence from which you never return. You can come to feel that you no longer even BELONG in this world.

3. The Streets are Dangerous!

You are very likely a soft, li'l suburban pup like me, suddenly thrust into the middle of a social setting filled with some of the craziest characters this side of the nuthouse, and some of the most violent characters this side of the Federal Penitentiary. (And where do you think most of the people in the joint or the looney-bin ended up being dumped after they've been released? Why, on the streets, of course.)

Sometimes, you're not even allowed one mistake on this level. If you fuck up — if you trust the wrong person, or just end up at the wrong place at the wrong time (and there are many such places and times on the streets) — it could have disastrous consequences. For you.

One trait that will serve you well, beyond almost all others, is the ability to read people: to keenly appraise human nature. But can this trait be taught? If so, please send me a book that does so. Because so far, I've had to pay for each lesson with chunks of my hide.

What does Joe Average American do to avoid being a victim of violent street crime?

1. He avoids the poor urban neighborhoods where most of the violent crime is taking place.
2. He rarely, if ever, goes out after dark. And
3. He locks himself up inside his apartment and stays there.

Unfortunately, these are three options not afforded the average street person.

1. You will very likely get shunted off to the crummiest of urban neighborhoods.
2. By the very nature of street life, you will probably end up living a fairly nocturnal existence, staying up late into the night. And
3. Needless, to say, there's no way to lock yourself into your sleeping bag at night.

Probably no person is more vulnerable than a person asleep in a sleeping bag on a city street. It's absolutely essential that you learn to find crash spots that are fairly safe. Of all the limiting factors of Urban Camping, this is one of the most severe, even more so than the illegality factor.

As for the violent street crazies out there, personally, I've found the best way to deal with them is to be

1. Fairly large,
2. Male, and
3. Slightly weird-looking. This always worked for me.

If you can't arrange for that, then you might want to start hanging out with a fairly large, slightly weird-looking male to protect you. But the problem is, those are the very types who are most likely to attack you in the first place. So what can you do?

It also helps if you can project a vaguely malevolent vibe. A look that says: **I-may-in-fact-be-crazy-as-you-so-you-might-want-to-think-twice-about-fucking-with-me-pal-P.S.-Fuck-You.** After a couple months on the streets, you will be able to project this vibe easily and naturally.

4. Overexposure to The Elements

Without those four walls as a buffer between you and the world at large, you end up underprotected and overexposed. To *everything*. You get too much sun, too much wind, too much rain, too many bugs, and (most deadly of all) too many people!

After my latest four-year stint of outdoor living, my skin — which was never all that hot to begin with — began taking on a decidedly leathery texture.

Living on the streets is a war of attrition. It's not the major disasters that do you in (though these make for great gossip and comic relief amongst the street denizens). It's all the little things that wear you down, drip by drip. It's a cumulative effect, which makes it hard to gauge. And even harder to protect yourself from. You usually don't notice it while it's happening. You only notice the end result, after the fact, when it's too late to do anything about it.

During the rainy season, you can easily go four months without a single decent, uninterrupted night of sleep. Many of the street people you see staggering around are simply suffering from (no, not drugs, but) chronic sleep deprivation. You get progressively tired-er and tired-er. And then you're *more* tired.

It's absolutely essential that you develop a healthy, on-going relationship with Mother Nature. Ironically, if you do this right, this can turn out to be one of the great and glorious by-products of street living. You can develop a very real relationship with nature, something that many city dwellers, living in artificial man-made environments, never develop. And probably need.

The first section of the morning newspaper that you read is the weather report. Like the business freaks monitoring the *Wall Street Journal*, you begin to painstakingly monitor the shifting patterns of rain, wind and temperature, as well as the changing seasons, and the cycles of the moon and the sun. And that's a good thing. For this is your fortune.

Of course, you don't want to over-romanticize this Back-to-Nature shit, especially when you're lying in a wet sleeping bag filled with natural fungus. At such moments I was often reminded of an episode of the sitcom *Taxi*, where the city slickers are stranded out in the wilderness.

"How would our ancient forefathers have handled this situation?" asked Tony.

"They would have built cities and moved into them," answered Alex.

Being overexposed to other street people can also be a serious problem. Because, let's face it, some of them are flaming assholes. They batter against you like the rain, leaving your soul just a little more damp and soggy from the experience of them.

When I lived in an apartment, I didn't realize how much I dealt with people by *smiling, smiling, smiling;* and then rushing off as soon as possible to lock myself safely inside my apartment. On the streets, it is very difficult to get away from other street people — the scene is just too small and you're constantly bumping into each other. It's a lot like prison life, except instead of worrying about a con sticking a shiv in your back, you have to worry about an asshole ramming his mind-fuck into your soul.

You can only run so long, because you can't get away from them. At some point you have to learn to face them and deal with them. Otherwise, they will continue to invade your space. I've learned from painful experience that it's better to just cut to the chase right from the beginning and call the asshole on his shit and get the ugly scene over with right off the bat, rather than just postpone it, and then end up having the ugly scene anyway.

You are dealing with some fairly dysfunctional personalities. Many of them understand nothing aside from, "Go away." And if that doesn't work, resort to "Go away, **OR I WILL HURT YOU!**" That usually works. But not always, alas. I probably got in more physical fights in one month on the streets, than I did in my previous fifteen years of apartment living. On the other hand, if you *like* fighting, you might find street living an enjoyable experience.

5. Drugs and Alcohol

Drugs are waiting for you on the street scene. They are everywhere. And they are getting more powerful and more deadly every year. If you have any weakness in this regard you could get swept up into all sorts of shit very quickly.

Not only that, but you have all this time on your hands (to "kill") and very few checks on your social behavior. You can easily get locked into a social scene that revolves around nothing but drinking and drug taking. This is inevitably the most volatile scene on the street, and disasters and calamities follow in its wake everywhere it goes.

If that wasn't bad enough, drugs are also *illegal,* which makes you even more vulnerable to cop leverage than you already are. On the streets you can be jacked up at any moment, under almost any pretext. On top of that, unlike apartment dwellers, you're carrying all your shit around with you everywhere you go. There's nothing more disheartening than hearing a cop say, "Empty out what's in your pockets!" while you're frantically trying to remember exactly what's IN your pockets, and wondering if it's anything that could change the course of the next couple of months — or even years! — of your life.

That said, I have a real beef with the sloppy cause-and-effect logic that keeps positing *"drugs-and-alcohol"* as one of the prime reasons people end up homeless. This is a cop-out that lazy minds use to avoid considering the brutal underlying Real Estate shifts of the last 30 years that are the true underlying causes of homelessness (yes, we'll be getting to this in later chapters!).

Drugs and alcohol are prevalent in society at large. If anything, they're only *slightly* more pervasive on the street scene (maybe). The only real difference is, it's more obvious with street people because they're getting fucked up out in the open.

Which isn't to say that drugs aren't a major problem on the street scene. Especially the central nervous system drugs like crack and speed — they'll tear through your body in record time — and especially shooting up drugs. Some people, you actually see them disintegrating right in front of your eyes, and that's sad.

If you're a newcomer on the street scene, and drugs seem like good fun to you, you might want to take a closer look at some of the old-timers, some of the long-time drug users that litter the streets like ghosts. Those that are still *alive*, anyway. And ask yourself if you really want to become one of them.

6. Bad Associations

One of my favorite *New Yorker* cartoons was this one with these two grizzled, old bums sitting on a bench. One bum looking at the other bums and saying: *"It's not WHAT you know, it's WHO you know. Who do I know? YOU!"*

If you're on the streets, you are very likely fucked up on some level. Very few people *choose* to end up on the streets, at least not as their first choice. Most of them end up *driven* there because of some personal problem or some character flaw.

The problem is: As you try and deal with your personal problems, you find yourself surrounded by people who are just as fucked up as you, if not more so. How's THAT for a frightening thought? From these associations you will pick up every manner of bad habit, as if by osmosis. For example, I managed to pick up smoking cigarettes at age 40. Could anything be dumber than that? Everyone around me was smoking and I just sort of fell into it.

In the same way, you subconsciously begin to pick up the value system of the people you're hanging with. Alas, it's largely a value system that perpetuates failure. The people you turn to for advice and counsel will very likely be the same people whose *own* advice and counsel has led them to be sitting in the gutter begging quarters from strangers.

It is very difficult to find people who can help you pull yourself out of the mess that your life on the streets often becomes. You are surrounded by people who are going DOWN, and if you latch onto them you could very well go down with them. You are surrounded by people who are wasting their lives, and they'd be more than happy to waste yours, too.

The-teen-runaway-sitting-at-the-bus-terminal-with-her-suitcase-while-the-big-bad-smiling-pimp-approaches-her-with-his-offers-of-"help" is a stock image ingrained in the public imagination. With good reason, for it is an apt metaphor for the dangerous associations that await the unsuspecting street novice.

Just the other night, I passed this little street waif, this newcomer to the scene, and she was obviously lost and confused and didn't know where to turn. She was crying. And these hardened street chicks were surrounding her, trying to console her. I heard one of them sort of sneer at her, "You think those people you're hanging out with are your *friends*, but they don't *care* about you!" And I could see from the look on the waif's face that she was not so sure that these chicks were really her friends either.

But who else is she going to turn to after midnight? Other street people, that's who. You can make an appointment to see a social worker from 9:45 to 10:15 on a Tuesday morning, but the rest of the time you're on your own, kid.

Whatever weaknesses you start out with, will very likely be exaggerated by the harshness of the pressure-cooker street environment. It is all too easy for your very soul to be twisted like a pretzel into a grotesque thing in this world of gargoyles. Hating society, hating the world, and hating yourself: These can all become seemingly normal, common sense values, when every person you hang out with seems to share them and validate them.

7. Life in General is Hard

The general lot of human life is basically misery, suffering and confusion. And the additional turmoil of street life may be all it takes to finally drive you round the bend.

The Buddha said, *"Life is suffering,"* and the Fat Boy knew what he was talking about. The street person must endure all the other hardships and tragedies that befall the average person (if such a person exists). On top of that, he's on the street, with all the bullshit that entails.

Let's say you fall prey to an illness. Well, at least, you're "sick in bed." The street person is "sick and in the gutter."

Let's say you get rejected in your love life — it can make you feel like a loser, psychologically. Well, when that happens to you on the street, you're not only a psychological loser, but, from your vantage point in the gutter, everything around you confirms that you ARE a loser, period.

In a sense, the street person has been stripped of his last line of psychological defense. For many, the streets take on aspects of a Last Stand. And when they lose that battle, many of them go into a free fall from which they never recover. They start falling apart, and keep falling, until they've fallen right off the face of the Earth.

8. You are Totally Unprepared for This Shit

Until now, you've never had a fabulous book such as this to prepare you for the exacting art and science of street life. I've always felt every high school should offer, at the least, a mandatory four-year course on "How To Pay The Rent — 101." Wouldn't that knowledge have been at least as valuable as, say, Trigonometry?

Most kids get thrown out into the real world without having a clue. I'll tell you another thing; we, as a society, are doing an increasingly poor job of preparing our kids to make the transition from adolescence to adulthood. The ever-increasing population of homeless street kids attests to that fact.

You want to know who the vast majority of these homeless kids are? If I had to make one sweeping generalization, I'd say they're mostly kids from broken homes, or highly unstable homes. They've been shunted from grandmothers, to relatives, to orphanages, to foster homes, to juvenile halls, to prisons, and, finally, to the streets.

Now consider this startling fact of modern life. The average adult child in America doesn't move out of his parent's home until the ripe old age of 26. You know why? Because modern American life has become so complicated, so sophisticated, and so overwhelming. Not to mention so expensive. In the Bay Area, you need close to $2,000 (for first/last/and deposit) just to move into a crummy one-bedroom studio apartment. If you can even FIND one. This is a VERY difficult adjustment for the average young person to make, even one with the financial and emotional support of two loving parents and a stable upbringing.

Now consider the average kid from a foster home. At age 18, he's instantly considered an "adult" and booted out of the home, with no trust fund, no support, no nothing. A lot of these "institutionalized" kids probably don't even have a concept of what an actual home IS, having never experienced one first-hand themselves. And now they've got to figure out how to make one for themselves?? Right.

These are the kids that are ending up on the streets. If that wasn't bad enough in itself, on top of that they're constantly being told that it's their own fault for their plight because they're a bunch of drug-addicted, alcoholic, lazy bums/spoiled brats, etc. Shit, if I was them, I might want a drink myself at that point.

These are just some of the general problems that await you on the street scene. In the coming chapters, we're going to look in detail at all of these, and much, much more. And you are going to learn how to kick ass on every one of these potentially fatal problems. And graduate with honors from the *School of Hard Concrete*, because the point of this book is not only to survive the streets, but also to THRIVE on the streets. Well… Let's just see if we can fucking survive it first…

Chapter Two
Your Stuff

15

Chapter Two
Your Stuff

If you've just lost your home and are headed for the streets, the first question you'll have to ask yourself is: What will I need?

Many people end up hitting the streets with nothing but the shirt on their backs. They often get off on the wrong foot and never quite get their balance.

If you've ever gone on a camping trip for the weekend with a backpack stuffed with provisions, then you can imagine the dilemma one faces: how, after all, does one prepare for a camping trip that could last for the rest of your life?

1. Your Sleeping Bag

The one most indispensable item is a good-quality sleeping bag. On both occasions when I ended up hitting the streets for years at a stretch, I was blessed to start out with a good quality down sleeping bag, gifts from two friends of mine. Both bags ended up being worth their weight in gold. Besides keeping you warm, a good down bag is also lightweight and compact — absolutely essential traits when you realize you might be lugging each pound every step of your way.

I found my own bag to be such an essential piece of property that I did in fact end up carrying it with me, stuffed in my backpack, for the entire first year I was on the streets, as opposed to stashing it somewhere, where there's always the risk of it getting ripped off. One of the advantages of carrying your bag is it makes you highly mobile. You are ever-ready to crash anywhere a sleeping opportunity presents itself to you.

I also got in the habit of stashing back-up sleeping bags here and there, to loan out to friends in need, or to keep for emergencies.

A good down sleeping bag is the one item I would recommend investing money in. (Just about everything else I needed I was easily able to scrounge up or Dumpster dive.) It will save you endless grief in the long run. For a hundred dollars or less you should be able to find something decent.

And yet you'd be surprised how many street people can't be bothered with such a crucial factor. I've known many street people who would think nothing of blowing $100 (or more!) for a weekend of drugging and drinking, but would never consider getting themselves a good bag that could help them for years to come. Strange.

A crappy sleeping bag, on the other hand, can be an albatross around your neck. Not only is it bulky and heavy, but it's usually not that warm, so you have to bulk up even more with extra blankets and sweaters. A big bulky bag is also harder to conceal. To walk around with a visible sleeping bag everywhere you go is to be branded as a *Homeless Person*, which can have ramifications in and of itself (which we'll discuss in later chapters). Plus they take longer to dry when they get wet, and can start to smell of mildew, which gets on all your clothes. It's a mess. Take some time and try to scout up the best bag you can. In the long run, it'll be highly worth it.

If you can't find a good bag, then double-bagging two crappy ones can often do the trick.

2. Matting

Matting to put under your bag when you sleep is also essential. I found a thin plastic matting that worked perfectly. And I usually put a piece of hard plastic under that. Keeping layers between your bag and the ground is important. It you can't scrounge up plastic matting, at the very least make sure you have some cardboard to sleep on, especially if you are sleeping on cold, hard cement. One winter night I made the mistake of sleeping directly on the pavement. After about an hour, it's the equivalent of sleeping on a block of solid ice. Even worse, the cold tends to freeze up and numb the muscles in your back. When you stretch your back in your sleep, you can easily tear one of the muscles. I ended up hobbling around for a month with a painfully fucked up back. And, considering that you're on your feet all day, often lugging a heavy pack on your back, one problem can easily compound another problem and snowball into a major problem. Keep that in mind as I offer up these boring little common sense tips. Life on the streets can get very harsh very quickly. And an ounce of prevention can save you a pound of total misery.

3. A Backpack

This is your one other crucial item, particularly if you plan on being mobile. I generally kept a large green backpack stashed up in the woods at my crash spot, stuffed with clean clothes and miscellaneous supplies. And I kept a smaller backpack with me always, filled with the items that I would need during the course of the day, or valuable items that I didn't want to risk losing.

For a while, I lugged my large backpack around with me. As I said, there can be a certain stigma involved with this. But I felt almost defiant about it. Many street people simply take the attitude: *"Yeah, I'm a street person, you don't like it? Then fuck you!"* which may do wonders for your self-esteem, but it can still end up a limiting factor in various social situations.

You wanna talk "social stigma"? A good friend of mine actually works at the Oakland law firm that sued Denny's restaurant (successfully) for $40 million when they refused to serve some customers because they were Black. I went into a Denny's last year with a backpack and the waitress refused to serve me. She said it was company policy not to serve people with backpacks. It's a clear-cut case of class discrimination, but what are you going to do? It just drives the point home that you, as a visible street person, are in many people's eyes the '90s version of the "nigger."

In "liberal" Austin, Texas, they actually enacted a "camping ban" where the cops could give you a ticket just for walking around with an "oversized backpack" or visible camping equipment.

Another advantage of keeping a backpack full of supplies stashed somewhere is that you are ever-ready to hit the road at a moment's notice. This also highlights an important point: The importance of being ORGANIZED. It's one thing to live in an apartment with a cluttered closet full of crap. On the streets, you carry that cluttered closet with you, every step of the way.

This is also the beauty of life on the streets. The forced simplicity imposes a discipline on you. Because, quite simply, you can no longer afford to be loaded down with material crap. Every time you pick something up, you have to weigh in your mind, pound-for-pound, exactly how much you really need that item. And you find, to your glee, how easily you can live without most of the crap that at one point seemed so essential.

When I first realized I was losing my mind and was headed towards the streets, I realized how much stuff I had managed to accumulate in fourteen years of apartment dwelling, anal-retentive pack-rat that I am. But now I was chained to it. I needed to flee, but all my stuff was like an anchor around my neck that was weighing me down. At that point, I began going through my boxes of stuff and separating the junk from the true value. It began a process of paring down my bloated, materialistic life to its true essentials, a process I'm still going through to this day.

4. Toiletries

I kept my soap, toothbrush, razors, and various other useful items such as a needle and thread, extra pens, can opener, scissors, etc., in a Chanel No. 5 perfume bag that I found somewhere. That Chanel bag was absolutely perfect for the job, aside from my having to field jokes about being a fag. It zipped up tight and was coated with waterproof plastic. I also took some ribbing for having a pink, compact mirror.

5. Clothes

Most street people go for the layered look. I developed this routine where, as the day heated up, I would progressively peel off layers of clothes. Then, as the evening gradually chilled down, I would begin putting more and more layers back on. A pair of leg warmers really helps for insulation under your pants. A scarf can be a good addition, too, and it takes up little space. Hooded sweatshirts are also recommended as a versatile piece of clothing. And I always liked to keep a thick, bulky jacket stashed somewhere for emergency cold weather, or for sleeping in during the peak of winter. Keep in mind you are LIVING outdoors. Your clothing is how you adjust the thermostat.

Hats are also essential. A baseball cap in the summer is mandatory, to protect your face from the sun. Remember, you are out in the sun constantly. My first summer on the streets, I didn't quite realize that, and ended up with a blistering red, sunburned face. Ski knit hats are also necessary for keeping warm in the winter, as your big fat head is where you will lose most of your body heat. Also, considering that toupees and expensive hair-weaves are beyond the budget of the average street person, hats are ideal for covering up those annoying receding hairlines.

Clean socks are another prized commodity on the streets, and I always tried to keep a couple fresh pairs handy. Socks and underwear were the only items I would actually buy.

6. Shoes

A decent pair of shoes is ABSOLUTELY ESSENTIAL, especially in the winter. If you've got a hole in your shoe and your socks get wet, you are very likely going to be walking around in cold, wet socks for the next few days. You might have all the other warm gear you need, but with wet socks you are going to be cold and shivering and miserable and very possibly sick. Bad shoes will be your Achilles heel. *For want of a good pair of shoes, many a street war was lost.* Keep in mind, you are not a normal person; you will very likely be living with your boots on, sometimes up to 24-hours-a-day (I have a friend who sleeps in his — he's afraid someone will steal 'em if he takes 'em off). No point in dying with them on, too, at least not just yet. Get good ones.

A friend of mine in Humboldt County — a very wet county — was sitting on a park bench airing out his bare feet. It had rained non-stop for two weeks, and this was his first chance to take off his shoes. I noticed his feet were covered with painful fungus from walking around for weeks in wet socks. He was the kind of guy who would spare-change endless amounts of money to get beer (to kill the pain of his fucked up feet, among other things), but he could never muster the initiative to hustle up decent footwear.

It's a common problem, this skewed sense of priorities, because let's face it; street people are the procrastinators of all time. For a couple of months, I was wearing this pair of sneakers I had found that were about a half-size too small. I figured they would stretch into shape, or maybe I was just too busy doing nothing all day to find a decent pair. But after a couple of months of constant walking — which was my thing — along with lugging around my heavy backpack everywhere, my feet were seriously fucked. (My heart goes out to all you women cramming your feet into tiny shoes.) The arches of my feet remained painfully sore for six months afterwards, and for a while I feared that I had permanently fucked up my feet.

Even more tragic was my doomed friend from the streets of San Francisco, Fearless Frank. One morning we were sitting in this gospel soup kitchen on Folsom Street getting our daily dose of hell-fire and damnation, plus coffee and stale doughnuts, and I noticed oozing, pus-filled sores all over his ankles. He was wearing ill-fitting hard black dress shoes with no socks, and with each step he took, the hard edges of the shoes cut directly into his bare ankles. Bugs were crawling in and out of the festering mess. It was horrifying to my 19-year-old mind. Even more horrifying, Fearless Frank, simply just did not give a shit.

7. Bags

Plastic garbage bags are incredibly helpful in a hundred different ways, especially during the rainy season. Here's a tip for you: Janitors in large buildings often keep extra garbage bags stashed in the bottom of the garbage can, underneath the bag that's already in the can (that way they have replacements handy every time they change the bag). You can take a couple per can and nobody'll notice. I went through hundreds of these over the course of the El Niño winter.

Different kinds of bags come in handy for all sorts of things on the street. Remember: Organizing and re-organizing your stuff is a constant chore.

(People would sometimes say, **"Get a job you bum!"** But what they never realized is: Surviving on the streets is often a full-time job in itself.)

I became obsessed with collecting different kinds of bags — backpacks, duffel bags, army bags, travel bags, tote bags, shoulder bags, you name it. It got to the point where I had this large bag filled with nothing but other bags! And then I found a bigger bag to put all of that into.

8. Miscellaneous Stuff

The only other items I regularly kept with me were bottles for coffee, a journal, and (for meditation purposes) incense, spiritual books and a photo of my guru. I always like to keep a supply of plastic bags of various sizes handy, for various ground-scored items. And the Priority Mailing envelopes that you can pick up for free at the post office are excellent for storing various things, as they are durable and waterproof.

There are many items that you might think you'll need, but by trial and error you'll discover how unnecessary they are. A flashlight, for instance. They're heavy to lug around and the batteries are always going dead, for one thing. And for another, I figured, if I really needed a flashlight to find my way to my campsite, then I was probably going too deep into the woods for my own good, anyway. Plus, a flashlight that illuminates your way also illuminates exactly where YOU are, something you never exactly want to broadcast when you're illegally camping.

Only once in my street life did I carry a weapon among my stuff, a razor-sharp knife that I mostly used to sharpen my pencils. It ended up being used against me, pressed up against my own throat.

Some street people get their stuff down to the absolute bare minimum. One guy I know carries nothing but the shirt on his back and a toothbrush in his pocket (and, occasionally, a syringe in the other pocket). When his clothes get dirty he just throws them in the trash and gets a new set from the free box.

Other street people load themselves down like pack mules, with shopping carts crammed full of stuff. This one grizzled old Black guy on Shattuck Avenue was famous for that. He'd load one shopping cart to the brim with stuff, then strap another shopping cart to the back of that one. And when that shopping cart got filled, he'd strap another one to that. And so on. Until he was pulling around this huge caravan of five or six fully loaded shopping carts, all brightly decorated with huge colorful collages of paintings and pictures cut out of magazines and flotsam and jetsam of modern life that he would find in his travels. Eventually, the load would get so big that the carts would tip over and he wouldn't be able to move them. So he'd just abandon the whole mess right there, and start all over with a new shopping cart.

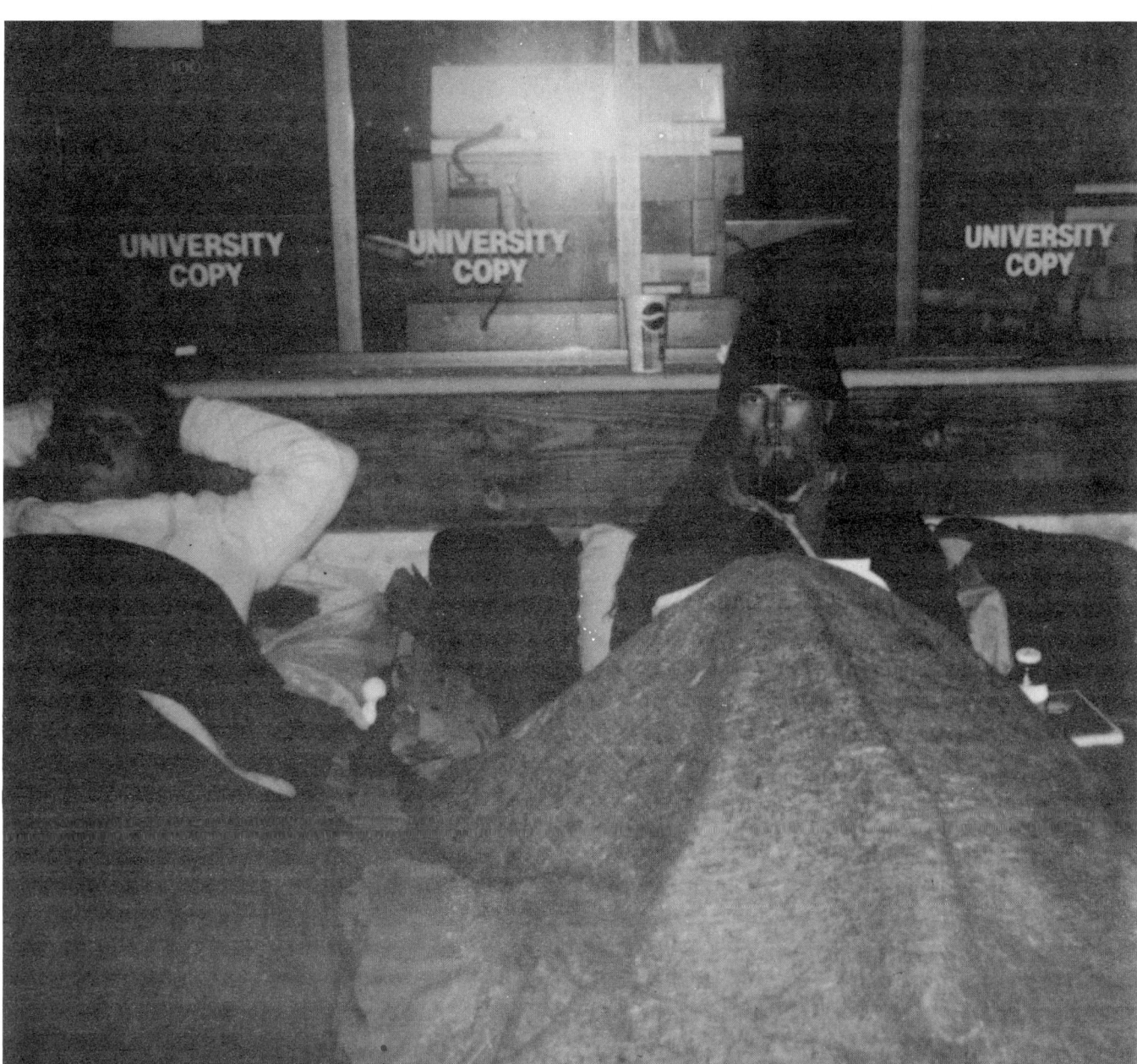

Chapter Three
Where to Sleep

It's easy to find a place to crash at night. It's dark and there aren't many people around. This trick is to find a place you can wake up to in the morning.

There are many sleeping options available to the average homeless street person, most of them bad. Let's examine a few of them:

1. Doorways/Alleyways

This is the first and most obvious choice for many urban campers. Many dispirited street people can't seem to organize themselves much beyond staggering two or three blocks from their panhandling spot on the sidewalk to the nearest available doorway. They sleep there until they inevitably get rousted by the cops. Then they stagger to the nearest free meal joint. Then stagger back to their panhandling spot. And then back to their doorway home. And that's life as they know it.

Doorways offer one distinct advantage — they're out of the wind and rain. And I generally had a few choice doorways scouted out for emergencies such as torrential downpours.

The downside is you can quickly start racking up trespassing tickets at $125 a pop. In a supreme irony, a friend of mine got a sleeping-in-public ticket for camping out in a doorway of the local Homeless

Chaplaincy. When he complained to the "dynamic" director of the Chaplaincy, she explained that there was nothing she could do about it, of course, but that she felt endless compassion for his plight.

Another disadvantage of doorways is you're vulnerable to anybody coming up and fucking with you at any moment. And you literally have your back against the wall.

2. Highway Off-ramps

These are one of my favorite crash choices. Off-ramps illustrate a key point for what you look for in a crash spot, something I call "tweener" spaces. Tweener space is a little pocket of unused space that exists in between the spaces that people are using. An off-ramp exists as one of these nebulous pockets of space, existing in between where people are coming from and where people are going to.

You'd be surprised how many of these little free-zones exist, even amidst the most congested urban settings. The sharper you become at recognizing and claiming these spaces as your own, the more breathing space you will carve out for yourself. I may not have a deed to these properties, but in my mind I've put my flag on them and claimed them in the name of the Republic of Backwords.

The key of course, is to find space that nobody else wants. Nobody is going to plan a picnic with the kids on the ole off-ramp. Nobody is going to build a store on the ole off-ramp. Very few people are going to even be walking through the maze of freeways to get to them. Once you've darted under the shrubbery you might as well be in your own personal Fortress of Solitude.

3. Downtown Parks

I'm talking here about those little one or two block plots in the center of town. These are a very poor choice. Probably 90% of the indignant letters-to-the-editor crying, "We've got to do something about those damn bums ruining our city!!!" stem from these park dwellers. To the average tax-paying citizen living amidst urban concrete, these downtown parks, these little oases of manicured grass and trees, are the crown jewels of his environment. To see it being despoiled by drunken bums is almost too much for his blood pressure. It's particularly alarming for Average Urban Mother taking her little tots to the swing-set only to see some grizzled old troll pop his head out of the bushes. It just brings back too many bad Jethro Tull acid-flashbacks of Aqualung eyeing little girls with bad intent. Avoid these parks.

4. Parks on the Outskirts of Town

On the other hand, these parts are great, my first choice always. On the downside, I have to walk a half hour every night to get to my campsite in the Berkeley hills. But this is also the upside, for it weeds out all the lazy fuck ups who can't make the effort.

As a general rule, if cops see you walking *away* from the center of town, they will rarely stop you. Because they know if they turn you around, you'll just go back downtown, which is the last place they want you. That's where the cop is getting all the heat from the merchants and residents.

You'd be surprised at the splendor of these spots. I regularly wake up to what I fondly call "million-dollar views." Despite urban sprawl, we've still managed to maintain pockets of actual quasi-wilderness, a mere stone's throw from the most overdeveloped city streets. My neck of the woods has packs of deer, skunk, foxes, and raccoons (watch out for those surly bastards, they can fuck you up), and even an occasional mountain lion. The downside is, you have to know what you're doing camping in the middle of nowhere. Mother Nature is playful, but she can play rough. To give an example, one night I camped in the high grass on top of a hill. As I was walking into town I felt an itching sensation in my sides. As I scratched myself I realized, to my horror, that it was a blood-sucking deer-tick just beginning to burrow its head into my very guts. Yes! A harrowing encounter with a blood-sucking tick! I heroically pulled the thing off me and squashed him with my very own foot. Man triumphs over nature. Life on the streets is a saga after all. But you are reminded how easily and unpredictably you can get seriously fucked up. I know people who are still dealing with the after-effects of their tick encounters 20 years later.

5. Squatting

I don't like squatting, but it's more a personal preference than a criticism of squatting. I know many people who have squatted comfortably and even luxuriously, for years and years. Some abandoned buildings even come with running water and electricity.

Squatting is a prime choice of many of the artist and bohemian elites of the streets. Due to their fairly straight appearance, they can blend into the nice neighborhoods and the prime squats. Conspicuous bands of mohawked gutter punks, on the other hand, often get shunted off to the crummiest neighborhoods and the most trashed-out buildings.

The key to squatting, even more so than with most other urban campsites, is invisibility. It just takes one loudmouth asshole to ruin the whole gig. And on the streets, alas, there are no shortages of this type. A great squat was recently ruined when a local crackhead began using it as his personal launching pad. But what can you do? Give the guy an eviction notice? And if you try to beat his ass, the resulting noise and clamor will likely just bring the heat on you anyway.

One ingenious squatter friend of mine got rid of an unwanted intruder by posing as the owner of the building, and scaring him off. He even put his own lock on the door.

On the downside, there can be a claustrophobic feeling from being trapped inside a boarded-up building. Also, too, the walking-on-eggshells feeling from sneaking in and out can wear you down psychologically.

Some street people squat in buildings that are in use. Having scammed a key from somewhere, they crash on rooftops or basement laundry rooms. These situations are even more tenuous and day-to-day.

6. Motor Vehicles

Many street people live in their vans, buses, or cars. They often don't consider themselves homeless; "My car *is* my home!" The advantage is, they're mobile and they have a place to store their stuff. The downside is the perennial problem of parking tickets. Generally you look for "in-between neighborhoods" to park in. The *nice* neighborhoods will have the cops run your ratty jalopy out in a minute. The shitty neighborhoods will steal everything but the frame of your car.

The ideal is to rent out a driveway from a friend where you have access to a bathroom, and sometimes even electricity and running water.

The city of Berkeley tried an experiment a few years back to set up a legal parking lot where car dwellers could live. Unfortunately, the fledging community was plagued with problems, not the least of which was two teenage DeadHeads getting bullets in their heads and their bodies dumped in the Bay. As a general rule, avoid camping in groups of street people. Many of them may be even as fucked up as you.

7. Homeless Shelters

I've never slept in a shelter, primarily because I'm not an "institutionalized" type of person who is comfortable in that setting. On the positive side, shelters offer a warm bed, a shower, and often a hot meal. Plus, you get a modicum of stability in the otherwise unstable street life. For women, in particular, shelters can offer safety from the violence of street life.

On the downside, what man really wants to be a ward of the state, dependent on others for his shelter? Another problem is, most shelters have fairly rigid schedules — some of them you have to show up at five in the evening in order to be admitted — and this can be a problem, what with the free-form nature of life on the streets.

Another problem is you're surrounded by a room full of fellow street people — not always a joyous experience. My friend Blue — a somewhat refined, college-bred, suburban pup — spent a year sleeping in the Berkeley shelter, often the only White boy surrounded by a room full of Blacks, most of whom had just been released from the joint. After enduring verbal abuse, punches, and kicks, he finally just jumped up on top of his bed one night and shouted: "IF ANY OF YOU NIGGERS WANT A PIECE OF THIS WHITE BOY, HERE I AM!" A whole bunch of them took him up on his generous offer, jumped on top of him and pounded the crap out of him. But after that, they left him alone. "For some reason, they respected me after that," explained Blue. They don't exactly teach you how to properly deal with situations like this at the University of New Hampshire.

8. Couch-Surfing

If you happen to be a Beautiful Loser who's a "perfect lodger, a perfect guest," this may be the gig for you. But the rest of us tend to handle this delicate living arrangement with less than aplomb. Be forewarned; couch-surfing has a way of incubating and pressurizing resentments that can permanently ruin friendships.

I've seen this one from both sides. As an apartment dweller I've had different street people start storing stuff in my living room — first just a box here, then another box there, and before I knew it, my living room was a storage locker. And then, when I became homeless, I ended up doing the same thing to some of my apartment dwelling friends.

If at all possible, try to avoid the old "Is-it-okay-if-I-come-up-and-use-your-shower" routine. As much as possible, try and carve out a street existence that isn't dependent on the kindness of strangers. Self-sufficiency is the key. It's the battle you are fighting daily, and largely losing. Couch-surfing, at best, is nothing but a temporary and tenuous holding pattern.

9. Day-Sleeping

Many street people stay up all night and then sleep in the grass or on the sidewalk during the day. The advantage is, it's safer sleeping during daylight, and it's warmer. Plus, if you're hanging with a group of street people, you'll blend in with the crowd and not get ticketed by the cops. Most street people are so inactive; it's hard to tell if they're awake or asleep.

In many ways, the nocturnal life of many street people can be seen as a public service that we perform to help alleviate the crowdedness of city life. We've volunteered to go on the night shift and sit out the daytime action. It's also another way to claim unwanted space, for at night, entire blocks, entire neighborhoods — particularly the warehouse districts and financial districts — can become the private personal playground of the street crew.

10. Cracks

Street people are like water pouring into the cracks in the city structure. And many of them are absolutely ingenious at finding these little nooks and crannies, and carving out their personal space. This one friend of mine spent a year sleeping in this little nook right in the lobby of this big movie theatre complex downtown. She used to panhandle outside the theatre. When it rained she got into the habit of holing up in this little hallway in the lobby that led to a dead end. She was out of the way and didn't bother anybody so the security guy let her hang out in there. Eventually, they let her sleep there overnight, locking her into the lobby when they closed up at night. So, for a year, she practically lived there. She had a safe, warm, and dry spot all to herself, right in the heart of the city. She spotted the space, and claimed it for her own.

Now that I've given you a general overview of some of your sleeping options, let's take a more in-depth look at some of the specific spots I chose over the years, and why I chose them.

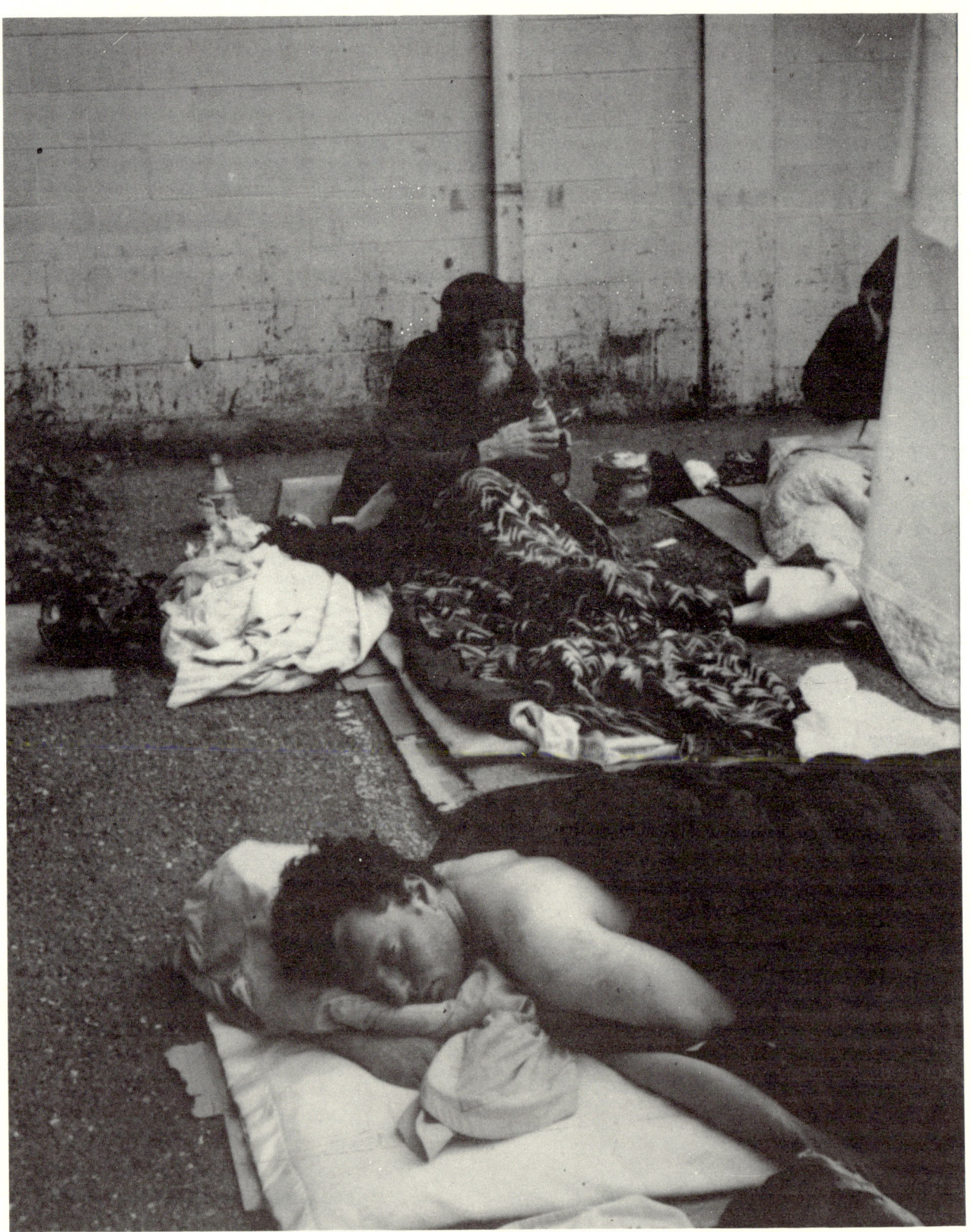

*Chapter Four
Your Homeless Home,
Be it Ever So Humble*

Chapter Four
Your Homeless Home,
Be it Ever So Humble

Man, like most creatures, has an inherent need for a stable, secure nest, and Homeless Man is no exception. In fact, it's the lack thereof that most drives Homeless Man nuts.

Most homeless people have great difficulty finding and maintaining a stable, long-term sleeping spot. Instead, they end up getting rousted and run off of one spot after another with dreary regularity. This is no way to live. At the least, it does a major number on one's already shaky self-esteem.

Finding a "home" when you're homeless *is* difficult. But it *can* be done. I've done two different extended periods of homelessness, and in both cases I managed to carve out a stable homeless home that I lived at for years at a stretch with relatively few hassles. So you might want to listen closely to what I'm saying here, because I know what I'm talking about (as opposed to some of the other chapters where I'll be talking out of my hat).

The Streets of San Francisco
(No, not the banal TV show but my dismal youth)

I first hit the streets at the age of 19 in San Francisco in 1976. Jimmy Carter was just about to be elected, it was the Bicentennial summer, and San Francisco was still inhabited mostly by white people.

Surviving On The Streets

The term "homeless" hadn't even been invented yet (we were just "bums" back then). It seems like another world, as I look back on it from this vantage point of 2001, and indeed it was.

My first attempts to find a homeless home illustrate some of the common — and sometimes fatal — mistakes that the novice street person makes.

The first place I went to was the Haight-Ashbury, looking for remnants of the fabled Summer of Love, and finding mostly boarded-up buildings and burned-out acid casualties. I camped in the Golden Gate Park at the foot of Haight Street. (The lead singer of the Dirty Rotten Imbeciles actually camped there for many months in a tree fort he built, before the band started raking in the royalties.) But it was crawling with crazies, so I pushed deeper into the Park, sleeping at the other end near the Pacific. One morning, I woke up to find two cops standing over me — not the best way to wake up. One of them was nudging me with his boot.

"Oh, this one's still alive," said the cop casually. "We find dead bodies around here all the time."

I'm not sure if he was telling the truth, or if he was just trying to scare me off of that spot, but I took the hint and went looking for another spot. (A few months later, I did in fact, read in the paper about a decapitated body of a street person found near where I had been sleeping. They never found the head.)

Many street people spend their entire homeless tour playing and replaying the dismal scenario of getting rousted by the cops from one spot after another. It's a terrible loop to get stuck in. You begin to feel like you're being pushed off the face of the earth. A lot of the problem stems from simply failing to identify a suitable, long-term crash spot in the first place.

The Golden Gate Park had several factors working against it:

1. ***It's too public.*** It's a public treasure that will inevitably generate citizen complaints, and then cop heat, when they see it being despoiled by the tramp sites.

2. ***It attracts too many other homeless.*** By all means, if you can, avoid running with the pack. Where two or three homeless are gathered together, police sweeps are never far behind.

Next, I moved downtown and camped in the bushes of the off-ramp on 5th and Bryant Street. This was the warehouse district, so it was fairly deserted at night. The problem was, it was right off the sidewalk, and I was vulnerable to anyone sneaking up on me while I was sleeping, as I was to find out.

One night, I was fast asleep in my sleeping bag, when I suddenly woke up and literally jumped out of my sleeping bag as if pulled by some subconscious defense-mechanism (you learn very quickly to sleep with one eye open). This guy with one leg was coming at me fast. He was almost right on top of me when I jumped up. He stopped on a dime. Swiveled around on his crutches, and sped off in the opposite direction, swinging wildly back and forth on his crutches. He screamed over his shoulder:

"NOW I KNOW WHERE YOU SLEEP!! I'M GONNA GET YOU!! NOW I KNOW WHERE YOU SLEEP!!"

I stood there in the night air, as his voice gradually faded off into the distance, wondering if this had all really happened or if I had just dreamed it all.

There's a surreal quality to much of street life. It's similar to life in prison, or in a war zone: Long stretches of boredom, punctuated by unexpected moments of absolute bizarreness. You suddenly have these weird scenes jammed into your brain, which you have no precedent for dealing with, and only the slightest clue as to how you're supposed to react to them. Mostly, you just push these bad scenes into the back of your mind — undigested and unresolved — and stagger onwards, to the next bad scene.

*Chapter Four
Your Homeless Home,
Be it Ever So Humble*

A month later, my doomed friend Fearless Frank, had an even unhappier encounter with the one-legged man. One morning, Frank showed up at the gospel Soup Kitchen with a horribly battered face; two black eyes, huge purple splotches, and crusty scabs. He explained:

"You know that guy with the one leg that's always cursing and screaming? The one that got his leg blown off in Vietnam and now he's mad at the whole world? Well, last night he took it out on me. He snuck up on me while I was sleeping at the off-ramp on Fremont Street underneath the Big Phillips 76 clock. His arms are strong as hell from lugging himself around on those crutches all day. He pinned me down in my sleeping bag and raped me. And then he beat the hell out of me with his crutches."

This story illustrates a fatal flaw in a potential crash spot: *You cannot have someone sneaking up on you while you're sleeping.* There are simply too many assholes lurking around in this world of ours.

I finally struck gold with my third spot. I ended up living there for over a year, and, in every sense of the word, it was my home. It was a beautiful spot on top of this man-made hill at the foot of the Bay Bridge overlooking the entire East Bay.

First and foremost: **It was difficult to get to.** First you had to walk up the wrong way on the off-ramp. And then you had to walk across a narrow, heavily weeded path with the beams of the Bridge on one side, and a 50-foot steep incline on the other side.

1. *It wasn't accessible.* It wasn't a place where a passerby would be wandering around at night in the dark. And if by chance they did, you would hear them coming, thrashing around in the darkness, long before they got to your campsite.

2. *It was only accessible from one direction.* You do not want anyone sneaking up on your back. Also, equally important, being familiar with the terrain, I knew several escape routes where I could flee down the hill, if need be. You want only one entrance to your campsite, but you also want several potential exits, because you don't want to be trapped with your back to the wall.

So the safety factor — always a prime consideration — was there.

The next crucial question you have to ask is: **Who will care that you're there?**
In this case, no one.

1. *Merchants/residents heat:* This is a "tweener" spot, nestled in between the end of the warehouse district and the beginning of the financial district. So it was practically deserted after working hours and on the weekends, which was when I mostly inhabited the spot.

2. *Cop heat:* The cops might not like it if, by chance, they happened to see you walking up the off-ramp while they come speeding down the ramp. But you'd be long gone into the bushes by the time they wended their way back through the freeway maze, if by chance they really wanted to stop you, which they don't. The cops — contrary to the belief of many street people with big-time persecution complexes — can generally tell when you're keeping out of people's way. And they're usually (but not always) more than happy to let you go. But again: It's up to **you** to learn to recognize these cop-free zones.

The next factor was dealing with the elements. This was during the Drought Years. But the few times that it did rain, I just jumped over the fence and slept under the Bay Bridge.

The other problem was the fierce wind that whipped off the Bay. But I dealt with this by putting up some boards along the exposed side of the mattress that I slept on.

On top of that, this spot was absolutely beautiful, on top of a cliff overlooking a spectacular urban vista. I can still remember those lonely nights of my youth, lying on top of that hill, staring out at the stars, and the panoramic view of San Francisco Bay (cue up Otis Redding song for soundtrack), as the chilly, gray fluorescent water swirled in the wind, and the city lights of Oakland and Berkeley twinkled off in the distance, as I tried to figure out what this crazy life was all about, and what it had in store for me. I'm still trying to figure it out.

Keep in mind, too, I managed to carve out this isolated, peaceful little spot in the midst of the most congested, urban setting. Not 40 feet above me, literally millions of people rushed by me on the Bay Bridge, commuting on their way to and from The City, totally oblivious of my homeless presence below them.

The spot was so hidden away, that only once, in the year that I camped there, did someone stumble into my turf at night. I heard him coming from a distance, so I stood there and waited in the inky darkness until he was about five feet from me and I said, "Hey, what's up?" Scared the poor guy half to death. He jumped in the air, letting out an involuntary yelp of surprise and fear, and fled off in the opposite direction at amazing speed.

The spot was so secure, I even set up a little campfire with a grill for cooking hamburgers and heating coffee. I no longer recommend this for city campers. Fire will inevitably bring heat on you.

Overall, the spot proved to be a real home, in every sense of the word. It offered me a safe haven from the storms that raged on the streets, and the storms that raged in my head.

At one point, I decided to get off the streets and rent out a room in the Tenderloin. After three days of enjoying this "home" indoors, I nearly had my head sliced off by four Black muggers lurking in the hallway. I realized I was actually much safer sleeping outside than locked up in some of these inner-city death traps, which raises an ironic question about what actual constitutes a "home" and what it really means to be "homeless?"

The Berkeley Hill-Billies (No, not the dull sitcom, but my exciting middle-aged years)

My second prolonged stint of homelessness began in 1995 at age 38, and continued for most of the late '90s. After a bit of bumming around, I finally settled on a beautiful spot up in the Berkeley hills, fairly deep into the deserted woods. Gurgling creek. Wild flowers. Flocks of swooping blue jays cawing and singing to the sun. Families of deer frolicking up the hill. An occasional blood-sucking tick. It was a veritable Heaven on Earth. It was my home, in every sense of the word, for several years.

Can you imagine sleeping in the deep, dark woods like an animal for years at a stretch? It's a trip.

It was about a 30-minute walk from downtown, which is good, because it takes you away from the homeless masses, who usually center around the nearest free-food joint and fans out from there.

In terms of human predators, like my first spot, it was a fairly difficult trail to follow at night without a flashlight or without making enough noise to awaken me. And I rigged the trail with a few strategically placed potholes and branches to make sure an intruder would make even more noise. You don't need to booby-trap the trail leading up to your spot so that a noose slips around the intruder's ankle and catapults him across the horizon. But you might want to take a few precautions.

Chapter Four
Your Homeless Home, Be it Ever So Humble

The first thing I did when I moved into this spot was clean up all the litter and trash. There are several reasons for this. First of all: you, as a street person, are going to be blamed for any mess in the area anyway, so you might as well clean it up.

I remember one gutter punk complaining bitterly to me:

"I was just sitting on the sidewalk panhandling, minding my own business, and I was sitting next to these orange peels *that somebody else had left behind,* and this **fucking pig** comes up and gives me a ticket for littering. It's so unfair, man. *What can you do about something like that?"*

Well, you could pick up the fucking orange peels, idiot. It's not like you're doing anything else with your time.

Secondly, the litter will give you a good idea of the history and the habits of the place. It doesn't hurt to play at being an archeologist sifting through the ruins, or a detective searching for clues at the scene of the crime.

On the one hand, if there's a lot of litter around, that's a bad sign because that means that a lot of people come trampling through this spot. On the other hand, it's a good sign that it's outside the jurisdiction of city workers or maintenance people, who would just run you out of there eventually.

At this spot, there wasn't that much litter (which was a good sign) and what there was, was old newspapers from several years ago, and ancient, rusted beer cans and bottles (which was an even better sign because that indicated that not many people had been through there recently). There were also a few *old* hypodermic needles (*fresh* needles are always the sign of a bad scene in the making).

There were also a couple of trashed-out, abandoned campsites. I waited a couple of weeks to make sure the previous occupants weren't returning and then cleaned them out. It's a weird feeling to be sifting through the remnants and the ghosts of Street People Past. You can't help wondering what happened to the previous occupants. What had caused them to be pushed to the very outskirts of human society? To be sleeping in the bushes like animals? Had they regrouped in this spot? Or had they fallen completely off the edge? And you realize you are the latest in a long chain of social outcasts, just as somebody would replace me after I left this spot.

Also, you might consider the energy or the vibe that the previous occupant left behind. I know you hardheaded realists scoff at superstitions such as haunted (and blessed) spots. But consider this: In the apartment building where I lived for many years, a man had committed suicide in the room right across the hall from mine. His body laid on the floor for several weeks before it was discovered, leaving a permanent stain on the floor. The next guy who moved in there also died in that room a year after moving in. He had a heart attack and his body was found several weeks later, lying on the floor in almost the exact same spot where the first guy died. I kid you not.

The third reason for picking up litter is purely psychological. One thing that plagues many street people is a sense of alienation — a lack of connection with the world around them. As I began picking up litter in my spot, and the surrounding area, I began to claim the spot as my own on a psychological level. I was the one taking care of the grounds, after all. So I began to think of it as mine.

Pretty soon, I began carrying a garbage bag with me and cleaning up all the trash along the way of my 30-minute walk to and from downtown. I began taking great pride in the pristine condition of my world.

Try it. Don't do it out of a sense of trying to be a do-gooder, because nobody is going to applaud you. Do it for the simple reason that it very well might make you feel good.

Also too, most street people don't pay taxes or make great contributions to society, while many of them sponge off the social services that society provides. Any way that you can even out this balance of give and take will benefit YOU more than society. Picking up litter is one way that anybody can make a contribution.

Surviving On The Streets

Remember, too: Nothing will get you run off of your campsite faster than if you start leaving big messes behind. It's tough enough just to *find* a good, stable crash spot in the first place, but it's pointless if you don't learn how to maintain it.

Turf Wars

In terms of human predators — we'll get to critters later — this spot was pretty secure. First of all, it was hard to even find the trail that started off the main road because the entrance was largely obscured by a fallen tree blocking the path. Secondly, the trail didn't lead to anything except increasingly rugged, hilly terrain (*one entrance*). Thirdly, it was a very spooky trail at night. I camped at a worse — more visible — spot across the street for many months precisely because it was such a spooky trail to walk into in the blackness of night. And the gnarled, old trees gave a haunted feel to the place. The feeling, on entering at night, was akin to climbing into a long, dark cave. *"Come into the enchanted forest, my pretties! Ah-HA-HA-HA!!"*

You might laugh, but you'd be surprised at how many big, strong street people end up huddled in a skuzzy doorway downtown precisely because they're squeamish about strange things that go bump in the night, and not entirely without reason. They'd rather sleep downtown on a cold sidewalk under neon lights in the very midst of some of the most evil and dangerous human predators that walk on this earth, than risk sleeping in the dirt "with creepy-crawlers!! UGGHHH!!"

Once I saw this crew of big, tough East Oakland-type gangbangers strutting cockily through the woods. One of them almost shit his pants in terror when he was suddenly startled by a squirrel rustling in the bushes under his feet.

At any rate, this was the kind of trail that hardly anyone would be stumbling into at night.

Actually, my biggest concern wasn't someone sneaking up on *me*, but that I would sneak up on somebody who had inadvertently crashed out for the night in my spot. Keep in mind, in the inky darkness of the woods you can't see more than a few inches in front of your face until your eyes being to adjust to the darkness. You don't want to accidentally step on somebody's head. It doesn't pay to startle weird street people from a dead sleep in the pitch darkness of the deserted woods. So every night I would cautiously creep up to my sleeping spot by the creek, hoping nobody was already there.

However, twice there was somebody there.

The first time, I happened to come across a young hippie couple who were fucking in their sleeping bags right on "my" spot. Now I put "my" in quotation marks, because this spot really isn't "mine." Like all animals, there's a tendency to get territorial about your turf, but the fact is, I don't pay rent on this spot, after all. In the eyes of society, NONE of us have a right to be sleeping there. So the hippie couple might very well feel they have as much of a non-right to sleep there as I do, and first-come-first-served, etc. You have to remind yourself of this dynamic constantly, because, after a year of camping at a spot, you begin to think that it's "yours," whether it is or not.

At the same time, there IS a certain street decorum — there are certain overall turf rules — in regards to people's crash spots. But don't kid yourself if you think there's some kind of overall *CODE OF THE STREETS*. There's little general consensus to street life. Whatever rulebook there is, the "rules" vary widely from person to person, and from situation to situation. In most cases, the only rule is: WHATEVER YOU CAN GET AWAY WITH.

*Chapter Four
Your Homeless Home,
Be it Ever So Humble*

For example, you'll hear some street people decrying and condemning "snitches." And then, in the very next breath, you'll hear them screaming: *"You touch me and you're going to jail, bitch!"* and go running off looking for a cop.

Now in the incident of the hippie couple, I would have quietly relinquished my spot for the night and then come back in the morning to reclaim my spot (lest they had any plans of moving in permanently), except for one niggling detail: My sleeping bag and my gear were stashed in the bushes directly on the other side of the humping bodies, and I needed that bag.

I called out softly, "Uh, excuse me, I hate to interrupt, but this is my usual crash spot."

"Oh, we're sorry," they replied, mid-thrust. "We'll move."

"That's okay, you can stay here tonight. I just need to get my sleeping bag from those bushes."

"We'll be out in the morning," they said.

And the situation resolved itself happily. Proper street protocol was demonstrated by both parties, and a potentially sticky situation worked itself out easily.

The second incident did not work out quite so happily. Same basic beginning: I got to my crash spot around midnight to find somebody already sleeping there.

"Uh, this is my crash spot," I said.

"Oh."

"That's okay. You can stay here, **tonight**." I emphasized the word "tonight" hoping he would get the point.

The next morning I come back to reclaim my turf. He's gone, but I immediately notice he's left his stuff stashed in the bushes. Not a good sign. Shortly thereafter, he comes back lugging several more bags of stuff.

"Do you know any good places to crash around here?" he asked.

"No," I said coldly. "There are some good spots right up the road." HINT. HINT.

But the big lummox doesn't take the hint. He hops across the creek and lumbers up the hill, and I hear him setting up his campsite about 20 yards from mine. Even worse, to get to his newly chosen campsite he has to tramp in and out of *my* campsite. This is totally unacceptable. This is a major breech of street protocol (at least according to MY rules). You quite simply cannot have some total stranger stomping through your campsite in the middle of the night with his big fat boots only inches away from where your soft, melon-like head is sleeping. Oh no.

What's really going on here, beneath the surface of our casual exchange, is: This guy is trying to bully me out of the prime spot that I have claimed as my own.

In other words: **THIS MEANS WAR!!!!**

Now, in a situation like this, you cannot go running to the cops to back you up, or file a complaint with the local rent board, or even write an indignant letter to your Congressman. The only thing you can rely on is whatever personal power you can muster. This actually can be one of the beneficial aspects of street life, because similar to prison life, it strips you down to the basic core of your being. When you are alone, facing off against some big asshole, in the deep, dark woods, it can take on a primal aspect akin to the caveman days.

In truth, it's probably not all that different from the brutal power game that Real Estate sharks play out in their nice, clean three-piece suits while they tear each other new assholes with their stylized, bloodless financial power plays. Which reminds of another myth: *The street person as noble loser.* The fact is, the

Surviving On The Streets

average street person is just as much a greed-head as the Wall Street millionaire. The only difference is, we just don't happen to be as GOOD at it.

What makes these street people turf wars even more confusing is that there are no clearly defined borders between my space and your space. Technically, NEITHER of us has any space of our own. The only space you can claim as your own is that which you can carve out by the dint of your will and your ingenuity. It's a fundamental issue, because, on the streets, *all* you have is your personal space. And you have no four walls to protect it, only the walls you can construct with the force of your mind.

It's like sitting on the end of an empty bus bench minding your own business, and somebody comes along and, instead of giving you some breathing room, sits down right next to you, practically right on top of you. They may not be touching you, but they've violated your personal space nonetheless. They can say: "This is a public space; I can sit here if I like!" And that's true. As far as I know, there are not yet laws against being an asshole. But assholes have to be dealt with nonetheless.

As space becomes increasingly limited by our ever-expanding population, these turf fights are going to intensify, especially on the streets, where we've already been squeezed almost completely out.

I've seen fights break out over:

"HEY MAN, THAT'S **MY** GARBAGE CAN!"

"WHADDAYA MEAN **YOUR** GARBAGE CAN? I DON'T SEE YOUR **NAME** ON THAT GARBAGE CAN."

"THAT'S **MY** PANHANDLING SPOT RIGHT HERE BY THAT GARBAGE CAN."

"OH **YEAH**?! SAYS **WHO**?!"

It might strike you as the ultimate absurdity that a man would be willing to fight to the death over the right to sit by a garbage can. But keep in mind, that spot by the garbage can might be all the poor guy has in the world.

Even worse, I've seen many fights start up over people just LOOKING at each other:

"WHY ARE YOU **STARING** AT ME, MAN?"

"I'M NOT STARING AT **YOU**. YOU'RE STARING AT **ME**!"

"OH **YEAH**?!"

"**YEAH**!!"

Nowadays, people don't even have the spare space to park their eyeballs. Get your eyes out of my space, man.

The message always is: You're getting too close to me, man. And out of such squabbles, world wars erupt. This syndrome is even more tragic in our congested prisons, where every move you make bumps up against somebody else's movements.

So anyway, the next night, in the middle of the night, I'm awakened from a dead sleep by the sounds of this guy pounding nails into a tree at his campsite. **GRRRRR!** This lummox has invaded my Paradise, my Eden. Keep in mind, every sound in the deserted, quiet woods, travels for miles as if it's rattling around right inside your skull.

Around 4 a.m. I'm awakened again by the sound of his hacking and coughing. **THAT'S IT!** I decided to force the issue. I started throwing big logs and rocks in the general direction of his campsite. Then I took out my guitar and started screeching out the loudest, most abrasive chords I could muster. Anybody who's heard my guitar playing, even on a good day, knows that I can make one helluva noxious racket. You don't want to hear me when I'm TRYING to sound bad.

This penetrates his dim cranium. He comes staggering down the hill. I'm sitting there in the lotus position with my incense and my altar to my Guru, practicing a little voodoo on his psyche.

"Do you know what time it is?" he asks casually.

Chapter Four
Your Homeless Home,
Be it Ever So Humble

"I HAVE **NO IDEA!**" I said harshly.

He walks by me, down the trail. I hear him slipping in the mud on a few branches I had placed strategically on the trail, and then he's gone.

I climbed up the hill and investigated his campsite. His backpack was hanging from a rope that he had nailed between two trees. He had already stashed quite a bit of stuff up there; there was a ratty mattress, cans of food, and garbage strewn everywhere. On top of being an asshole, he was a slob, which means sure doom to your campsite. Remember always: **Invisibility is next to godliness when it comes to maintaining a long-term campsite. It's called "no-trace camping."**

It's bad enough that these fellows shit in their own nest. The problem is when they start shitting all over yours. But, as with most street situations, you must learn to handle these situation with finesse and delicacy. Because you are already standing on shaky ground. Any kind of violent scene or major commotion will likely only ruin the campsite for both of you. And remember, too, the guy now knows where you sleep, and where you stash all your stuff. You can run him off now, but he can always come back later, when you least expect it. Many of these street losers are like tar babies, *any* contact with them only covers you with their tar and you lose. You must handle the situation delicately. But, alas, most of us on the streets are crude and indelicate.

The next morning I built a huge wall of branches and logs across the path leading up to my campsite. An unmistakable message: **KEEP OUT!**

Later that evening, when I came back to my spot, I noticed he'd torn a path through my barricade. And, to add insult to injury, he broke several of the sticks in half and rammed them into the ground right where I sleep. His answer: **FUCK YOU, TOO!**

It was shocking how quickly the situation was escalating and deteriorating. I figured there was only one way to handle this.

So the next night, while he was sleeping, I snuck up to his campsite, bashed his head in with a big rock, and buried his body in a shallow grave on the other side of the hill. And, since he was a transient street person, probably nobody will even notice he's missing for years to come.

No, of course not. Actually, the story had a rather anti-climatic ending. The rainy season began — El Niño. It started raining that night, and didn't stop for 20 days, and that was the last I ever saw of him. But he did leave a huge mess of garbage behind for me to remember him by.

How would I have handled the situation if nature hadn't taken its course? It's hard to say. Each street situation is unique. Like I said, there is no rule book — you just have to react to each moment as appropriately and as spontaneously as you can. You must be firm, and you must draw certain lines in the sand, otherwise you'll just get run out of one spot after another. But you must be flexible, too.

Usually — but not always — you can bluff people off with the THREAT of violence. Most people are cowards, really. But keep in mind: Some people LIKE violence. To them, your bluff is an invitation to dance. You don't want to waste your time with pointless, macho posturing that escalates into violent confrontations, simply because violence rarely works in the long run on the streets.

It's inevitable that you will run into some dysfunctional assholes on the streets who are nothing but walking time bombs. There's nothing macho or impressive about being around them when they explode. Sometimes, the only reasonable course of action is to just get away from them as quickly as possible, though, inevitably, you will find yourself in borderline situations where you must decide whether it is worth it to run or to take a stand.

In truth, most of the dysfunctional street assholes are more like walking *stink* bombs. You don't lose a limb; you just get covered with their stench.

Generally, if a person is an asshole, the best course of action is to just get away from them. The problem was: it often turned out that *I* was the asshole. And I learned, from painful experience, that, as much as I tried, I simply could not get away from myself. And at that point, I finally began to learn something.

Chapter Five
How to Deal With the Cold and Rain

Chapter Five
How to Deal With
the Cold and Rain

Move to some place warm and dry.

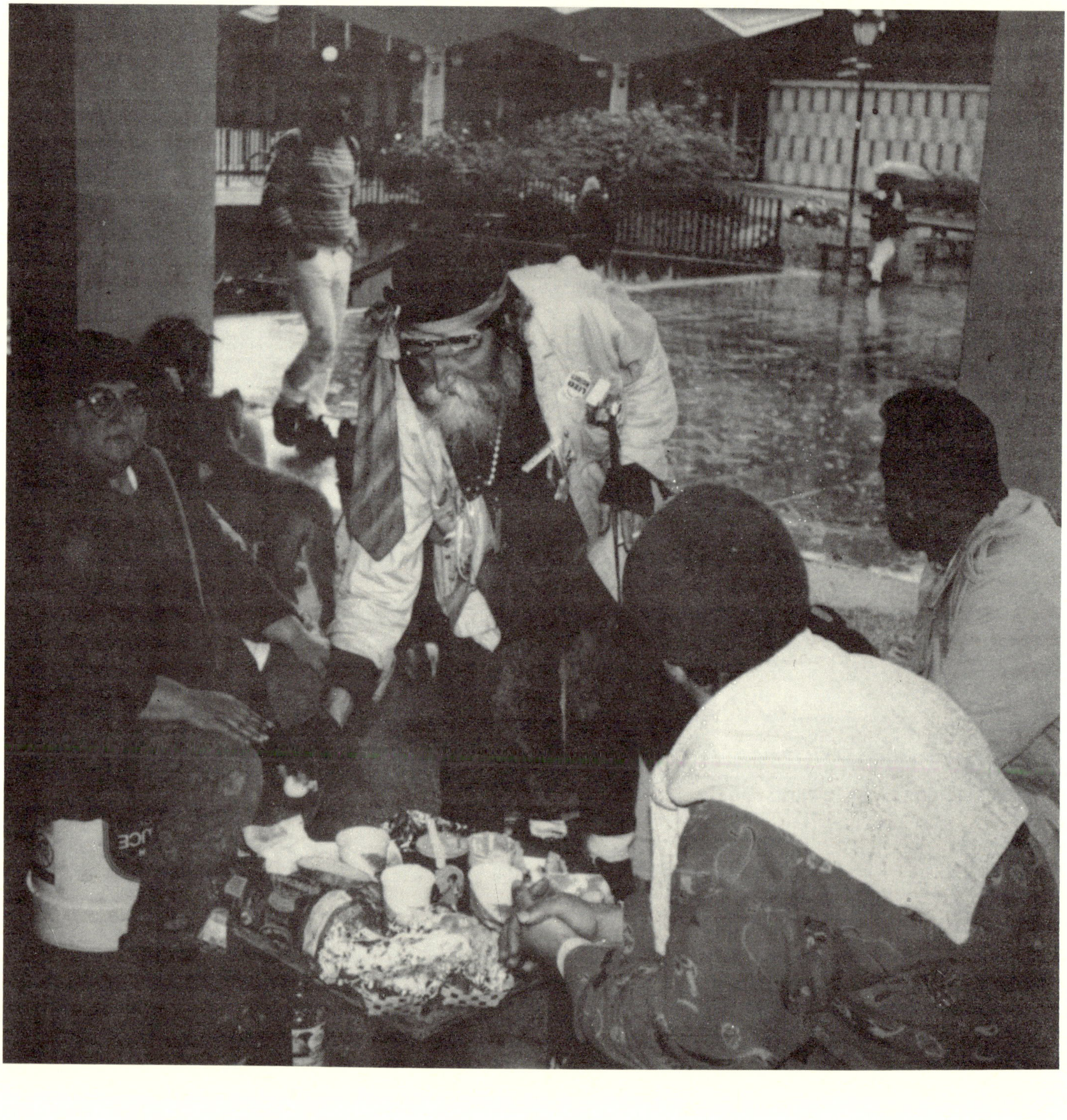

Chapter Six
Still Dealing With the Goddamn Cold and Rain

In truth, I don't know how street people survive the sub-freezing winters on the streets of Minnesota or New York. Or why.

I know that some street people live deep in the bowels of the New York City subway system, and that others sleep on top of the heating grates, etc. But it would take a more advanced treatise than this humble, little course in **Introduction to Homelessness: 101** has to offer to learn how to survive those kinds of extreme weather conditions. And I only hope I never have to write about it.

Due to the transient, mobile nature of street life, many street people are able to follow a general migratory pattern to keep one step ahead of the extreme seasons of heat and cold and rain. On the west coast, you'll see the troops come flocking in and out, from Portland — to the Bay Area — to Southern California — to Tucson, Arizona — and then back again.

But no matter WHERE you live, if you're living outdoors all year long, you have to learn to deal with the elements, because they will fuck you up if you don't watch out for it. You begin to monitor the daily weather reports as avidly as the Wall Street freaks monitor the stock reports.

Surviving On The Streets

One of my abiding premises is: **Mother Nature is basically playful, BUT SHE PLAYS ROUGH!** Therefore, like my 7th grade shop teacher Mr. Burnie used to say after Joey got his finger sliced off on the electric drill-saw: "BE PREPARED! BE PREPARED!"

There's probably not a lot I can tell you that won't sound like banal, common-sense advice: i.e., when it gets cold, dress warmly, etc.

One thing I always tried to do was to keep a dollar stashed in the back of my pocket for emergencies, so that I could always buy a cup of coffee somewhere and get indoors, out of the elements, for an hour or six, if need be.

Libraries and used bookstores are another great refuge — especially those that stock all those great Loompanics books that you have no address to order by mail. One winter I enjoyed what amounted to a self-made university, courtesy of the many hours spent wallowing in those great shelves of books. (If this chapter is getting too boring and technical for you, you can always skip ahead to the exciting chapter on How to Deal with Sex-Crazed Teenage Nymphet Runaways.)

The Cold

The coldest I ever slept outdoors was 22 degrees, on the road in Northern California near Willits. And I slept quite nicely, thank you, in my two sleeping bags, three jackets, four shirts, three pairs of pants, and three hats. I woke up in a field covered with frost, and white clouds of exhaust billowing out of my mouth.

Any temperature below 22 degrees would have been beyond the endurance level of my equipment. I certainly couldn't have handled it on a regular basis. You can get away with these extreme weather conditions once or twice, but remember: It's a long-term, cumulative effect that gets you. Eventually, you get worn down by it, and die an early death. You must learn to distinguish between conditions that are merely *unpleasant*, as opposed to those that are *debilitating*. This can sometimes be a very subtle distinction, as the effects often aren't apparent until it's too late.

On the one hand, your body has an amazing ability to adjust. Conditions you once thought of as unthinkable, you learn to shrug off with nonchalance. I once saw a photo of Australian aborigines, sitting comfortably in a circle on the ground in sub-freezing temperatures, wearing nothing but tiny loin cloths. The body adjusts. But keep in mind, they were born into that milieu, whereas you've been ripped out of the soft and warm insulation of modern society to face the harshness of Mother Nature head on. Like a skin diver that suddenly goes too deep too quickly, you can become debilitated from the bends.

The cold can fuck you up seriously, even if you know what you're doing. One time back in 1976, I ran into this old hobo on the road in Ukiah. He was a certified street expert; he'd been riding the rails since the Great Depression. He was truly the last of a dying breed.

Anyway, I had been stuck on this off-ramp for about eight hours trying to hitch a ride. The ramp had piled up with about twenty other hippie types who were also stuck there, so if any driver dared to stop, he'd immediately be gang-swarmed by twenty desperate freaks. It was a hopeless situation. (This was in 1976, after all, and the memory of Charles Manson was still fresh in people's minds, especially in little towns like Ukiah where American flags flew proudly on every other lawn and the populace was notoriously hostile to counterculture types, not entirely without reason. It's funny; when I would hitchhike back through some of these same towns 20 years later, it would be the rich, hippie pot-growers who were running the town, living in the big houses, and driving the expensive trucks, and electing the mayors and police chiefs. It was like the scene at the end of the movie *Back to the Future* where the entire context of reality has changed virtually overnight. But I digress.)

So anyway, I'd probably still be stuck on the damn off-ramp if that old hobo hadn't taken me down to the train yard and shown me the ins and outs of hopping freight trains. It's a beautiful way to travel actually, if you know what you're doing (no, I'm not going to teach you). Unlike traveling on the freeway, where you see nothing but shrubbery and Chevron stations, the trains cut right through the backyards of all of these little towns, and you get to see a fascinating slice of Americana.

So anyway, (this is my one and only *Hopping-Freight-Trains-With-Old-Hobos-From-the-Great-Depression* story, so forgive me for being long-winded) as we were winding through Norman Rockwellville, the old hobo told me about one of his near-fatal encounters with The Elements. He had hopped a ride on this flatbed lumber car, the kind with no walls where you sit right out there in the open on top of the lumber. Well, sir, the wind in his face felt really good for about fifteen minutes, until he realized he'd fucked up. The train wasn't heading south to Los Angeles like he thought, but north to Canada, and right through a serious snowstorm. On top of that, the train didn't make the stop he thought it was scheduled to make, but kept going non-stop for two days.

By the time that train finally stopped two days later, they had to carry that old hobo off the train, literally frozen in a seated position, frozen solid! He laid in a hospital bed for two weeks, shivering and teeth chattering, until he finally began to thaw out. It was a miracle that they didn't have to amputate some limbs.

This story illustrates just how slim your margin of error can be on the streets — especially when you're on the road — even when you know what you're doing. BE PREPARED. FOR ANYTHING.

The Rain

The rain is a source of constant dread on the streets. It complicates everything. Your already-limited street existence becomes even more limited. Now there are even fewer places where you can hang out and still stay dry.

But — like with most yin-yang aspects of life — there's a surprising counter-balance. One of the great unexpected benefits of the rain is, most everybody else is indoors, so you end up with much more space and privacy for yourself than the other months.

Another surprising revelation: The rain may be annoying — or worse — but generally speaking it won't kill you (though every winter there will be a few old timers who don't make it through the rainy season).

You catch a cold after the first rain, and never quite shake it for the next six months.

When I first hit the streets I got some excellent advice from Scooter, a street veteran of many winters, when I asked him how he dealt with the rain: "When your stuff gets wet, just throw a couple of quarters in the dryer at the Laundromat," he shrugged.

In truth, it's not the rain that does you in, but walking around, day after day, in wet clothes, and sleeping in wet blankets. But you'd be surprised how many street people never get around to scrounging up that quarter. Instead, they try to keep warm by investing in endless bottles of cheap malt liquor.

Ponchos are great for keeping dry. Plus, they're loose enough to fit over the biggest backpacks, and they're airy and not as stuffy as conventional raingear (keep in mind you may already be steamed up with four or five layers of clothing). I had a pair of rain pants, but I never found them necessary. If you're getting your pants soaked, you're probably already doing something wrong.

And PLASTIC BAGS! PLASTIC BAGS! PLASTIC BAGS! They will save your ass in a hundred different ways. At the very least, a plastic garbage bag can be made into a make-shift poncho in case of an emergency.

I also kept a good supply of umbrellas handy. Umbrellas are easy to ground-score, because many people junk them as soon as the rain stops, or if they get the slightest tear, which you can easily repair.

Which reminds me of a funny attitude that is prevalent amongst many street people. It might be right in the middle of the rainy season, but if it stops raining for twenty minutes, they immediately toss their raingear into the garbage. The logic is: "It's not raining now. What do I need this shit for?" Like it never occurs to them that it may very well start raining again at some point, like tomorrow. Many street people are notorious for living in the moment, and not planning ahead. It's often why they ended up on the streets in the first place. Me? Maybe I'm weird, but I meticulously planned out my falling apart, months in advance.

Another odd scene you'll see: It'll be right in the middle of the worst torrential downpour of the year, and you're huddled safely in a doorway, and yet, at that exact moment, you'll invariably see some hapless street person trudging down the street, his sopping hair matted to his forehead, as if he urgently has to get somewhere at that exact moment. Where is he going? By all means, wait out the storms. Try to stay as dry as possible. An ounce of prevention is worth a gallon of water drenching every single possession you own.

One of the nice things about the rain, actually, is that it slows you down, it forces you to sit still. This was especially nice for a jumpy person like me. I remember one night being stuck under an awning with ten other street people. It was obvious the storm was going to continue for the next six hours. You realize, there's really nowhere to go. Ever. It's just an illusion that something better is happening down the next block. So the ten of us just cooled our heels for the duration and had a great party. This might not seem like much, but it was a nice contrast to so much of street life, which usually has this herky-jerky, transitory quality of people being here one second and gone the next.

I stored my stuff in the bushes inside plastic bags, inside plastic bags, inside plastic bags. And then I put it inside another plastic bag. And yet, no matter what I did, raindrops and moisture would get in somehow. The problem is, when water sits inside a sealed bag, it doesn't evaporate; it sits there forever, wreaking havoc. There's nothing worse than reaching into your bag to get your last bit of dry clothes, only to find the entire bag has become infected with mold and mildew. You must open and air out these bags on a regular basis — something that is not always easily accomplished during times of constant rainfall.

Homeless Shelter from the Storm

I tried sleeping in a tent for a while. These are actually handier in the summer if you're camping in the middle of mosquito country. But, unless you have a really expensive one (which is doubtful), they're not much use for long-term camping in the rain. Like with plastic bags, the water will always seep into your tent somewhere, and stay there.

I had much better luck using a long piece of hard, transparent plastic. It was about twenty square feet, with ropes attached to the side of it. If it suddenly started raining at night, I would just grab the tarp and roll myself up inside it.

Chapter Six
Still Dealing With the Goddamn Cold and Rain

If I wanted to get more involved, I could easily wrap the tarp around low-hanging tree branches and fashion a makeshift tent, with walls, floor, and double flap. Also, the tarp was strong — it wouldn't tear — but it was also lightweight, and folded up very compactly, making it easy to pack up and store in the morning.

As a general rule, I recommend against constructing permanent — or even semi-permanent — homeless structures. They're a magnet for unwanted attention. If at all possible, pack your campsite completely away in the morning. But I found during the peak of the rainy season that almost nobody went walking up into the woods anyway. So I felt confident leaving my tarp-tent set up, sometimes for a month at a stretch.

On the subject of homeless structures, I've seen some amazing ones: teepees, tree forts, tin shacks; there were even some intricately built, two-story squatter-cabins built on the legendary abandoned Albany Landfill, with shower facilities and everything. Nearby my campsite, I once stumbled upon what looked like a human-sized gopher hole, burrowed deep within the thicket, where some guy had fashioned a cozy-looking, rainproof sleeping compartment.

El Niño

I spent the entire "El Niño" winter on the streets. El Niño set an all-time record for the most rainwater drenched on the Bay Area. It rained constantly for eight months, and I slept outside every night of it. In fact, I remember one stretch where I went twenty months straight without sleeping indoors in a bed once. There are some street people who have gone DECADES without sleeping indoors. Can you imagine?

The rain seemed to go on forever. At one point, during the month of February it rained 26 out of the 28 days. And I don't remember the two days when it didn't rain.

Dealing with the rain, wind, and the cold becomes a constant preoccupation. You sometimes hear people say, "WHY DON'T YOU BUMS GET A JOB!" Which is fine. But, like I said, what they don't realize is: **Living on the streets IS a full-time job**. Whereas most people work at a job to get a piece of paper to buy their food and shelter, for the street person, finding his food and maintaining his shelter IS his job. In a way, that's part of the beauty of street life, for it is more basic and real than many other aspects of this increasingly computerized and artificial society of ours.

One of the surprise benefits of living outdoors is that you develop this on-going, profound relationship with Nature. You become constantly aware of the painful interactions between You and Nature, which ironically, expands and deepens your sense of connection with it. You *have* to pay attention to this relationship, because, if you don't it'll kick your ass. Your relationship with Nature is akin to a relationship with a demanding dominatrix; if you learn to please Her, she will reward you extravagantly.

You begin to relate to the sky as if she was an intimate, long-lost friend. For the sky is your ceiling. Let's just say you begin to feel plugged into Nature in a way that people who live in a box, go to work in a subway box, stare all day at a computer box, and then come home to watch their television box, can never know.

I was never the type that could go off into the woods and just sit there. Boring. But when you're living in it, for years at a stretch, you begin to develop an appreciation for the rhythms of the beast. (Yes, all this musing is leading up to yet another *homeless anecdote*.)

I remember one night during the peak of El Niño. It rained all night, but I slept snugly and peacefully inside my tarp, as the raindrops beat out a *rat-tat-tat* rhythm against the plastic all night long. As morning broke, the sun was just peeking out dramatically from behind the dark clouds. The woods seemed fresh and clean from the rain, and bursting with awakening energy from every direction. My flock of blue jays

Surviving On The Streets

were pirouetting and dive-bombing in the sky. The deer were gracefully chewing on leaves and romping in the wet grass. The gurgling brook was filled to the brim with fresh, churning rainwater, adding a throbbing rhythm to the morning air. There was probably not another human being around for a mile in any direction (could anything be more blissful than that?) I took a big pull off of my bottle of chocolate-flavored coffee and wolfed down the apricot pastries I had saved from last night, throwing my leftovers to my blue jays on the other side of the creek. Then I lit a stick of incense and began my morning meditation.

Later that day I ran into a couple of my apartment dwelling friends downtown.

"ARE YOU ALRIGHT?" she asked frantically. "We were so worried about you last night, stuck outside all night long in the middle of that horrible rainstorm! HOW COULD YOU STAND IT!"

I assured them I was bearing my misfortune with heroic stoicism. When I asked them how *their* night had been, they told me they had spent the evening in their cramped little apartment on the second floor of a shitty, crack-infested neighborhood in Oakland, listening to the sound of gunfire not too far in the distance outside their window, as they tweaked out all night long in front of the tube, watching re-runs of *Love American Style* and the *Brady Bunch*.

Perhaps I should have been worrying about THEM.

Which isn't to say I want to paint too pretty of a picture of this rain shit. For — like so much of street life — when it's good it's GREAT, but when it's bad it can be very bad indeed.

Another night I was sick with a fever. There are few things more unpleasant than being sick as a dog and having to trudge off to the woods to sleep in a rainstorm. I was all set to call it a night and crawl inside my nice, dry tarp-tent, but first I had to pour off all the big pools of rainwater that had accumulated on top of my tarp. Unfortunately, I accidentally poured the water all over the inside of my tent, drenching the floor and my sleeping bag! Shit! There was nothing I could do now, but huddle in my sopping bag and shiver through the night.

The next morning I noticed my sleeping bag had ripped. ONE FUCKING THING AFTER ANOTHER! It looked like a pillow fight gone bad: White, down feathers were strewn everywhere, on the muddy floor, in my hair, in my beard. I lay there in my wet bag, in the mud puddle that my tent floor had become, and contemplated the sheer misery my life had become.

I figured, fuck, there was only one way to deal with this: masturbate. The way my mind works is (and this is embarrassing to admit): When I'm feeling totally miserable, the only antidote is to try and add a little pleasure to my life. So I figured what the hell, I'll just lay here in the mud and dirty down feathers and masturbate. The problem was, as soon as I started jacking off, all the wet, muddy down feathers that were stuck to my hand began sticking to my dick. And the harder I tried to get it off (no pun intended) the more it stuck to my member. It looked like I was yanking off Big Bird's dick. I would describe the scene as a "comedown" only that's a pun too lame for even Ron Jeremy.

It's moments like this when you wonder just how pathetic your life can become. Very pathetic indeed.

The rain can sneak up on you sometimes. One night, it started out raining lightly, but as the evening wore on the storm gradually picked up in intensity to the point where I was getting nervous about whether my raingear would hold up. At that point, from way off in the distance, I faintly hear the sound of a man's voice crying, coming from the woods on the other side of the road. Gradually, the voice got louder and louder, as he walked towards the general direction of my camp. Some hapless homeless guy had been caught out in the rain. Horrible, loud shrieks and sobs of absolute despair, anguish, and pain. And then,

Chapter Six
Still Dealing With the Goddamn Cold and Rain

gradually, the voice got fainter, as he trudged off in the direction of the long walk back to town, or wherever he was going, if in fact, he was going anywhere.

There are many moments like this on the street scene. Moments of absolute, heart-wrenching sadness. For it is the sound of ruined, shattered lives.

One night I really got caught in it. I was camping in Arcata in my tent, deep in the Redwood forest, about a half an hour from anywhere. This was the last time I used a real tent, actually, because the storm was so fierce that it pretty much wiped it out by the time it was done. Now anyone who's spent a winter in Humboldt County can tell you about the rain. It comes down in solid SHEETS, for days at a time with no let up. According to my journal entry, the night went like this:

December 8, 1996:

Made a BIG mistake last night pitching my tent in the Redwoods. It started raining just as I climbed inside. And did not stop. All night. Hour after hour. I woke up several times with that sinking realization that my tent was not going to hold up, that the ship was going down, and that I was going down with it. It was like being submerged at the bottom of the ocean with this tiny pocket of air, my tent. There was no hope of fleeing, for the woods were too dark and stormy to navigate, even if I had anyplace to go to, which I didn't. I was stuck.

I could only hope my tent held, as the wind buffeted it back and forth. The floor of my tent rapidly filled up with water. That sickening feeling when you roll over and feel this huge, wet puddle, and your sleeping bag is sopping it up like a sponge. You turn the other way, right into another puddle under your ass, soaking your pants which are now clinging to your pink, little butt. And knowing it's going to be a *very* long night, that you have nowhere to go for the next eight to ten hours, except to lie there on this shivering block of ice that is your bed. Slipped in and out of this weird dream-state, except that it was unlike any dream sensation, it was more like a half-dream/half-waking hallucination, like slipping into a coma. Just when the zombie nightmare was getting unbearable, I got a lucky break as the rain finally stopped for twenty minutes, giving me a chance to pour out the gallons of water from the bottom of my tent. Then I got the idea that saved my ass: I untied the shower curtain that I kept on top of my tent. The fierce wind had already wind-dried it, so I wrapped myself in it inside my sleeping bag. This provided a protective layer between me and the sogginess of the bag. Managed to actually sleep soundly for a couple more hours as the rain continued to rattle and drum against my tent. Finally — after several Eternities! — the light of morning approached. It had been a long and unpleasant night, and yet it was also a strangely meaningful experience. There's this lesson you learn when faced with unavoidable pain. It's like the body's natural defense mechanism kicks in — you begin to detach yourself from your feelings. The unpleasant sensation of lying in a puddle — it sucks, but once you accept it, it becomes just another vibration, another sensation. You have no choice *but* to endure it, so you do. You think, over and over, of the glorious future — which seems like it will never come — when you'll be sitting in a warm coffee shop eating a delicious ham and Swiss cheese sandwich. But you also know that the future won't really be all that great, just as the present moment really isn't all that bad. It's this sense that you can't escape the present moment, so you might as well dig it. And if you can dig even this nightmare, then you've passed some kind of test.

The "Breaks"

My first winter on the streets of Berkeley I copped a great "break." I was chosen to coordinate the annual Homeless Christmas Card project sponsored by the local Homeless Chaplaincy. This gave me access to a deserted office in the basement of a local copy shop. Among other things, the office gave me a place to get out of the rain, and to hang my wet clothes and sleeping bag, and to store my backpack. I couldn't stay there at night, but occasionally I'd turn the lights out during the day and catch a nap on the floor. For a homeless person, these are all great luxuries.

This highlights an important point: **GET INVOLVED WITH THINGS!**

Getting involved will invariably open up unexpected doors and opportunities. You can never tell for sure where these new involvements will lead, but I can tell you where sitting on your ass all day doing nothing will lead you.

There's a real danger of becoming ghettoized within the narrow confines of the street scene. Many street people, the only people they see or relate to are other street people. You almost get forced into this position because your daily life is so singular and so unrelated to "normal" existence. You almost have to force yourself to break out of this subworld and get involved with the mainstream. If you don't, you'll be limited to fighting for the same crumbs all the other street people are fighting for. Also, at some point you'll probably want to get off the streets, and that's nearly impossible if you haven't made some connections with the Real World.

The other point is: **YOU MAKE YOUR OWN BREAKS**.

The reason I got that "break" of having that office in the first place was because I had already been involved with many other homeless-art projects. It wasn't just some lucky fluke that landed in my lap, but the result of previous efforts.

Now, on the streets — as in life in general —there is great conjecture on the subject of the "breaks." Many a street person has been heard to moan: "I *NEVER* GET THE BREAKS, MAN!" They ascribe their bad "luck" to some mysterious, unseen Cosmic Hand that exists solely for the purpose of preventing them from ever achieving personal happiness.

The other day I heard this homeless kid complaining bitterly about his lack of breaks: "Everybody I know gets some kind of check or trust fund. Where's *my* free money?"

Let me assure you; as The Man said: *"What you reap is what you sow."*

One of my favorite Buddhist lines is: *"If you want to know about your past lives, just look at your present circumstances. If you want to know about your future lives, just look at your present actions."* In other words: the breaks you get — both good and bad — are in fact your richly earned karma.

I'm taking the time to lay this out for you, because the one thing you will have to survive on the streets, most of all, *is your own attitude.* A bad attitude — like a chip on your shoulder, or an unwillingness to make an honest effort, or a refusal to take responsibility for your own life — has ruined more street people than all the other dangers of the streets COMBINED.

Remember: What you get out of life is EXACTLY what you put into it. If you don't like what you're getting, then you might want to start by taking a closer look at EXACTLY what you're putting into it. Can you think of a better place to start? (I suppose you could start by blaming the government. Let me know how far this approach gets you in terms of reorganizing *your* life.)

Chapter Six
Still Dealing With the Goddamn Cold and Rain

A Second Break: Why, What a Lucky Bastard I Am

The next winter I got a second break that helped me survive the rainy season. One night I noticed that the padlock on the backdoor of this boarded-up women's latrine down the road from my camp, was just hanging there unlocked. Ten stalls all to myself, plus running water!

The first thing I did was clean the place up, and then kept it clean. I did this for two reasons:

1. to keep the maintenance people from snooping around, and
2. to keep track of whether anybody else used the place.

Nobody did. As far as I could tell, it was only in use about five times a year when the Cal Bears had a football game at the stadium below it.

Also, I took great care never to be seen by a passing car actually walking into the latrine (just as I never wanted to be seen taking that crucial step when I veered from the road to the trail that led up to my campsite). Sometimes I would walk by the place two or three times before I felt it was safe to dart in there. And I was careful to leave the lock propped up back on the door when I left first thing in the morning.

In truth, you only get so many "breaks" in life. The trick is to be able to spot the opportunity when it presents itself to you, and then to be able to take advantage of it and maintain it. (What's the point of getting one break after another if you just blow them?)

Living on the streets requires a willingness to take *calculated* risks. For, due to the quasi-illegal nature of so much of street life, virtually every move you make will involve some kind of risk: some minor, and others more serious consequences. You must ask yourself constantly: *"What's the **worst** thing that could happen if I do this? What are the **odds** of that happening? And how does the **risk** weigh against the potential **benefits**?"* The street people who are sloppy in these kinds of advance calculations are the ones who seem to have one "bad break" after another inflicted on them.

In a strange bit of timing, the very day the rainy season finally ended, I noticed that somebody had locked the padlock back on the latrine door. It gave me this weird feeling like some mysterious, unseen Cosmic Hand had been looking out for me all along.

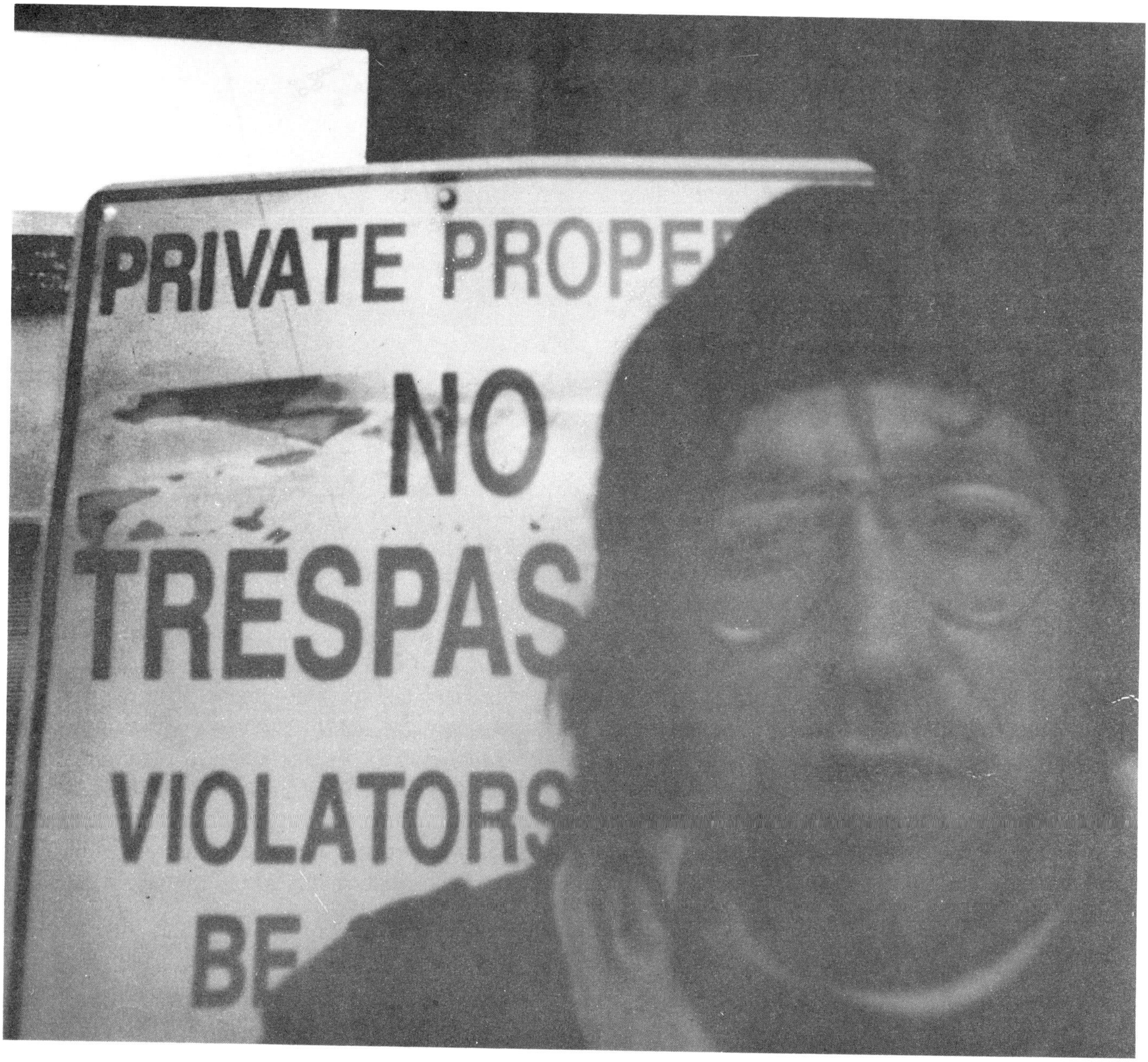
PRIVATE PROPE
NO
TRESPAS
VIOLATORS
BE

Chapter Seven
The Rain as a Metaphor for a Bunch of Philosophical Shit

It's common knowledge that money, fame and success don't necessarily bring happiness. It's not as widely known that the flipside of this equation is also true: That poverty, obscurity, and failure don't necessarily bring unhappiness.

Out of all the brutal lessons that I learned during my stay on the streets, this was one of the more pleasant. The reason for this strange paradox regarding "success" and "failure," I believe, is because losing — when it doesn't warp you — has a way of building character and humility in the same way that winning seems to breed arrogance, egoism and smugness. And street people are all intimately acquainted with losing. We've all been humbled by life many, many times. Without wishing to perpetuate the "beautiful loser" stereotype, there is, in fact, a deep soulfulness to many street people.

"You learn from your mistakes," said Linus, trying to comfort Charlie Brown after his latest monumental fuck up.

"THEN THAT MAKES ME THE SMARTEST PERSON IN THE WORLD!!" cried Charlie Brown in anguish.

But it's true.

My understanding is that we've been put here on this Earth to learn something. Whatever level you are on, the Universe will continually manifest that lesson until you finally learn it. What we perceive as "mis-

Surviving On The Streets

takes" are really nothing more than the things we still need to learn for our spiritual evolution. You'll find that you easily master most aspects of being human, but there'll be that one mistake, that one banana peel that you keep slipping on over and over. It's not a "mistake," it's just the thing you still need to learn.

In truth, The Universe doesn't make mistakes. It's simply too intricately ordered for that.

I didn't always feel that way. For much of my life I felt that something was seriously "wrong," that the world was a mistake that needed to be fixed, and that my life was a problem that needed to be solved.

I spent the first twenty years of my adult life being almost constantly depressed. For twenty years I tried and tried to make something of my life, and only succeeded at getting more and more miserable. It was the main reason I finally ended up on the streets, actually, because finally I just gave up on trying. And at that point, oddly enough, I finally began to find some happiness.

One of the first things my Guru said that really turned me around was: *"Everything that happens to you is for your own good."*

Everything.

You might be amazed at what a difference this outlook can make. Because, face it, many things happen to you in this life that seem very, very bad, indeed, if not horrible. And your mind will not be at peace — it will race to and fro — until you finally find the understanding that reconciles you to this sad fact. (And no, don't misinterpret what I'm saying here as some kind of Pollyanna, look-on-the-bright-side kind of bullshit, because, on one level, I happen to be one of the most bitter, cynical people you will ever meet. You'll know when you hit on The Truth, for it will soothe your soul, it will get you ALL THE WAY OFF, while Pollyanna wishful thinking will only cock-tease you to distraction. Let that be your guide.)

What helped me towards this understanding was realizing that what seemed to be "misfortune," what seemed to be "mistakes," could actually turn out to be quite "fortunate" indeed. And vice versa (just ask King Midas).

In other words: The bad stuff is good, too. Or, as Ram Dass put it: "Suffering is grace." For it's suffering (i.e., losing) (i.e., mistakes) that forces us to learn something. Which is the whole *point* of this spin on the cosmic wheel, remember?

Success or failure? I'm reminded of that old Zen story about the hunchedbacked old man whom everybody in the village felt sorry for because of his "misfortune." Then one day, war broke out and all the healthy young men were enlisted in the army and went off to die. But the hunchback was spared because of his "unfortunate" condition. And all the healthy young trees were chopped down for wood. But the gnarled old "useless" trees were spared. What was misfortune turned out to be fortune.

These are the things you think about when you're in the unfortunate position of sitting in a ratty doorway in the middle of the night in the middle of a torrential rainstorm with twelve cents in your ratty-ass pocket. For there's nothing like sitting in a rain puddle for three or four hours at a stretch to get you in touch with the fundamental philosophical verities.

One such night I remember well. It was New Year's Eve, the last night of 1996. I had been flushed out of my campsite by a torrential downpour, and was huddled in the doorway of an abandoned maintenance building up the road.

New Year's Eve has a way of making you take stock of where you've come from, and where you're going. For twenty years I had tried to be a success. But now here I was, the ultimate failure, a bum in a doorway in the rain. But like I said, I was just starting to get inklings of a greater kind of success.

This turned out to be one of the biggest rainstorms to ever hit the Bay Area. Soon, the main road that headed back into town was flooded over and turned completely into a raging river of rainwater. Fortunately, I lay there in my sleeping bag in that doorway, protected from the wind and rain by those three

Chapter Seven
The Rain as a Metaphor for a Bunch of Philosophical Shit

walls, and content in the knowledge that I was elevated high enough so that no water could possibly get into my nice dry doorway. Man triumphs over the streets yet again! I drifted happily off to sleep.

About an hour later, I woke up with a start. My sleeping bag was soaking wet! My doorway had inexplicably become flooded with water! In a flash I realized I had been sneak-attacked from my flank. Water was pouring on me from *inside* the building! The building had flooded and there were several feet of water on the floor, and it was now pouring out of the crack under the door and all over my sleeping bag. Just when you think you've got all the angles covered, on the streets you learn to expect the unexpected.

I staggered down the main road back towards town, trying not to get swept into the churning currents of the river that the road had become.

At the end of the road, the river came to an abrupt end, roaring majestically like a waterfall into the air, and pouring into the football stadium below with a booming crash.

But here's the weird thing. As I staggered down the road, soaked to the bone, I noticed that I was euphorically happy. It was so out of context with my wretched conditions, that I really had to wonder if I had finally completely lost my mind. For twenty years, I had reacted to these kinds of calamities with a raised fist and a grimaced curse at The Fates: "WHAT THE FUCK ELSE COULD POSSIBLY GO WRONG!!"

But something had changed. And it wasn't just excitement at being unexpectedly thrust into the middle of a Real-Life Adventure. Or awe at the shocking, cataclysmic power of Nature. It was more the sneaking suspicion that this, too, would turn out to be for my own good.

And sure enough, the violent power of the flash flood ruined the gravel road that led up to my campsite, tore it to shreds, and they had to barricade it off with roadblocks, giving me the whole place to myself for the next year-and-a-half.

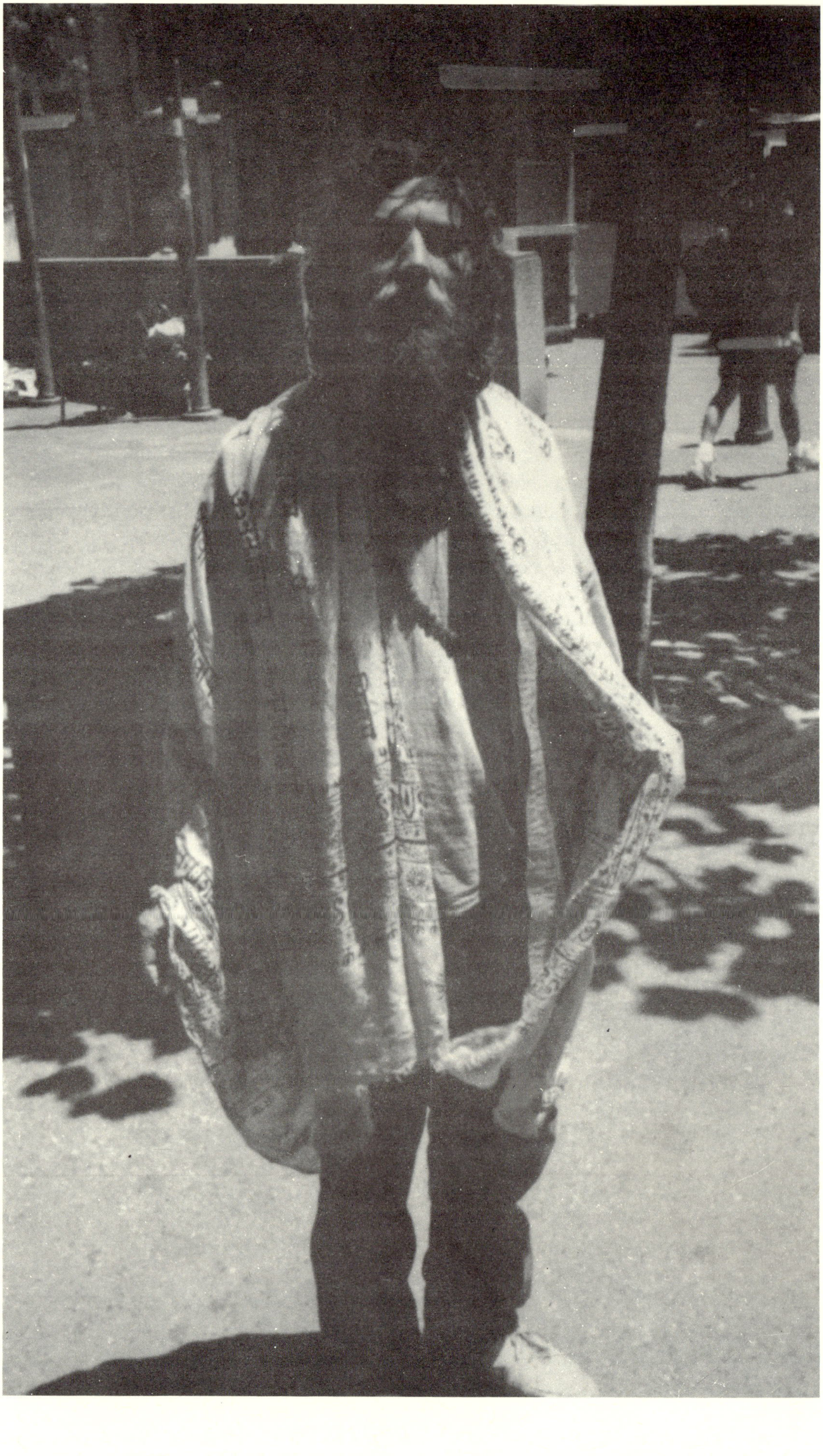

Chapter Eight
Wild Critters

I'm not trying to make myself out to be Nature Boy here. But you sleep under a tree for two years in the dark woods, and it changes you somehow.

It is an odd and profound experience. A two-week camping trip doesn't begin to approximate it. It's the difference between being a tourist in Nature, and feeling yourself as one of the wild flowers growing out of the soil. Two years of sleeping in the dirt will do that to you.

How can I say this without sounding like an air-headed hippie? You live outdoors for a couple of complete cycles of the seasons — exposed to the wind, the rain, the sun, and all the rest of it — and pretty soon you start feeling like just one more of the wild creatures that are crawling all around you in the woods.

I developed a strong affinity with the wild animals that were living alongside me. Simply because of how I was living was more similar to them than to my fellow humans: I slept in a nest in the bushes, I foraged for food in garbage cans, and I mostly ventured out late at night to avoid being run off by human beings.

Compared to the people around me — riding in BART trains and staring at computer screens on the 40th floor and living in temperature-controlled boxes — I lived more like a wild raccoon than a human being.

I don't want to over-romanticize this Back To Nature stuff. Because I never quite adjusted to it. But it wasn't the living outdoors part that was the problem, but the fact that I was so out of sync with the rest of indoor living society. In truth, how I was living was probably more akin to how mankind has existed throughout the centuries than the queer modern lifestyle that most people consider normal.

The interactions I had with the wild animals was one of the unexpected treasures of my homeless experience. Before this, my only encounter with animals was with domesticated pets such as dogs and cats, who live more like humans than animals. Living in the woods, it was the other way around; I was definitely on their turf, and I mostly adapted myself to them.

Now, again, it wasn't as if I was fending for myself in the wilds of Borneo wrestling in the river with crocodiles. My campsite in the woods was only a half mile from the nearest house in one direction (and miles and miles of woods in the other). Still, for a life-long city boy this was a major adjustment for me.

Every night when I left the main road and ducked under a tree branch to head up the rocky trail to my campsite, it was akin to plunging into Another World. For in the inky darkness of the tree-enshrouded woods you could barely see the hand in front of your face. There is something undeniably spooky about being alone in the dark woods. All those gnarled, old trees, and strange, creepy sounds. Moanings in the wind. It was one of the reasons I had the woods all to myself. Most people would be afraid to venture in there alone at night. (And if they knew I was lurking in there, maybe for good reason.)

While there's no doubt that the most dangerous critter in the woods is Man, it might be instructive to look at some of the other creatures of the night you might meet:

1. Raccoons

Now there's no question that you, as a human being, are on top of the food chain. And most of the creatures in the woods intuitively respect that. You go **"Boo!"** and most of them go scurrying for cover, for our reputation precedes us.

But the raccoons, on the other hand, are an exception to this. They stomp around in the woods like the Neighborhood Bully. At first I had assumed that the raccoon was nothing more than a cute, little, over-grown squirrel. I soon learned they were more akin to a grouchy, surly bear cub with the claws and agility of a big cat. It's not uncommon to hear of a dog cornering a raccoon — *"Now I gotcha, Rocky!"* — only to have the raccoon slice the dog to ribbons. They can definitely do some damage. And they're smart too. Homeowners will tell you of raccoons getting into their kitchen and opening their refrigerators and helping themselves to the potato salad and beer.

And they're strong, too. One night I woke up in my sleeping bag to see one of the bastards lugging off a big bag of my food.

It's a weird feeling to wake up in your soft little sleeping bag in the middle of the night, and see this gang of masked raccoon-faces popping out of the bushes staring at you with those glowing blank eyes of theirs, studying you.

I would jump up and shout at them — ***"BWAH!! GET OUT OF HERE, YOU STUPID RACCOONS!!"*** — thinking that should do the trick. But the raccoons would just sit there, looking at me with those blank, quizzical eyes. And they'd keep creeping towards me like an advancing army that had me surrounded.

No, they do not fear you one bit. It wasn't until I began beaning a couple of them on the heads with rocks, that they got the message and retreated back into the woods.

One night I woke up just as a raccoon was going for my pack. The startled raccoon scampered straight up the tree like a shot. You are impressed by how quickly and powerfully the hairy beast can scale that tree. So now, I've got this big, hairy raccoon trapped on a tree branch directly over my head while I'm trying to sleep.

I figured, fine, eventually, he'll go away, so I laid back down. But then, this other raccoon began advancing towards me, snarling and hissing at me. Evidently it was the treed raccoon's mate, for there was a little baby coon alongside her. So now the Mama coon was jumping into the fray to rescue her Hubby, growling at me as if to say, **"YOU MESS WITH MY JOEY AND I'LL TEAR YOU A NEW ASSHOLE, MOTHERFUCKER!"**

And then she'd turn to her mate up the tree and make these sort of soft cooing sounds to him, like: *"DON'T WORRY, HONEY, YOU HANG IN THERE, I JUST CALLED 911 AND EVERYTHING'LL BE ALRIGHT."*

Then she'd turn back to me and growl, **"ONE FALSE MOVE AND I'LL KILL YOU!"**

And then back to cooing to her Hubby.

It was the coolest thing, to actually experience this kind of interspecies communication. I got up and moved my sleeping bag to another tree. Far be it from me to break up their happy home.

Eventually I reached a détente with the raccoons. When I left my campsite in the mornings, I'd leave a bunch of food for them. During the day they'd clean it out while on their scrounge routes, and by the time I came to crash at night, they'd be long gone.

2. Deer

It's a nice thing to wake up in the morning, and the first thing you see is a family of deer grazing on the side of the hill, nibbling on the tree leaves for their breakfast. Often I'd see a family, a mother and father, and two little awkward fawns following them in the rear. It's a nice way to start the day. And what was the first thing YOU saw this morning when you woke up, my friend?

3. Gophers

Another nice way to wake up was one morning when I turned my head just as a gopher was popping his head out from the dirt from the hole he'd been digging. He looked at me twice right in the face, as if to say: *"What the fuck?! Let me take another look at that damn map!"* And ducked back down into the dirt. I guess it wasn't quite as nice for him to wake up to me.

4. Skunks

Less pleasant was the time I woke up in the middle of the night to a skunk. I had stupidly left a bag of greasy pizza right by my head where I was sleeping. I woke up suddenly when I heard something rustling around beside me. Unfortunately, my sudden movement startled the skunk who was checking out the pizza. He turned and fired. A direct hit. I got a jet stream of skunk piss (or whatever the fuck it is) right in the face. YUCK!

But you know, even that was cool in a weird sort of way. For it was a unique experience. Most of the time on the streets *nothing* is happening. This was a bit of an inconvenience, but you've got plenty of time to kill, after all, and nowhere you have to be in the morning, anyway. So you start to dig *everything* that happens to you as An Experience, as opposed to a hassle that gets in the way of what you're supposed to be doing. You're not really doing much of anything, actually, so at least it's something to do.

So I staggered down the road to a nearby swimming pool, washed my face, shirt, and sleeping bag off, and enjoyed a moonlight swim.

5. Blue Jays

The blue jays were my favorite, and I enjoyed bringing up special treats to feed them every morning — rice, popcorn, croissants, etc. I became quite attached to them, and them to me. Sometimes, when I would leave town for a week, when I got back they would seemingly whoop with joy at my imminent arrival. There are very few times in my life when my imminent arrival was met with whoops of joy. So it was cool.

I also enjoyed watching their pecking order squawkings, squabbles and commotions. It was sort of like a burlesque routine acted out for my enjoyment every morning. When they were fighting they could never move fast enough to actually peck the offending party, so the best they could do is sort of goose each other in the ass, and the goosed bird would jump in the air and squawk and parade around in a huff with his dignity intact. It all gave me a perspective on the squawkings of the humans I would encounter during the course of my day.

I don't know if this was my imagination, but the packs of blue jays would swoop down from the sky and caw out a warning to me whenever an intruder was invading my campsite. Just call me Namor, Prince of the Pigeons. Fighting crime with the help of his flock of birds who follow his every command!

6. "The Screeching Weasel"

I had one other odd interaction with a wild critter of the night that inexplicably began assaulting my campsite.

It started the night after I had done a radio show about Timothy Leary and the just-released "Timothy Leary is Dead" documentary. I referred to the good witch doctor over the air as "one of the great mindfuckers and soul rapers of our times," among other things. I happened to have been on acid at the time — my final acid trip. And I had a lot to get off my chest. For I had suddenly realized, in a rare moment of psychedelic coherence, that acid had deranged my brain. Instead of deepening my understanding of reality, LSD had led me down a false path into a hall of mirrors of illusion and delusion.

Later that night, as I was trying to sleep, this weird creature descended on my campsite, like a demon specter out of an LSD nightmare. I was lying in my sleeping bag when this creature in the dark woods began shrieking at me — this eerie, piercing, high-pitched shriek directed at me. It went on for hours until it finally went away.

The next night the creature was back, shrieking at me again. And it continued like this for weeks and weeks.

I couldn't figure it out. For I had been camping at this spot for a year with no problem. It wasn't like I had invaded the creature's nest. I was here first, and all the other woodland creatures had come to accept my claim on the territory.

Chapter Eight
Wild Critters

After awhile it really started to get to me. Not just that it woke me up every night. But that the sound of the shrieking was a strange mixture of agonizing pain and a very definite sense of anger and hostility that was very definitely being directed at me for the express purpose of intimidating me and driving me out of my spot. It was relentless. And the creature would keep circling around me through the course of the night. It would be silent for a while, and then the howling would come at me from the other side of the woods. And so on.

Finally, I would jump out of my sleeping bag in a rage and run after it into the woods in my bare feet, slicing my feet up as I hurled rocks and sticks in the general direction of the shrieks. Sometimes I would get close enough to actually hear the creature scurrying off as it fled into the distance. But I could never get a look at it. And then it would continue its shrieking at me from the top of the hill, just out of range of my barrage of rocks. I would stand there, panting and cursing, screaming:

"**WHAT THE FUCK IS YOUR PROBLEM??!!**" and wondering: "**WHAT THE HELL *IS* THIS THING??!!**"

I became obsessed with the thing, which I referred to as "that Screeching Weasel!!" Every now and then I would catch a glimpse of it silhouetted against the moonlit sky. It seemed to be some kind of cross between a polecat and an otter or a hyena.

I became convinced that the creature was the soul of Timothy Leary, reincarnated as a tormented, demon beast of the netherworlds for his soul-crimes against humanity. In fact, Kabir — one of the great Indian mystics, circa 1400 — maintained that false prophets were not spared by the law of karma and were sent into lower species to suffer and atone for their deeds: *"...to be born as swine and dogs, in the vicious circle of lower species, they'll rotate and rotate, suffering misery."*

Indeed, Leary had been haunting the town of Berkeley for years. In fact, his first wife had committed suicide in a house just down the road from my campsite; she "turned on" the gas in the garage while Leary, the great psychologist, slept peacefully in the bedroom upstairs. And Leary had come within inches of taking me down with him — just as he had taken countless other doomed souls down with him. And now, here he was, back in Berkeley, reincarnated as the Dog from Hell, coming at me for one last shot at me and my soul.

Yes, you could say it was getting personal between me and the Screeching Weasel.

I would regale my friends with dramatic accounts of my latest battles with the Screeching Weasel, and my latest theories regarding Timothy Leary's dearly departed soul. And they would look at me as if I was nuts, which was a very real possibility. I would grill my acid-head friends about any possible soul traveling encounters they might have had with Leary. One friend told me about a dream where he was standing alone in a desert, and Leary appeared on the horizon leading a battalion of tanks, and as he got closer and closer he stuck his head out of the tank and sent a beam of light out of his eye and zapped my friend directly in his eye, and then smiled and said, "GOT YOU!"

One night I decided to ambush the fucker. The Screeching Weasel's first assaults were always the boldest because he figured I was asleep, so he'd sneak up within ten feet of my sleeping bag before he fled out of range of my rocks. He would tease me and taunt me like that.

So I laid out my sleeping bag, and propped up my pillow so it looked like I was in it, and hid in the bushes about twenty feet away, with my hands filled with rocks. And waited.

Sure enough, five minutes later I heard it approach my campsite and start screeching at it. I jumped up and charged at it from behind, totally surprising it. I began spraying rocks in its general direction. It darted off in retreat, screeching up a storm in a frenzy and panic. I picked up a huge rock and flung it in the direction of the shrieks, and heard a distant THWAAACKK sound of rock connecting with weasel flesh. And the piercing shrieks suddenly stopped, mid-shriek. Bull's eye!

And then it got very quiet. I jumped up in the air, giving out imaginary high-fives to imaginary comrades. DEATH TO THE WEASEL! VICTORY IS MINE! NOBLE HUNTER OF THE FOREST! Etc.

I climbed back into my sleeping bag and quickly drifted off into a blissful sleep.

About 30 minutes later I was awakened by the sounds of the Screeching Weasel's return! And his shrieks were louder and angrier and more demented and haunted-sounding than ever. It was out for blood now. SHIT. FUCK. PISS. What IS this thing?

This went on for several months, until one night, when it kept screeching at me all the way into the early morning. As daylight approached, I decided to see if I could track it down in the morning light.

When it heard me coming after him, it rushed off as usual, but this time I was able to keep following him. It stopped and turned around, from what it *thought* was a safe distance to continue it's screeching, and was shocked to see me right on its tail. It let out a yelp of panic and took off in high gear through the woods, trying to escape me. I spotted it up ahead, crossing the main road, and scurrying up the dirt trail that led up into the Berkeley hills, with me in hot pursuit.

It jumped into a dry, rocky, creek bed and tried to ditch me by scampering up the rocks and disappearing around the corner. I jumped in after him. Unfortunately for him, the dry creek bed led to a big dead end, this big stone slab wall that was the bottom of a waterfall when the creek was running. Dead end. The end of the line! Cornered at last! Trapped like a rat that it was!

I braced myself for the possibility that the rabid beast might come lunging at me like a bat out of Hell. Instead, it just lay there, completely unmoving. Even its eyes were tightly shut. It was as if it was trying to blend in with the gray rocks.

I looked down at it. It didn't look up at me. It wasn't a weasel after all. It was a little gray fox, with fairly thick, almost wolfish hair. This creature that sounded so fearsome from a distance in the darkness of the night. And now, here it was, laying there at my feet, frozen, unmoving, eyes closed, as if totally surrendering to my mercy.

I gave the damn thing a hard, long look, and let him know that I could bash his fucking head in if I wanted to. And then I turned and walked back to my campsite.

And I never heard from the Screeching Weasel ever again after that. To this day I have no idea what that was all about. If any of my readers know, let me know, okay!

Part Two

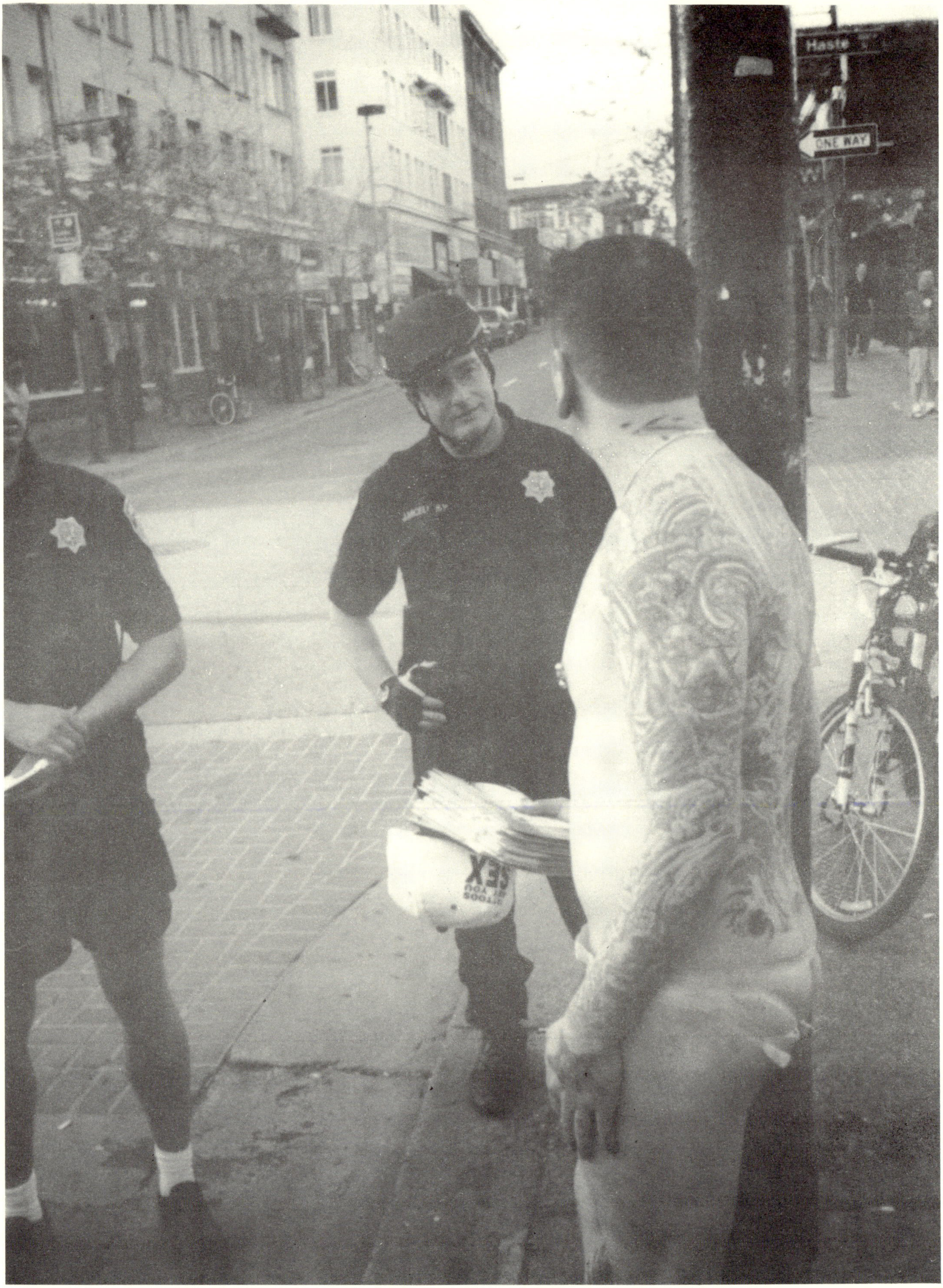
Haste
ONE WAY

*Chapter Nine
Dealing With the Cops
(and Being DEALT WITH by the Cops)*

Chapter Nine
Dealing With the Cops
(and Being DEALT WITH by the Cops)

When sleeping, eating, drinking, shitting and pissing, and even SITTING become quasi-illegal acts, it's not surprising that street people come into a certain amount of conflict with the police.

When you are homeless, there's no question that you are on the *other* side of the law. And that fact is impressed upon you in a hundred different ways.

Most street people just try to take the attitude that cops are an inevitable inconvenience of street life — like the rain, or bugs in your dreadlocks — and try to stay out of the cops' way as much as possible.

But some unfortunate street people take the attitude that cops are *The Enemy*. And they wage this secret battle against *The Cop* every step that they take. Which is fine, except that it's a battle that the street person invariably loses.

Many street people — particularly those of the young-and-male variety — have a problem with authority figures to begin with, and not entirely without reason. Many of them have ended up on the streets in the first place, precisely because they've been recently fucked over by parents, teachers, bosses, social workers, etc.

To the street person, The Cop can come to symbolize all the unseen faces of a society that's been fucking with him for years, man, and he's had a goddamn 'nuff of it! **GRRRR!**

Surviving On The Streets

The Cop comes to represent The Enforcer of a society that's been actively working AGAINST him all of his life. All the mysterious and unexplainable forces that have ruined his life now reach a visible flashpoint in the face of The Cop, The Persecutor.

After all, the politicians who enact the laws to run you out of town, and the citizens who put pressure on the politicians to enact these laws, are mostly off-stage and unseen. But it's the cop — it's HIS big, fat, ugly face — that gets pushed right into yours, as he throws your ratty backpack into the garbage and hauls you off to jail in handcuffs. And many street people milk these dramatic arrest scenes for all they're worth: The street person as Christ being martyred by the Romans.

You might be able to save yourself from playing and replaying this dismal scene by considering, for a moment, the cop's perspective on all this.

Four Things That Will Draw Cop Heat

1. *Complaints and pressure that the cop receives from residents/merchants/politicians/media.*
It's important to remind yourself that it's not personal with the cop. Usually, he's just the hapless middleman caught between the warring forces of the citizenry and the street people. And usually the cop is going to side with the side that's paying the taxes and paying his salary (hint: that's usually not the street person).

Granted there will always be a few cops who are just assholes — who use their badge as an excuse to act out their bully-boy leanings and personal psychosis, just as you find people who are assholes in every other walk of life (it might be a novel theory for some of you to consider that cops are actually people in the first place). But most cops do not get any particular thrill out of rousting some little old bag lady from a doorway and confiscating her meager possessions.

It's important for people on both sides of this conflict — the street person AND the citizen — to realize that, on the issue of homelessness, the cops are neither the problem NOR the solution. At best, the cop is a social garbage man, called in to clean up the mess that society has created. In truth, society has no clue, no general consensus, about what to do about the homeless problem, even as they keep screaming at the cops to do *something* about it.

The cop, after years of being caught in the middle of this mess, knows he has no solution. I've seen with my own eyes the futility of this whole charade. I've seen cops roust a motley crew of gutter punks from their hangout on the sidewalk, only to have the punks pick up their backpacks and belongings and trudge across the street and plop their asses down directly on the *other* side of the street.

It's THAT pathetic, this whole game: The cop has received a complaint; the cop has told the punks to move; the punks have moved. And an incredible amount of time, effort, and manpower gets squandered on these pointless maneuvers, and nothing really gets accomplished. About the only general consensus society has come up with for dealing with the problem of homelessness is: "GO SOMEWHERE ELSE." The problem is, as cops well know, most people are on the streets in the first place precisely because they HAVE nowhere else to go. And yet that's basically how we've chosen to deal with the homeless problem.

Best way to deal with it: Usually, if you keep your ears open, you can sense where the heat is coming weeks and months before the cop sweep comes down. The best move is to simply avoid those neighborhoods until the heat dies down. Unfortunately, some street people get defiant, taking the attitude: "I can stay here if I want!" Often, they find out they can't.

Chapter Nine
Dealing With the Cops
(and Being DEALT WITH by the Cops)

2. *People who stand out, who look like they don't belong in a certain environment.*
Face it; you are the square peg in the round hole. You, as the street person, are quite possibly a little eccentric looking, and are usually lurking about late at night, in places where you don't belong. Naturally, this is going to attract the cop's attention. Again, it's not personal, it's not some vendetta to track you down like an animal and pounce on you when you make your first wrong move, though it can certainly FEEL that way.

Compounding the problem, many street people quite simply do not feel they belong in this world in the first place. They lurk from place to place like Cosmic Orphans, like refugees trespassing in a hostile and alien world that they don't fit into. This vibe alone is enough to get the cop's attention. (One of the best pieces of advice I ever got was: Just act like you belong, and everyone will assume you do.)

You're probably not doing anything wrong in the first place — which only increases your sense of self-righteous anger. But keep a lid on it, Sid (see point #3). The last thing the cops want to hear is some angry harangue from some bum telling him: *"Don't you have anything better to do, like going after REAL criminals instead of fucking around with innocent people like ME!!"* The cop has to take angry harangues all day long, from noisy assholes who actually have power over him. It may be very tempting for him to NOT take it from someone like you who has no power over him (cops are people after all, remember?).

But it *can* be tough to take.

I remember vividly, the night when I finally blew my top. It was the last time I ever did acid, so my psyche was already a bit shattered. On top of that, it was one of those days where people seemed to be constantly fucking with me all day long, the culmination of a *lifetime* of people fucking with me.

So it was 2 a.m. and all I wanted to do was crawl into the bushes up in the hills and be left alone to sleep in peace. Unfortunately, as I cut through the deserted Berkeley campus, I noticed a cop car was slowly following me about 30 feet behind me. When I stopped and turned around, the cop car would stop. And then when I started walking again the cop car would start following me again. Finally, when I got halfway up the hill, I just turned around and glared at the cop car with my hands on my hips. When the cop pulled up to me, I started yelling in his window:

"WHY ARE YOU FOLLOWING ME? I HAVEN'T DONE ANYTHING! WHY DON'T YOU JUST LEAVE ME THE FUCK ALONE!!? "

Not a particularly brilliant maneuver for dealing with the cop on my part, but there was a certain momentary satisfaction from the outburst. The cop was so flustered by my unexpected rage that he immediately called for a back-up. The cops quickly surrounded me and explained to me *The Situation*: Since I wasn't a student or involved in university business, they could technically stop me at any time for trespassing — they can ALWAYS get you, *technically* — and furthermore, it was obvious that I was going off to sleep illegally on campus property, etc. In other words: HAVE WE MADE OURSELVES CLEAR, BOY? Quickly sizing up my options from within the frazzled nerves of my acid-drained brain, I switched gears to my *"Yes sir, no sir, I'm just a good American like you temporarily down on my luck"* mode, and talked my way out of it. But it gets to you. For it is a relentless pressure.

Best way to deal with it: Make an effort to blend into the scenery. Avoid lugging around bulky backpacks and sleeping bags. Find an environment that suits your personality. I like to hang out on college campuses because I like books and carry a notebook. Also, it's relatively easy to blend into a college environment because it's largely a scene of strangers and constantly new faces. Also, too, college students are a fairly low-income group which makes it easier for the impoverished street person to fit in. And, unlike most other poor neighborhoods, the crime rate is relatively light. On the other hand, if you're the type who likes to tear apart the engine of your '56 Chevy, you might blend in easier in the warehouse district. On the other hand, if you're a homeless black guy trying to camp in a largely white suburb, you

Surviving On The Streets

can plan on getting stopped by the cops at least twenty times a week. On the other hand, a white guy trying to camp in a largely Black urban area, you can plan on getting jacked up to five times a day.

(But, just to show you there are exceptions to every general rule of homelessness, there was this one famous bag lady who, for reasons known only to her, ended up camping in this ultra-rich suburb in trendy Marin County. She stood out like a sore thumb as the town's one-and only *Homeless Person*. The result? The entire town practically adopted her. She became the total focus of the towns' do-good impulse as their one-and-only charity case. And she, and her dogs, ate nothing but gourmet handouts, five meals a day, and lived like queens.)

3. *People who challenge the cop's authority.*
This will arouse the full fury of the cop's force more than any other single thing. For the cop's whole livelihood depends on his ability to assert his authority. "Anti-authoritarian" types, who can't switch gears into the "respect" mode, often bear the full brunt of the cop treatment. There are many unfortunate people who have spent months, and even years, of their lives locked up for no crime greater than being constitutionally unable to "take shit" from cops. Many of these "rebel" types get locked into this futile, pointless power struggle with The Cop — a struggle they inevitably lose. And, while I'm impressed with their "sense of honor," I'm less than impressed with their sense of stupidity. Like dealing with street assholes, you should view the cop as a walking time bomb; there's nothing particularly impressive or macho about tinkering around with it crudely, and blowing yourself up in the process.

Remember: The cop has guns, clubs, handcuffs, pepper spray, and cages built specifically for people like you, *plus* the entire weight of society backing him up. At the very least, have some respect for *that*.

There's an odd scene that I've witnessed repeatedly over the years. The cops are jacking up some street person and the guy decides to resist. It's as if he's thinking: Maybe if I fight back against these ten cops with their clubs, guns, handcuffs and stun guns, maybe *then* they won't arrest me. No. You only have two choices, to go easy, or to go hard. There is no third choice. And yet still, a surprising number opt for the hard way, with their face rammed into the concrete, and a 250-pound cop's knee jammed into their back, and their arms pulled all the way back to just about the breaking point (and sometimes beyond).

I should say, on the subject of police brutality, in all my years on the street scene, I have only witnessed one real incident of police abuse with my own eyes. This wino in San Francisco had passed out on top of the marble steps of this bank near St. Anthony's Dining Hall. This cop grabbed him by the ankles and drug him down the steps. And his head went *ka-BONK-ka-BONK-ka-BONK* on every step. And they threw what was left of him into the back of the paddy wagon and drove off.

I'm not saying this stuff doesn't happen. But I've also seen a lot of people get carried away on this subject. I remember once doing a radio show on the subject of police and the homeless. My friend Moby, one of the nicest, most mild-mannered guys you could meet, was delivering an impassioned speech on the subject of "The Pigs!" and "police oppression of the homeless," etc. I cut him short:

"Moby, in the two years that you were homeless, did you ever get hassled by the cops?"

"Uh… No."

"You know why?"

"Why?"

"Because you didn't cause any trouble, that's why."

*Chapter Nine
Dealing With the Cops
(and Being DEALT WITH by the Cops)*

One thing that helped me with my relationship with cops (well, "non-relationship," actually, as I strove in all ways to not talk to cops, to not look at cops, to not appear in any way, shape or form as even a blip on the cops' radar) was that I have a basic sympathy, and even respect, for the cop, an attitude which perhaps is not widely shared in the street community. For one thing, my older brother was a cop for a while, so I saw firsthand what a tough job it was, and have little desire to make their job tougher. I'll never forget riding around with my brother one night in the squad car, in this rough little town in Jersey, or the looks you get from some of the blacks and some of the street people, when you ride by them and they turn around and look at you as they get caught in the glare of your headlights with the look of Pure Anger. Far from being the all-powerful bullies that most street people seem to perceive the cop as being, most cops see themselves in considerably less grandiose terms. As my brother put it, shortly before he quit the force to become a banker: "Most cops either become cynics or drunks. Or both."

Best way to deal with it: Don't waste your time getting macho with the cops. *Macho* is the cops' *business.* They very well may be better at it than you.

4. *People who are actually committing actual crimes.*

While this rarely seems to be the cops' number one priority, if you commit enough crimes, you will eventually attract the attention of the cop. As I said, the mere fact of living on the street is enough to garner cop heat. If you're also walking around with car stereos under your arm, you might as well be dead meat. Your margin of error is already slim to none. Why push the odds?

The Criminalization of The Homeless

Which isn't to say there won't be problems, even if you stringently follow these four handy guidelines. I'll give you a clear cut example of how the mere fact of being homeless puts you on the other side of that line.

For the twenty years that I was an apartment dweller, I considered myself a social drinker; I would occasionally share a beer with a friend at my apartment, or maybe once a month, I would go out to a bar with my pals and tie on a good one. When I hit the streets, without thinking about it, I continued this same general drinking pattern. Only suddenly, I began racking up all these *Drinking-in-Public* tickets at an alarming rate (at 220 bucks a pop that's a very expensive swig of Budweiser!)

Now you can cry and scream at the unfairness of it all. You can also curse at the rain and piss into the wind. The point is: It's *you* who has to adjust to the cop, not the cop who has to adjust to you.

Part of the problem is, most of the laws with regards to public vagrancy were written long before the reality of modern homelessness kicked in. And most of our recent laws — written in an attempt to deal with homelessness as a criminal problem — have been equally inappropriate and ineffectual.

Another thing that is a jarring wake-up call to reality of homeless life: You know those search warrant laws that you take for granted will protect you in the home where you live? Well, don't kid yourself that they also apply to the car, the crash spot, or the backpack, that you, as homeless person, live in. As one cop put it: "There's a law or regulation pertaining to virtually every facet of the automobile. For instance, if your mud-flap is a half-an-inch to the left of regulation, I have a pretext to stop you and to check you out if I want."

Surviving On The Streets

You're Under Arrest

To understand just how vulnerable the street person is to the arm (and foot) of the law, one only has to consider that, in the eyes of the law, the very act of *sleeping* is a criminal offense — something the average, irresponsible street person does at least once every 24 hours, and sometimes even more often!

Believe me when I tell you, when you're on the streets it is ridiculously easy to start racking up tickets, and most street people do. The street person, being a classic procrastinator and all-around fuck-up, usually doesn't get around to taking care of his tickets, even if he had the money to pay them — which he doesn't — or the motivation to do the community service — which he also doesn't. And even if you opt for community service, you still, usually, have to pay a $20 paperwork fee, which the street person doesn't have. So usually, the street person doesn't get around to taking care of his tickets. So then a warrant goes out for his arrest. This is the point of the whole exercise.

The warrant is the tool that the cop uses to control the street person, as well as his excuse for running your name through his computer and keeping tabs on you. While technically, the cop can't stop you and arrest you in America simply for the crime of being poor, the warrant gives him the basic tool to do it anyway. *Now,* thanks to the miracle of the warrant, the cop can legally stop you and fuck with you under any pretext. *Now,* the most uppity, loud-mouthed, rebellious street person becomes meek and compliant in the face of *The Warrant*.

It's not uncommon to see cops going up and down the main drag, stopping various street people who are just hanging out: "I know you got a warrant out, Jack. I better not see your ass on this street or else I'm running you in." Perfectly legal, and not a damn thing you can do about it.

Many cops assigned to the street beat, are known to keep a daily, updated list of all the street people with outstanding warrants. And they've got nothing better to do, apparently, than go up and down the Ave looking for them.

This is particularly galling considering this little tidbit that I read in the *San Francisco Chronicle* last week. In the state of California alone, there are 2,600 outstanding warrants… **FOR HOMICIDE!** These are warrants that the cops aren't even bothering to look for. They've basically given up on these warrants, the reason being that they just don't have enough time or police manpower to do anything about those homicide warrants. But believe me when I tell you: They always seem to have plenty of time to take care of every single Sleeping-in-Public or Open-Container warrant.

It's a clear-cut case of selective enforcement. But good luck explaining it to the judge. It's a running joke on the street scene that maybe we should start killing people so then the cops would leave us alone.

Now it's important to understand the cops' motive in this strange dance. Some street people mistakenly assume that the cop is primarily motivated by a desire to run the street person off the face of the earth, when in fact, all the cop *really* wants is a modicum of control over you.

Keep in mind, the cop really DOESN'T want to arrest you. He doesn't want your homeless ass cluttering up his already-crowded jails anymore than he wants you sleeping anywhere else (file this information away in the back of your mind).

What the cop *does* want is some degree of leverage, of control over you, *if need be*. Because, face it, the street scene is ever teetering on the verge of bursting out of control. (And the cop's the one who gets the shit from the citizenry when it does.) The key point to remember is: The cop really doesn't want to *use* that leverage. What's the point of giving you a ticket or arresting you? You can't afford to pay the ticket, and there's no room for you in jail anyway. And on top of that, you'll just be back out on the same streets in a couple of weeks anyway.

If you simply communicate to the cop your WILLINGNESS to submit to his control, he will rarely force you to demonstrate it. I'm not talking about being a suck-ass here. I'm talking about not being a *wise*-ass. Just show the cop you're not out to fuck with *him*.

Every now and then, a cop would stop me on my way up to my campsite. Usually it had nothing to do with me. A prowler had been spotted in the area. Or maybe the cop just wanted an excuse to check me out; it's his job to keep up with what's going on on the streets, after all. He'd pull me over in his car, shine a flashlight in my face, and bark:

"You can't sleep up here."

I'd say: "Oh, okay officer."

And I'd turn around and sneak back to my campsite from another direction. Everybody's happy. The cop has shown that he can stop me if he wants. And I've shown that I'm willing to go along with the cop game. And then I go off and do what I want. Which is the important thing.

What you *don't* want to do is force the cop to draw the line in the sand. You don't want to challenge his tenuous sense of control over you, because *then* he will be forced to demonstrate it. I have a homeless friend with a serious bad attitude toward the cops. He's the type that, if a cop casually asked him, "How's it goin', friend?", he'd respond, "I AIN'T YOUR FRIEND, FAGGOT!" and walk on.

One night my friend was confronted by that same cop on the way to my campsite:

"You can't sleep up here," said the cop.

My friend replied, defiantly, *"Are you arresting me? Are you detaining me? I'm not doing anything wrong (yet)! I'm just going for a walk! If you're not arresting me then you have no right to hold me here! I know my rights! I'm leaving!"*

And with that, my friend marched on up the road. He had called the cop's bluff and got away with it. *That* time. But believe me when I tell you this: The cop will remember. The *next* time. Eventually he will catch you. At *something!* Furthermore, your campsite will be marked off as a permanently off-limits spot, simply because you FORCED the cop to back up his authority.

As for me? That same cop may spot me heading up to my campsite a week later. But he won't bother to stop me, because he already knows — or thinks he knows — that he CAN stop me if he really wants to. You've given the cop what he wants: the *illusion* of control, which is all a man can really ask for in this uncontrollable world of ours.

The Legal Loop

There are few things more aggravating or infuriating than getting stuck in the middle of the legal loop. For this reason, I recommend taking care of your tickets as soon as you get them. At the very least, that saves you from the horrible feeling of looking over your shoulders and seeing cops everywhere, knowing that they could pop you at any moment. Who, after all, wants to see cops everywhere? Probably not even other cops.

I always opted to take care of my tickets by doing community service. But a surprising number of street people opt to do the time in jail (which can come out to about a day, or a week, or a couple of weeks, per ticket, depending on the offense, and your past record, and whether or not you're an asshole). Generally, they try to time it to take care of *all* of their outstanding warrants at once, preferably during the middle of the rainy season.

It's an odd story how I finally got enmeshed in the legal loop. I got busted at the annual Humboldt Hemp Fest of all places. The stoners rented out a big field in the Redwood Park. There were dozens of booths showing you all the different ways you can smoke pot. Dozens of speakers on stage telling you all about how great it is to smoke pot. Seven or eight rock bands singing all about how great it is to smoke pot. Hundreds of joints of shake got thrown out into the crowd. And, of course, hundreds of people were hanging out in the middle of the field openly smoking pot.

Being the discreet sort that I am, I picked up one of the joints of shake and went off into the woods to smoke it in private. Mistake. The cops, of course, weren't going to dare and try to bust any of the huge crowds of people who were smoking openly in the field. Instead, they snuck around in the back of the woods busting those people who were actually trying to be discreet. So after twenty years of taking virtually every drug I could get my hands on with impunity, I finally end up getting busted for a 50-cent joint of shake *because I was too discreet.*

So anyway, I was all ready for my day in court. Several friends recommended that I plead not guilty and contest the charge. This stratagem often works, because then they have to set a new court date, and the cop who busted you usually doesn't have time to appear in court as a witness to such a petty event, so the judge has to throw the case out. (This approach can backfire, sometimes, though, because if they DO decide to go through with it, they might go harder on you for forcing them to go through all the bullshit.) But the judge pulled a fast one on me. He was a real "friendly" type judge. Our exchange went like this:

The judge: "It says on your paperwork that you're a freelance cartoonist."

Me: "That's right, your honor."

Judge: "I notice you've been doodling in my courtroom. Are you going to put me in one of your cartoons?"

Me: "That depends on how you sentence me."

This got a big laugh from the people in the courtroom. Street tip: It is not good to get laughs at the judge's expense.

Judge: "Well, I'll tell you what, *Mr. Backwords*. If you plead guilty, I won't fine you any money, but merely require that you go to four, hour-long Drug Diversion classes."

That sounded pretty good, so I changed my mind and agreed to plead guilty. It wasn't until I went to sign up for the class a week later that they informed me: "By the way, you're required to pay $350 to sign up for the program."

DIRTY ROTTEN STINKING #@!!&*%#@!!!!!

I ended up battling the bureaucracy for the next six months over that damned 50-cent joint of shake. Finally, I ended up jamming the machine with a blizzard of paperwork, and the ticket ended up getting lost in the maze of their own computers (I think). The whole episode was a drag, to say the least. But I got the last laugh, because, one of these days, I'm going to put that damn judge in one of my cartoons, so he'll get his. DON'T FUCK WITH ME!

A Final Word on Dealing With the Cops

Good luck.

Chapter Ten
Street People vs.
The Merchants

The third wheel in the battle between cops and street people is usually the local merchants. The street people are drawn downtown for the same reasons as the merchants: It's where the money is. But the similarity ends there. In most every other way, the street person and the merchant find themselves working at cross-purposes.

From the merchant's point of view, the street person drives away their customers, degrades the environment with their raggedy-ass presence, steals their merchandise, messes up their bathrooms, and leeches off their tax dollars while contributing nothing to society.

From the street person's point of view, the merchant is a greedy, exploitive, capitalist pig, a bully who persecutes the weak, and an asshole who thinks he has more rights than everybody else simply because he has more money.

In truth, it's the *demonization* on both sides of this issue that is the most wearisome thing. As a homeless person AND a merchant (I work at a vending table) I got caught in the middle of all this. Usually I just concluded that both sides were right: we're *all* a bunch of assholes.

The Saga of Measure E

The story of Berkeley's infamous Measure E illustrates a lot of key points regarding the ongoing conflict between the street people and the merchants.

The whole thing started a few years ago when the merchants on Telegraph started getting alarmed about the swarming, and ever-growing gangs of street people hanging out in front of their stores. It was the usual complaints: drunken brawls, rampant drug use, garbage and litter left behind, broken store windows, scaring off customers, etc. In other words, the street people were behaving like motley bands of street people generally behave. And the merchants finally got sick of this shit and decided to take action.

With SOME justification, *okay, street people?* Like I said, I got sick of the demonization on BOTH sides of this issue. I got sick of hearing the street people describing the merchants as "evil, fascist monsters bent on destroying us for no reason at all, man!!!," as if the merchants didn't have some valid concerns. One poor merchant had his store window smashed **nine times** in a two-year period (I personally witnessed six of the smashings)!

I also got sick of the merchants endlessly scapegoating the street people for all their business woes. I used to crack up at the endlessly repeated claim that street people were "scaring off customers." The fact is, the sidewalks were usually so crowded with people, I often had to walk in the middle of the street just to get up and down the block. Hell, if the street people were scaring off customers, I wish they'd scare off a few more.

Even more galling, the merchants blamed the street people for all the "crime" that was making people afraid to come out at night and shop. There were, in fact, a long series of violent robberies during this period — including the abduction and murder of a UC student. But, to my knowledge, not one of the crimes was committed by a local street person. In fact, the suspects in virtually every case were the ubiquitous "young, Black male." But try to get anyone in liberal PC Berkeley to acknowledge *that* obvious fact. In the meantime, it's perfectly acceptable to dump all over street people, whether they're responsible or not. The fact is, there's more than enough stuff to blame us for that we *deserve* to be blamed for, without having to make shit up.

So anyway, the City of Berkeley, in response to the pressure from the merchants to *do something* about all the street people cluttering up the fronts of their stores, passed Measure E, which banned sitting on public sidewalks.

What followed was a year-long legal battle, where all the sides interested in *"doing something about the homeless problem"* expended an incredible amount of time, money and manpower. And when the dust cleared, the measure was amended to allow us the right to sit on the sidewalk "within five feet of a building." So the end result of this heroic struggle was that we fought and won the right to sit in the gutter. It's a triumph of the human spirit, I tell you!

At least the parasitic lawyers at the ACLU managed to take in a cool $100,000 in legal fees, so SOMEBODY benefited from the whole debacle.

This whole sorry episode is a classic illustration of the futility of our basic approach to dealing with the homeless problem, namely, endlessly attacking the *symptoms* after the fact, but doing almost nothing to address the underlying *causes* of homelessness in the first place. Could anything be more futile than dealing with the symptoms but not the cause? (We'll be getting back to this later.)

After Measure E got shot down in flames, the City of Berkeley — undeterred — designed a whole new series of measures to combat the growing street people menace. Things like, making it illegal "to have

Chapter Ten
Street People vs. The Merchants

three or more stationary dogs in any commercial district," and banning "lying on any commercial sidewalk," etc.

All these measures were designed, of course, to give the cops more ammunition to run the street people out of town, which is what the merchants really wanted. But mostly it just resulted in running us from one side of the street to the other, or from one city block to another, herding us around, back and forth, in this pointless circle.

All these measures are just a bad joke anyway. Because, as all street people know, Measure E or not, the cops can ALWAYS find some pretext to run us out of town if they really want to. And we don't need to pay the ACLU $100,000 to find that out.

The pretext that the cops ultimately used to run all "the bums" off of Telegraph went like this:

Now, just to set the scene, the merchants DID have a point. The street scene WAS spinning out of control. It was the peak of the summer of '98, and just about every night there were drunken fistfights, or crazed street chicks taking off their shirts and dancing in the middle of the street with their tits flopping around (well, this didn't happen *every* night, but the nights that it did were memorable). There were huge bands of crazy street people flopped in front of every store. Piles of dogshit everywhere. Bad scene after bad scene. Mostly petty shit, really — and, from my point of view, mostly entertaining shit; at least something was *happening*, ya know? — but it was the cumulative effect that was really starting to get to people.

One sunny morning I witnessed a typically bad scene. This little old lady was walking her poodle down the street when suddenly this street person's pitbull, which was lolling around unleashed, latched its jaws around the poodle's neck. The little old lady held onto her dog's leash for dear life, rolling around on the sidewalk in dogshit, while the street people kept beating on the pitbull's head trying to get him to release his death grip from Fifi's neck. From across the street, it looked like the little old lady was being mauled to death. *(Street tip: Clamp your fingers over the pitbull's nose — eventually he'll have to open his mouth to breath.)*

You could sense the growing outrage at these daily scenes of out-of-control anarchy. ("And not the *cool* kind of anarchy," as my friend Moby put it.)

A few mornings later, at the very same spot, a couple of White pot dealers got into it with some Black guys who had rolled one of their friends in the park earlier. As if the street scene isn't explosive enough, when the racial aspects get added into the mix, the intensity level quadruples, and near-riot situations often break out. Anyway, the Black guy ends up smashing the White guy into a store window, shattering that hapless merchant's window for the umpteenth time (in fact, the window repairman had just finished replacing it from when it was smashed the previous evening!). Then the other White guy retaliated by cracking the Black guy over the head with his skateboard with a skull-thudding whack. Two of the Black guy's buddies jumped into the fray, as well as some guys from the white guys' crew. After beating on each other for a while, they all went staggering off in opposite directions, moments before the cop cars made the scene.

Later that night, the whole dismal scene finally came to a head. It started when this cop tried to arrest this street hippie/junkie-type of guy for a warrant or something. As the cop tried to handcuff him, the guy started resisting, whining and screaming about some terrible pain the cop was causing to his injured leg.

There were large crowds of street people hanging out on both sides of the street, as was typical during that period. And when they heard their friend screaming in pain at the hands of the cop, they began surrounding the cop, taunting the cop from every direction. Soon, a crowd of at least 100 angry street people had encircled the cop, screaming and cursing and doing everything they could to keep their friend from being arrested. Right on cue, about ten cop cars came roaring into the scene, sirens blaring, to back up

Surviving On The Streets

their hopelessly outnumbered colleague against what was on the verge of becoming an unruly mob. Now if you've ever been in a near-riot situation, you know the kind of crazed, intense energy that crackles and sizzles in the air, like a fuse that's racing to its detonation point. Fortunately, the cops ignored the taunts, for it wouldn't have taken much to set off the whole scene. They finally managed to jam the screaming street hippie into the back of one of the cop cars and beat a hasty retreat. The street people pelted the cop cars with empty beer cans and general shouts of "FUCK THE POLICE!" and "YOU COPS WEAR THOSE CLUBS 'CUZ YOU HAVE LITTLE WEENIES!", etc.

This was followed by a mood of celebration. WE RULE THE STREETS, MAN!! A very *short-lived* celebration, I might add.

Like I said in the last chapter, nothing arouses the full force of the cops' fury like direct challenges to their authority. The next morning the police sweep came down.

Many of the very same street people from the night before were still flopped out on the sidewalk, after a long night of partying. The sidewalks were strewn with sleeping people in sleeping bags, backpacks, possessions, dogs, garbage, etc. One of the street people was actually heroically trying to clean up some of the mess, sweeping huge piles of beer bottles and garbage into the gutter with a big push-broom.

The quiet of the morning hangover was shattered by the sounds of waves of cop cars roaring back onto the scene like a motorcycle gang coming back for vengeance. Along with a huge garbage truck, which stationed itself in the middle of the street, engine running. It was like a military assault operation.

The cops rushed from street person to street person: **"YOU! GET UP OFF THE SIDEWALK! IS THAT YOUR BACKPACK? MOVE YOUR STUFF OUT OF HERE! YOU'RE BLOCKING THE SIDEWALK!!"**

Any gear that wasn't immediately claimed, the cops quickly tossed into the back of the garbage truck. Soon, the block was cleared of street people. The defiant street conquerors of last night had become docile and disoriented by this sneak attack. They straggled off the Avenue trying to save what they could of their meager possessions.

Later that week, the next phase of the sweep went into effect. The cops began to arrest the street people on any pretext, picking them off one by one. Most of them got popped for petty marijuana sales, slinging $10 bags, and shit like that. All in all, 70 different street people got hauled off to Santa Rita for several month jail terms. Most of the rest of the hardcore element of the street scene got the message and left the Ave. Most of them just moved a couple of blocks down the street to Shattuck, to start up the whole cycle again down there. Hurray, Hurray.

Like I said, the cops can always find some pretext to run us out of town if they really want to. And the street community (if such a thing exists) has to shoulder much of the blame, in this particular case, for making such a mess as to give them the excuse to do it. But there were two things about how the cops did it, about all the pot busts that were particularly galling:

1. The "liberal" Berkeley City Council, which encouraged this police action, has previously voted pot "the lowest police priority." God only knows how many of those very same political windbags are old potheads themselves. Further, in the wake of Proposition 215 — the medicinal marijuana ordinance which had been overwhelmingly passed by the California voters — marijuana was now being openly smoked everywhere in Berkeley. You could take a cross-section of virtually any segment of Berkeley society and find the same level of petty pot dealing, and yet it was only the street people who were getting thrown in jail for it.

2. Probably at least half of the very same Telegraph merchants who initiated this sweep in the first place were making money selling pipes, rolling papers, drug paraphernalia, drug books, or *High Times*

magazine, or the dozens of other cannabis magazines, or hemp merchandise, or books and records by authors and musicians who were famous for their glamorization of their own drug use.

But as one aging, hippie tie-dye vendor put it: "I don't care WHAT the cops do, so long as they run those bums off!"

Yeah! Back when I was a kid, we rebelled against authority in a respectful manner, unlike these punks nowadays!

Playing the Race Card

There was one other disturbing postscript to the whole mess. As if this issue wasn't muddied and emotional enough, in the midst of the whole media frenzy that this war generated, one of the merchants decided to play the dreaded race card.

The merchant — who was the merchant-of-the-perpetually-broken-window — certainly had some legitimate reasons to be pissed, and was one of the leading public advocates of Measure E and the whole *"we've-got-to-do-something-about-all-these-damn-street-people-who-are-ruining-our-nice-shopping-district"* camp. He also happened to be Jewish. In the midst of all this, he loudly began claiming he had become the victim of an "anti-Semitic hate campaign" because of his outspoken role in all of this.

EVIL HORDES OF NAZI STREET PEOPLE HAD ALLEDGEDLY SCRAWLED SWASTIKAS AND ANTI-SEMITIC SLOGANS IN CHALK ALL OVER THE SIDEWALK IN FRONT OF HIS STORE!!!

NOT ONLY THAT, SOMEBODY ELSE HAD PAINTED ANTI-SEMITIC GRAFITTI ON HIS MUCH-BROKEN WINDOW!!

A hasty Press Conference/Anti-Hate Rally was announced. A big, temporary stage was constructed in front of his store. And the entire block was suddenly roped off and jammed with every big-wig politician in town making their heroic speeches publicly decrying the heinous, racist street people responsible for this outrage! And just about every TV crew and reporter showed up to chronicle this great, great event.

Now I admit, I happen to have been shocked by this whole turn of events. I will say this: If somebody happened to have called *me* a bad name, I doubt very, very much that I could have immediately summoned the cream of the Bay Area's politicians and media to climb up onto a stage and publicly speak out in my defense.

Even more disturbing, the so-called "anti-Semitic" chalking turned out to be nothing more than a swastika in a circle with a slash across it, and a brainless appeal for the Berkeley cops to STOP acting like Nazis.

And the "anti-Semitic" window graffiti — the terrifying "golden cross" that was dramatically displayed in many newspaper photos — turned out to be nothing more than a mess made by a street tweaker who was frying on speed, he had a pen with gold ink that broke in his hand, so he stupidly smeared the ink all over the window.

It's a damn good thing the FBI was called in to get to the bottom of all this! Which they were, such a big, big deal this was.

As for the merchant-of-the-oft-broken-window... It's probably not my place to speculate on how much of this farce was motivated by a legitimate fear for his safety (street people *are* a little crazy, after all), and how much of it was motivated by a desire to sway popular opinion against the street community by waging a high-profile, media smear-campaign against them. But I will say this, the whole thing left a very bad taste in a lot of people's mouths.

Surviving On The Streets

74

Epilogue

As of this writing, most of the motley crews of street people that used to hang out on the Avenue are long gone. And this one particular "hip," bohemian, Berkeley café — which was famous for running off the throngs of street people who used to congregate on the sidewalk around their outdoor café, no longer has to deal with that shit. It's very quiet nowadays. Instead, this same café now has a very nice black-and-white photo exhibit hanging up on the walls, featuring artsy portraits of all the quaint and colorful gutter punk characters who *used* to hang out on the Avenue before they all got run off.

Chapter Eleven
The Homeless Activist

Chapter Eleven
The Homeless Activist

Wedged into the weird triangle of the street people, the merchants, and the cops comes a fourth wheel: The Homeless Activist.

It may be worthwhile to take a quick look at the Homeless Activist's role in all of this, because, on the one hand, he's one of the few people who is willing to work on behalf of the homeless (most people don't give a shit, after all). On the other hand, the Homeless Activist often speaks up on behalf of the homeless and presents himself to the world as a representative of *The Homeless* (a position most of us don't remember electing the activist to occupy).

This can cause serious problems for two reasons:

1. Many Homeless Activists have never been homeless themselves and lack understanding of the actual reality of homelessness. Because of this, they often misrepresent who the homeless person is, and underestimate (often with tragic consequences) the tenuous, vulnerable position the homeless person is in.

2. Many Homeless Activists have personal agendas and political/psychological issues that they interject into the already-muddied waters of the homeless issue.

On the positive side, the Activist fulfills a crucial role for many homeless people as a bridge between the homeless world and the mainstream world. Many people are homeless simply because they can't deal

Surviving On The Streets

with The System. They are baffled (and often frightened) by the world of banks, courts of law, welfare bureaucracies, and political red tape. The Activist, who is quite at home in this world, guides the homeless person through this maze, and translates the jargon into language that the homeless person can understand.

On the negative side, the Homeless Activist all too often uses The Homeless Person as cannon fodder to attack the people they hate (always done in the name of goodness, of course, for their "compassion" for the homeless knows no bounds). They view the homeless as symbols more than individuals. And because of this, they completely misread and misrepresent the reality of homelessness.

For example, in the '80s all the liberal Berkeley politicos *loved* The Homeless, because it was a club that they could use to batter the Republicans who they hated: "Just look at the suffering of these poor unfortunate homeless, all because of those greedy, scum-sucking pigs like Reagan and Bush!!!" But now, after eight years of Clinton/Gore, these very same liberals are singing the tune of: "We've been compassionate and tolerant long enough; now maybe it's time to give some tough-love to all these bums who are cluttering up the front of our stores!!"

Let's take a look at a few of the more common types of Homeless Activists, shall we, and see if we can make even more enemies.

1. The Cop-Hating Activist

During the recent Street people vs. Merchants war on Telegraph, there were many cop-hating activists who seemed to use the street people as battering rams to attack the cops. You'd hear them trying to rouse the street rabble to their anti-cop message (something that doesn't take much rousing for the average street person): "DON'T TAKE ANY SHIT FROM THOSE PIGS! FUCK THOSE PIGS! STAND UP FOR YOUR RIGHTS! DON'T LET THOSE PIGS TELL YOU WHAT TO DO! ETC!!!"

YEAH!

Thus inspired, the formerly apathetic street person rises up and marches right over to the "pigs" to straighten them out once and for all.

This is all well and good, aside from the dismal fact that those "pigs" *can* indeed tell you what to do, and they will in fact *tell* you what to do on a regular basis if you're dumb enough to press them on the issue.

What the cop-hating Homeless Activist never seems to consider is: while he goes home to the safety of his apartment after delivering his heroic tirade, the street person goes back to his quasi-illegal homeless existence where he is vulnerable to being jacked up by the cops at any moment for almost any reason. After all is said and done, it's the street person who ends up getting hauled off to jail, not the heroic, brave activist. Which is exactly how the Measure E debacle ended up playing itself out.

But the cop-hating activist doesn't give a shit about that. What he primarily wants to do is fuck with the cops, which he's succeeded at. The fact that all the homeless kids get rounded up and thrown in jail just gives the cop-hating activist more ammunition to show just how bad those damn pigs really are, man!

The fact is, many of these street kids have enough of a chip on their shoulders about Authority Figures *already*. They don't need the activist further pushing their faces into it, rousing them up, and couching it in terms of a challenge to their manhood to book ("STAND UP FOR YOURSELF, etc...!!") As I've said before, if you want to play the Noble Martyr, you'll have plenty of opportunities on the streets to have your head crushed like a bug into the dirt. But it's not a recommended ploy from my perspective.

Chapter Eleven
The Homeless Activist

This whole cop-hating/rabble-rousing routine reminds me of a classic story from the Berkeley People's Park Riots in the late '60s. Our now-"respectable" State Senator/then-"radical" SDS agitator Tom Hayden was trying to talk some Black Panthers into shooting down a National Guard helicopter that was patrolling over People's Park. Like many of the heroic activists of the day, Hayden had fantasies of enlisting the Black Panthers as cannon fodder, as sort of a street army to attack the cops and The System. Until one of the Panthers told Hayden: *"That's just like you, Tom: Get a nigger to pull the trigger."*

Or, as another Black guy put it: "When the '60s are over, all these white activists will just cut their hair and get a good job in the system. But I'll still be Black." Just as when the homeless battles are over, today's activist goes home, whereas the homeless person is often left hanging, more precariously than ever.

For some reason, Berkeley has always attracted a lot of these cop-hating activists who long to "confront the police state." This is odd when you consider that there are, indeed, countless brutal police states all across the globe. And yet so many of these activists seem to pick Berkeley — a town with one of the softest, most liberal police forces in the world — in which to wage their heroic battle. I guess they feel they can operate most effectively as far from the frontlines as possible.

In a related aside, in regards to the phrase *"Nazi police state"* (i.e., "Mayor Shirley Dean has turned Berkeley into a *Nazi police state!!!*"): After 50 years of listening to this talk, might I suggest a short moratorium, if only for the sake of variety, on the use of that phrase. Considering the endless other police states who no doubt also merit publicity, how about substituting something like, oh, *"Stalinist Russian police state"* or *"Idi Amin Ugandan police state."* Thank you.

2. The Professional Do-Gooder, Guilt-Tripper Activist

I've met some people who rise to the position of Professional Homeless Activist — quite often due more to their acumen at wrangling government grants, than due to any particular insights or gifts they may bring to the homeless issue. Often these types come from fairly affluent, upper-middle-class backgrounds, which left them with lingering feelings of guilt towards those "less fortunate," guilt they try to assuage with their acts of do-gooderism.

Quite often these types hate their fathers and use "the poverty of the homeless" as a club to batter their fathers: "Why, all *you* care about is money and your rich friends, you greedy bastard! Whereas *I* care about the suffering of the poor!" Usually it's a way to get back at their fathers for giving them material wealth, but no love. It's all very complicated, but what do I know, I'm not a psychologist, I'm just a bum on the streets.

Now, just for the record, almost anything you do that is motivated by a sense of guilt will be worthless. This whole idea of trying to get people to reform by convincing them that they are guilty sinners NEVER works. In fact, it has the opposite effect. You cannot shame a person into being good; it only reinforces his shamefulness. The person just figures: "Well, I'm a guilty sinner anyways, so what does it matter if I indulge in one more sin?"

One Professional Homeless Activist that I know was a classic of the type. To give you an idea of her thinking, I'll relate to you just one of her guilt-inspired brainstorms.

She got this bright idea to print up these things that looked like parking tickets, only instead they were appeals to donate money to homeless causes. She would target rich-looking cars and put the psuedo-tickets on their windshields. The car owner feels sour enough when he sees this ticket on his windshield.

Surviving On The Streets

Imagine how he feels as he reads the message, which, basically, says: "How dare you spend all your money on your rich, fancy car when there are people sleeping on the streets with nothing, you greedy, selfish bastard!" GUILT GUILT GUILT.

She even had this cute idea to target a different kind of expensive car on the different days of the week; "We could have Mercedes Monday, Ferrari Friday, and so on." Now doesn't that sound like fun? Well, actually, no.

In fact, many of the car owners — who worked long and hard to afford their expensive toys — were nonplussed to find this "ticket" on their windshield telling them that they were guilty of a "violation," and that they had no right to enjoy the fruits of their labor. Furthermore, they should pony up some of their hard-earned cash immediately to rectify their moral turpitude. And you can make the check out, care of Professional Homeless Activist, Inc.

In fact, many of the disgruntled car owners used the handy address and phone number on the tickets to register their complaints with the charity agencies that were sponsoring this act of brainless altruism. Later that week I heard the Professional Homeless Activist, at her Professional Homeless Activist Office, on the phone, trying to Explain Her Position to the enraged heads of these agencies, and assuring them that, no, she certainly wasn't planning to target any more expensive cars with her little paper guilt-bombs, and that, yes, in the future she would apprise them of any future projects she cooked up before they got beyond the planning stage.

Many of the Do-Gooder Activists come from a quasi-religious background. Many seem to be trying to buy their way into Heaven with "good works," a concept that has some merit in theory, but often seems to go awry in practical application. All too often, they merely replace the Financial Materialism, which they are rebelling against, with a form of Spiritual Materialism, which isn't much better.

Even worse, their main approach to dealing with The Homeless Problem is to project a useless sense of moral righteousness onto the issue. They see it as a battle between Good vs. Evil (with them as the good ones, naturally). They turn a highly complex issue, with infinite shades of gray, into a black-or-white affair.

One local homeless paper is famous for its endless depictions of the homeless as Noble, Saintly, Long-suffering Martyrs. And the landlords, merchants, police and politicians as the embodiment of Pure Evil. Issue after issue, tirelessly, they make and remake their one-and-only point: That

1. they, the Homeless Activists, have this endless compassion for the homeless, and

2. all these other people are bad because they lack such great compassion for the homeless.

Their only solution (aside from endlessly appealing for more money for social/welfare programs) is to point the finger at all these bad people (and their list is endless) who lack their great goodness, and try to shame them into rectifying their evil ways.

All I can say is, continue on with this approach for the next twenty or thirty years, and then get back to me and let me know how effective it was. Personally, I've never understood why some people feel the need to endlessly seek out a public platform with which to declare their goodness — perhaps because they themselves feel bad and guilty about something and therefore they need to convince the world in order to convince themselves? It's all very complicated, but what do I know — I'm not a psychologist, just a guy who pisses everybody off by sharing his thoughts in a book.

3. The Political Activist

Again, I'm not trying to run anybody down. I'm just trying to point out to some activists how *counterproductive* their approach can sometimes be, and how negatively it can impact the homeless they purport to help. To see the homeless as Noble Martyrs is just as offensive as seeing them as Worthless Bums, because it's a stereotype, a symbol, it's not real, and, hence, it's useless in dealing with reality. Homeless people, in fact, are no different, no better or worse, than anybody else. Plenty of them are assholes, I can assure you.

If you had some drunken, obnoxious asshole camped out in front of *your* doorstep, smashing your windows, urinating on your sidewalk, littering the area with his trash and garbage, and attacking you physically, etc., the LAST thing you want to hear when you start to complain that something needs to be done about this, is some self-righteous activist attacking YOU, telling you that there's something wrong with YOU for lacking the great compassion that he, himself, feels for this noble victim of injustice. It only makes you MORE angry at the homeless, not less. An anger that gets directed at us.

There was one Political Activist — a good guy, I should add, who really wanted to help — who got deeply involved in the Street people vs. the Merchants war on Telegraph. He would sit at his vending table and hand out leaflets decrying the "fascist" merchants who were persecuting and scapegoating these poor innocent homeless people who just wanted to hang out in front of their stores. Unfortunately, these very same poor, innocent homeless people got so obnoxious, crazy and threatening that the noble political activist had to pack up his vending table and move across the street to get away from them. He never seemed to see the irony that most of the other merchants couldn't deal with the problem by packing up their *stores* and moving to another block.

As one of the more reasonable merchants put it, in the midst of this battle, crying out in anguish and anger: "EVERYBODY ON ALL SIDES OF THIS ISSUE HAS THEIR OWN AGENDAS! THEY DON'T LISTEN TO ANYBODY ELSE! ALL THEY CARE ABOUT IS THEIR OWN FUCKING AGENDAS!"

The main agenda of the Political Activist is The Blame Game, and they never get tired of playing it. In fact, it's amusing to see these activists when they get together; the minute they run out of a Common Enemy to blame, they begin pointing the finger at each other, embarking on endless feuds and personal vendettas, which, at the least, exhausts some of their inexhaustible energy towards a worthy target; namely, themselves.

Many of the Political Activists — like their Religious Activist cohorts — seem to have unresolved Father-issues. They project the sins of their Fathers, who they hate, onto society at large, and the Homeless Person is cast as the abused, unloved, bastard offspring. It's all very complicated, but what do I know — I'm not a psychologist, just a guy who's part of the problem and not the solution.

One Christmas Eve, a bunch of Political Activists got together in front of the store of the-merchant-of-the-oft-broken-window and serenaded him with mock Christmas carols. The lyrics were changed to liken the merchant to Ebenezer Scrooge (How's that for subtlety?), and they cataloged his many "crimes" against homelesshood. Oddly, I don't remember any homeless people I know asking these activists to sing out on our behalf. And yet, there they were.

Another time, this woman activist tried to lead the downtrodden homeless in a rousing and inspiring chant of "WE'RE HOMELESS *NOT* HOPELESS!!" Round and round she marched, to the indifferent smirks of the handful of gutter punks who happened to be lying around on the sidewalk. Finally, the activist and a few of her cohorts — thus inspired — marched off to City Hall to confront The Oppressors!

Most of these Political Activists have serious axes to grind. Unfortunately, the average homeless person has little inclination to digest their dreary manifestos regarding the relative merits of socialism vs. capitalism and how it impacts on the homeless in regards to the proletarian underclass.

Personally, I'm no big fan of this multi-national corporate system of ours. On the other hand, I think some of these activists who are making their nice-sounding speeches about a better world, should be required to listen to all of the exact same nice-sounding speeches the Russian Bolsheviks made *before* The Revolution, and then take a good, long look at the actual Reality that resulted from those words. In other words, your words mean less than shit to me, pal. And if Trotsky ever comes back, I'll ram an ice pick through his *heart* this time, to make sure that vampire doesn't come back a third time.

4. The Real Deal

I should contrast this kind of tomfoolery with the many, many Homeless Activists who are doing great work, the Food Not Bombs people, for example. Cynics say that society has "burned out" on the homeless issue, but I can assure you there are countless people out there working on behalf of the homeless, and doing great work. I'm talking about all the concerned citizens working behind the scenes to provide food, clothing (we always need clean socks), blankets, money, hot chocolate on a cold night, toiletries, etc., to people who might not be able to provide these things for themselves.

And even most of the people I've criticized in this chapter have accomplished great, great things in their own way.

All I'm saying is this: After all the talk, all the speeches, all the bluster, all the effort, all the press coverage, all the appeals to compassion, all the proposed solutions, all the brilliant theories, and all the money spent, the fact remains that the homeless problem is as unresolved as ever, and getting worse and worse every year.

I don't think I'm doing anything odd here by asking you activists to spend a few moments questioning your own assumptions and perhaps even being a little critical of your own approaches. After all, nothing we've done has really worked. Yet.

Chapter Twelve
Food: Eating Low Off The Hog

Chapter Twelve
Food:
Eating Low Off The Hog

You want to know how naïve and helpless I was when I first hit the streets of San Francisco as a teenager? Well, when my money ran out after two weeks, I literally didn't have the slightest idea of how I was going to feed myself. Not a clue. I distinctly remember wandering around the Haight in a daze, wondering if I was going to starve to death; "What am I going to do NOW?"

Fortunately, in my hour of desperation, I ran into another street person who told me about St. Anthony's Dining Hall, where they served free hot lunch, five days a week, to the hordes of hungry bums. So I rushed downtown, got a free meal, and lived to see another day. It's a triumph of the human spirit, I tell you.

Nothing is more basic to survival than eating. So let's take a look at a few of your options, campers.

1. Soup Kitchens

Again, I don't want to make this book sound like too much of a saga. You want to know how a helluva lot of people survive on the streets? They heroically cash their welfare checks on the first and live off that until their money runs out, and then they spend the rest of the month eating at the free-food joints. And there are street people who have been doing precisely that for decades.

Surviving On The Streets

But, title aside, this book isn't just about *surviving* on the streets, but *thriving* on the streets. And the key to that is to be as self-sufficient as possible. For that reason, I don't recommend the free-food joints as a first option. Or even a second.

That said, I ate at them just about every day during my first tour of homelessness. And I want to thank all the great people who made those meals possible. I was so fucked up, I doubt I would have survived without them.

These feed-the-homeless programs vary from city to city, and they give a pretty good barometer of whether a town is homeless-friendly or not. In San Francisco, the enterprising bum can easily eat seven or eight meals a day. And some of them do.

On the other hand, a city like Reno is more hard-assed. When I went through there in '76, there was one mission that offered one bowl of oatmeal a month. After that, you're on your own.

One of the ironies is, the towns that are most willing to try and do something about the homeless problem by providing these free meals and homeless services are towns that get hit with the fullest brunt of the homeless problem. Street people will, indeed, flock to a town that has a reputation for being "homeless-friendly" (though the term "friendly" is relative here — NO town wants hordes of homeless descending on it).

The more a town is willing to offer food and services to the homeless, the more the homeless will come pouring into that town. So the more the town tries to do something about the homeless problem, the bigger the problem gets. How's that for a mind-fuck? This syndrome, more than anything else, ends up taxing the psyche of even the most "liberal" cities.

Indeed these free-food places are a life-raft for many street people. Aside from the food and services, they also provide a meeting place and a sense of community for many street people. In truth, it's one of the few places where street people are legally allowed to gather together. Which should give you an inkling of the kind of constant pressure that the average homeless person faces every day, and the nebulous, shaky zone that the homeless person exists in.

Also too, for many street people, the free-food places provide the only stability in their chaotic, haphazard day-to-day existence.

That said, I generally avoid the free-food places for several reasons:

1. It's good karma to live off of your own labor as much as possible.

2. There are usually strings attached to every gift. If you demand that society feeds you, then society has a right to make demands on you — demands that you may not want imposed on you. If you can't take care of yourself, then society has a right to take care of you.

3. Many street people have become totally dependent on these free-meal programs, and they may have gotten soft and lulled into a false sense of security. What happens if these programs lose their funding? You might find yourself left in the lurch without having developed the survival skills needed to fend for yourself. And when the shit hits the fan, it may be too late to learn them then. Also, it's human nature to take things for granted. Many street people have come to treat these programs like they're entitlements. You wouldn't believe the spoiled attitude of some of these bums, bitching about the quality of food or the service; this coming from some people who probably wouldn't think of lifting a finger to work on behalf of somebody else. Street people often live the lives of children who are simultaneously overly spoiled *and* overly deprived.

4. When you become a regular member of the Food-For-Bums circuit you end up having a social scene imposed on you, and one that very well may not be to your liking. Face it; there are a lot of dysfunc-

Chapter Twelve
Food: Eating Low Off The Hog

tional assholes on the street scene. And you might not want to be interacting with some of these jokers on a day-to-day basis and having them recognizing your face and name and getting into your daily business. As Bukowski put it: "What saved me was avoiding the crowd on Skid Row. For there were the winners and the losers down there, too, just like everywhere else."

Since the recent cuts in government welfare programs, it's been the churches who have pretty much taken up the slack.

Among them, the Catholics have a pretty good reputation for serving up the grub with a minimum of proselytizing.

The Gospel Soup Kitchens, on the other hand, are generally loathed. They usually force a captive audience of hungry bums to sit through an hour-long sermon/harangue, screaming at us for being a bunch of sinners, assholes, drunks, and sodomites, before they give us our soup. One friend of mine used to hold up an alarm clock (hint, hint) whenever a particularly long-winded preacher would go over his hour time allotment.

Food Not Bombs, on the other hand, are regarded as heroes of the streets. They are one of the rare charity organizations that was spawned from within the street scene itself; most Food Not Bombs volunteers are homeless, quasi-homeless, or part of the street scene. The success of Food Not Bombs gives hope that some kind of self-sustaining community could arise from within the street scene, as opposed to living off of hand-outs from others.

I should also point out that Food Not Bombs volunteers have courageously withstood endless hassles and pressures from the police and from the legal system for the crime of serving soup to hungry people. (Though I also suspect, for some of the FNB volunteers, the opportunity to righteously joust with the police is one of the fringe benefits of the job.) In "liberal" Arcata, California, a surreal scene played itself out every night at serving time. This Black cop, starring as The Man, would endlessly harass and videotape the mostly White street peasants, as part of the town's on-going legal battle to rid Food Not Bombs and the bums from their picturesque town plaza.

2. Ground-Scoring

Ground-scoring, also known as "scrounging," is my favorite form of feeding myself. To excel at ground-scoring food, what you need is

1. a love of walking, and

2. a sharp eye, both of which I fortunately possess.

Burned-out street person that I was, I basically spent five years of my life walking around in circles. And ground-scoring gave a semblance of purpose to my largely aimless wanderings. Plus, it's fun. Every discarded paper bag and crumpled box on the sidewalk was a potential source of treasures. And you'd be surprised how many of them were actual sources of treasures.

Most of the food that I ground-scored was bags of leftovers left in to-go containers on top of garbage cans by people who had finished their meal at a nearby restaurant. Generally, I don't go rooting around inside the garbage can. But if I see a neat-looking bag of something on top of the pile, I might reach in and check it out.

Surviving On The Streets

I'm constantly amazed at the food America throws out. The other day I found a $7 cheese-steak sandwich, untouched, still wrapped in the bag, still warm, not a bite taken out of it, just sitting there by the garbage can, ten feet from the cheese-steak shop. Why it was there I have no idea. You really do wonder: Why in the world would some guy spend $7 of his hard-earned cash to buy this luxurious food item, the likes of which 90% of the people on this planet only dream of being able to consume, and then suddenly decide: "Hey! This is a $7 cheese-steak sandwich! Why the heck did I buy this? I know; I'll cleverly walk ten feet and leave it by this garbage can."

Who can figger? You realize that many people have money to burn.

Now I realize that many of my readers are squeamish about this whole concept: Eating other people's leftovers. *"Eating out of the garbage,"* for crissakes. And I admit, even as I write this chapter I'm wondering if I'm some kind of total loser for having sunk down to this level.

But let's take a moment to contemplate the crux of the ground-scored biscuit, namely: What exactly is or isn't "garbage"?

Just five minutes ago that cheese-steak sandwich was a highly coveted, $7 value. Now I'm told that the exact same cheese-steak sandwich, simply by virtue of having been handled slightly and moved ten feet, has magically been reduced to worthless "garbage."

I don't think so.

If you, the Ground-Scorer, have any sense, you'll realize you've actually found $7 sitting there on the ground. And once you developed your scrounge-eye, you start seeing those dollar bills everywhere.

In a sense, this is the essence of this whole book right here: Learning how to survive completely outside the system, dependent on no one, and without ripping anyone off, merely by skimming off the fat of the land.

I would sometimes walk around for a month with the same $5 in my pocket, which I would never spend simply because I didn't have to. Virtually everything I needed I found merely by scrounging around. As weird as that sounds.

Probably the biggest benefit I got from this was the confidence that comes from knowing that I could be dropped, blindfolded, into almost any city in America, with nothing but the shirt on my back, and that I would be able to survive, *comfortably*, totally on my own.

Don't underestimate the psychological value of this realization, or the sense of independence that it can give. For I suspect that many, many people stay stuck in the hideous roles in society they've been forced to play out, simply because they fear the consequences of ever being cut off from society.

Of course, on the other hand, I'm a bum eating out of the garbage, so what do I know?

But I do wonder about the massive phobia that society apparently has about garbage and "germs." Take garbagemen, for example. Their job is looked down upon, right? Especially when you compare it to high status occupations like lawyers, right? Well, you want to know something? I think garbagemen do one of the greatest, most essential, most worthy-of-respect jobs in America. And if you don't think so, consider this: We could probably get rid of 90% of the lawyers in America tomorrow and this country wouldn't be diminished in the least by their absence. In fact, it would probably be improved. Whereas, if we lost even 10% of this nation's garbagemen, the entire country would probably degenerate into total chaos.

I guess it all comes down to the squeamish questions of "germs." And it's funny to see how even some street hipsters react to this. You'll see street people who wouldn't think twice about sucking deeply on a marijuana pipe that's been slobbered on by every drug degenerate in town. But heaven forbid they eat an expensive restaurant sandwich that somebody else had "handled." Or, heaven forbid, that somebody else had taken a bite out of! Horror of horrors. (You could just eat the unbitten half, ya know.)

Chapter Twelve
Food: Eating Low Off The Hog

Now I don't mean to downplay this "germs" stuff. I've seen some hapless street people pulling the most rancid, rotten dreck from the bottom of trash can and shoving it into their hapless mouths. It's guys like this who give the rest of us trash-eaters a bad name.

If you lack common sense, above all avoid ground-scoring your food. For example, if you're the type who finds a plastic bottle of fruit juice — postdated two months ago — and the container has expanded like a balloon from the pressure of some weird, mysterious biological fermentation process, and you say to yourself, "My, that's unusual. I'll bet that would make for an interesting, thirst-quenching experience.", then perhaps ground-scoring is not for you.

To do it right, you have to play detective. Every piece of food you pick up, you have to ask yourself, "Where did it come from?" and "How did it get here?" For instance, if you live 40 miles from the nearest McDonalds and you ground-score a bag of greasy Big Macs, the odds are they are not fresh.

By all means, BE PARTICULAR. When I first hit the streets with no money in my pocket, I was so worried about where my next meal was coming from that I started eating everything I found. Ended up gaining fifteen pounds. I thought: Maybe I better get a damn job so I can't afford to eat so well.

Be picky about what you grab, unless you happen to be starving to death. And if you're so unresourceful that you're starving to death in America, then there's probably nothing I could tell you here that would help you, anyway.

I will say, I know many street people who have fed themselves almost exclusively, for years and even decades, from ground-scoring and Dumpster diving, with no health problems. None.

On the other hand, I don't want anyone to read this chapter and go off and eat a bunch of garbage and get really, really sick and end up suing me for everything I've got. I might end up on the streets with nothing. Ha ha.

Here are a few basic food-scrounging tips:

1. If you're not sure, DON'T.

2. If you're not sure what something is, for god sake don't try to figure out what it is by tasting it.

3. If you're not sure whether the food's gone bad or not, don't try to figure it out by turning to a friend with an engaging smile and saying, "HEY! Are you hungry?"

4. If you discover some strange, unrecognizable food-stuff that, in color, texture and odor, is unlike any other food-stuff you've ever before seen on this planet, it's *possible* that its an exotic, gourmet taste treat that you've hitherto been unacquainted with. But it's also quite possible that it's not.

5. Generally, be very cautious of anything that's been left out in the sun, especially anything with meat or mayonnaise.

6. Be careful. Don't immediately gobble the whole thing down. Take a few speculative nibbles around the edges first. Check out a little of the rice and broccoli before you gobble down the marinated chicken.

7. And anything that's been taken out of its original container or appears to have been messed with in any way, pass on it.

8. Never drink yellow-colored ground-scoured beverages.

Surviving On The Streets

It's easy after awhile, once you get the hang of this, to get carried away, and start to feel like you're frolicking through a succulent and tasty forest with exotic taste treats hanging from every tree. (And they're free!)

You take a big gulp out of a strawberry milkshake that somebody left on a ledge (it's unmelted so you know its fresh). You munch on a banana that somebody mistakenly left in the bottom of their discarded bag lunch. You gobble down a fresh chocolate croissant (still in the bag) left outside the pastry shop. You sample a few bites of the exotic pasta dish left outside the Italian restaurant (Mmmm, chicken piccatta with white wine sauce). You decide to save the pasta for a friend and eat instead the nacho chips (still crunchy) with grilled steak and sour cream that you found outside the Mexican restaurant.

But you don't want to get sloppy. Once, during a frolicking foray, I came upon a fresh coconut, sliced in half, just sitting there on the ledge. Having lived a somewhat sheltered life, I'd never actually eaten fresh coconut before. So, without thinking (mistake), I picked it up and immediately started biting into it, scraping my teeth along the white meat in the same way that one might bite into a melon slice. But I didn't realize that, unlike a melon rind, the shell of the coconut is rock-hard, and I badly chipped one of my bottom teeth in the process.

That's the worst thing that's happened to me after almost four years of living on ground-scored "garbage."

One of the great ironies of my street tour is the fact that I actually ended up eating *better*, healthier food after I started eating out of the garbage. When I lived indoors, I would generally just open up a can of cheap chili or something like that, or heat up a bland, processed-to-death frozen dinner, or eat some lettuce and vegetables that had been sitting in my fridge for a week.

But now, on the streets, I was eating expensive, restaurant-quality food, freshly purchased and prepared that day, three meals a day. And it was free. Weird.

To give you an idea of the quality of food I eat, this Italian restaurant on my route would sometimes accidentally burn the bottom of their deep-dish calzones, rendering them unsellable to the fussy customers. So they'd put them in a pink box, still warm, and leave them on top of the can outside. I'd scrape off the charred part, and happily walk off with $20 worth of restaurant food. You're welcome to consider this "garbage" so long as you leave it for me.

A few more ground-scoring tips:

1. Bus stops are great. People are munching and drinking and then the bus suddenly shows up and they rush off, leaving their food behind.

2. Sporting arenas and concerts are a great place to scrounge around, too. The trick to getting into the building is to time it so you're going in right as the crowds are leaving — the ushers are too swamped with people at that point to notice you. After every Cal basketball game I'll take a quick sweep around the stands and collect about twenty bags of barely eaten salted peanuts, unopened bottles of soda, Crackerjacks, candy, hot dogs, etc. Go Golden Bears!

3. Catered group events where they give out bag lunches is my all-time favorite score. Boy, do I lick my chops when I see bag lunches. People are finicky eaters, see. One person won't eat his sandwich. Another won't touch his orange. Etc. When I see one of these events in progress, I'll hit every garbage can within the vicinity of the group, collect about 50 discarded half-eaten bag lunches, and stock up on enough sandwiches, fruit juice, candy bars, apples, hard-boiled eggs, etc., to last me for weeks.

4. Another favorite gig is the promotional free samples that companies hand out on street corners. As I write this chapter, in fact, I'm munching on some of the 40 cans of Pringles potato chips (in assorted

flavors) that I scored the other day, as well as drinking from the packets of Nescafe Gourmet Instant Coffee that I scored on another day (what the hell, I'll give 'em a free plug since they gave me the freebies). Often, you can walk back and forth seven or eight times before the guys handing out the goods starts to recognize your face. And you can find dozens of more free samples that pedestrians took and then discarded in the nearest garbage can. In the past, I've stocked up on dozens of bottled orange juice drinks, different flavored cold coffee drinks, cases of Mountain Dew, yogurt, Power Bars, etc.

After all these years of eating out of the garbage, about the worst thing that's happened to me, aside from chipping a tooth on a coconut, is that once I took a gulp out of a ground-scored cup of coffee and noticed a cigarette butt in the bottom of the cup.

Hate Man told me he once took a gulp out of a bottle of ground-scored water and noticed, to his horror, that there was a syringe in the bottom of it.

On the other hand, the only time I've ever experienced food poisoning or any adverse health effects from anything I've eaten was this time when I ate a hamburger at this swanky restaurant THAT I ACTUALLY PAID FOR.

Overall, I consider ground-scoring a righteous occupation. It doesn't hurt anyone or put a burden on anyone. And you're eating off of your own effort: The more you search, the more you find. And in a way, it's a very spiritual endeavor. For all of the food that magically appears in front of you can come to seem like a gift from God. Which it is.

3. Dumpster Diving

I'm not too big on Dumpster diving. Mostly because I find too much food already. Plus, face it, there can be some yucky stuff in those dumpsters, and I only get about one shower every six months, so I can't afford to get any more dirty and smelly than I already am.

But I do know many people who have been living quite well for years from hitting the Dumpsters behind restaurants and supermarkets. For a fuller treatment of this subject, I recommend as a companion piece to this book, *The Art & Science of Dumpster Diving,* by John Hoffman, available from Loompanics.

4. Table-Scoring

This is another one of my favorite eating resources. Table-scoring food off of restaurant tables is a subtle art that requires a bit of finesse to be done properly. Table-scoring is akin to finding a crash spot; it's easy to get away with it once — to grab and run — the trick is to be able to go back into the same restaurant and get away with it over and over.

The first time I tried it was a complete disaster. I spotted this half-eaten burrito just sitting there at an empty table in this Mexican restaurant. So I rushed into the restaurant, grabbed the burrito, and was headed for the door, when this woman came out of the restroom: **"WHAT ARE YOU DOING WITH MY BURRITO?!!"**

Oops.

All I could do was hand her burrito back and slink out of there with my tail between my legs.

Surviving On The Streets

The second time I tried table-scoring, I fucked up for a different reason. I spotted an almost-untouched plate full of eggs, ham and home fries at this coffee shop. But this time I decided to play it cool. So I waited and waited, to make completely sure the patrons weren't coming back to claim their leftovers. But just before I grabbed the food, the busboy came by and hauled off all that great food into the trash.

These two stories illustrate the inscrutable, contradictory, Zen koan of table-scoring, namely: ***"Look before you leap, and yet he who hesitates is lost."***

To deal with these problems, I developed a few basic table-scoring techniques.

First and foremost, remember always the mantra of so much of street life: **Invisibility is next to godliness**. The mistake most table-scorers make is, they march into a restaurant and immediately start grabbing food off of the plates. The worst table-scorers are the drunken gutter punks who come clanking in with their chains and purple Mohawks, scrounging loudly from table to table. Remember: The one point where you're most noticeable is when you make your *entrance*. People's eyes are naturally drawn to a moving target after all. So that's the make-it-or-break-it point where you have to be as unobtrusive as possible.

After making my inconspicuous entrance, I would sit down at the table that I was interested in scoring. But I wouldn't sit down directly in front of the plate of leftovers I wanted to score. If at all possible, I would sit down in the chair *next* to it, and put my backpack down on the chair directly in front of the plate. Then I'd perform a little pantomime, pushing the plate away, as if I was clearing a space while I waited for my own order to arrive. Next, I would take out a newspaper or my notebook and kill about five minutes. This gives me some time to scope out the joint and make sure nobody's onto my act before I strike. Usually, after five minutes, I've blended in with all the other faceless diners, most of whom by that time will have forgotten that I wasn't the original occupant of that table. Only at that point will I start eating from the plate of leftovers.

This little act serves two basic purposes:

1. By waiting five minutes I can make sure that the original diner isn't going to come back and reclaim his plate of food. Nineteen times out of twenty he doesn't come back, but that 20th time can really kill you. If he does come back, I can just say, "Oh excuse me, I thought you had left," and move to another table.

2. Putting my backpack on the seat *in front of* the plate of leftovers while I'm waiting, fools the busboy into thinking that the original diner has merely stepped out temporarily and he'll be back. So the busboy won't haul the plate away when he's making his rounds.

It all sounds very complicated and ridiculous when I try to explain it here. On the other hand, I've been eating expensive restaurant meals for free for four years now, so what the hell.

The best time to strike is when the restaurant is fairly crowded and the workers are too busy and preoccupied to notice you. But *not* when it's so crowded that you're getting in people's way.

Cafeteria-style restaurants where you order food at the counter are the kind you hit. Don't even consider going into joints with waitress service. If the waitress sees some bum hovering over her table full of tips, she'll come after you with a butter knife. Or worse.

The art of table-scoring is akin to performing a magic trick; the key is the diversion of people's attention. You have to be acutely aware of what every person in that room is noticing, especially the employees. The amazing thing is, how little people really notice. For example, you might be sitting in a room somewhere right now, and you might not even notice the wall right in front of you, even though your eyes are staring right at it. You only notice it now that I bring it up. In that way, you can learn to control what people notice. Or don't.

Chapter Twelve
Food: Eating Low Off The Hog

One of the best pieces of advice I ever got was: Just act like you belong, and most people will assume you do. Most people are too preoccupied with their *own* feelings that they don't belong in this world to notice whether you do.

Another favorite place to table-score is sports bars. Usually, the sports fan just buys his food as a prop to play with while he watches the big game. And when the game suddenly ends — especially when his team loses and he's too heartbroken to eat — he usually rushes immediately to the nearest exit, leaving behind plenty of half-eaten, extra-large pizzas with everything on 'em.

Catered events are another great place to score. If, say the Optometrist Society of America is having a convention — hey, I got glasses, you got glasses — I'll grab a plate at the head of the buffet table and blend in with the crowd. These are usually groups of strangers, so strange little you will blend right in.

Also, after these events are over, they usually leave behind tray after tray of leftovers, most of which are deli-fresh delicacies, which you can discreetly grab after everybody has left. Again, it's all in the timing — there's that crucial moment when the people have just left, but before the janitors have arrived. These trays of food make for great late-night street feasts with your crew of street pals.

Occasionally, but only rarely, I'll get busted. One time I was all prepared to help myself to a plate of food at a Cal Alumni buffet, when this guy behind me tapped me on the shoulder and said, "I'm sorry, this is a private affair."

To which I was tempted to say, "Hey, I'm a private person, what's the problem?" and leave with my dignity intact. But sometimes it's better to just leave.

The key to crashing these restaurants and parties, of course, is the ability to blend in anonymously with the crowd. Which brings up an important point of street life. Many of the tips I'm laying out here are not for everybody. Like all the creatures in nature, you have to adapt and develop the particular survival techniques in accordance with your own nature. And what works for me, might not work for you, and vice versa.

For example, if you sport a beard down to your belly, wear four layers of overcoats, and are lugging five big bags of crap on your back, it is highly unlikely you'll be able to successfully crash the Young Republicans annual picnic.

On the other hand, around Christmas time, all the do-gooders will be actively searching for people that look exactly like you so that they can shower you with turkey dinners, gifts, and cash, while a bland anonymous-looking person like me will miss out on that one. Make your weirdness work for you.

Some table-scoring tips:

1. Table-scoring is only a victimless crime if you're not hurting anybody. If you're annoying the customers and hurting the business, then you're doing it wrong.

2. Don't mess with the busboys. If the choice is between getting in the busboy's way and getting your food, pass on it. Generally, the busboys are poor like you, and sympathetic to your plight. But not if you're an annoying bum complicating their job.

3. College campuses are great. Thank God for dinky little co-eds with rich parents. They'll take three bites out of an expensive meal and then freak out about ballooning up ten extra pounds and generously leave the rest of the meal for you.

4. If you can afford it, buy something cheap like a cup of coffee first. That affords you the all-important cover of being a Paying Customer Who The Employees Have To Be Nice To. Plus, you can sit there and casually scope out the joint at your leisure before you strike.

Surviving On The Streets

5. If you can, leave a nice tip in the tip jar at the counter. There's something classy about scrounging a table full of expensive leftovers that were just going to end up in the garbage anyway, and then leaving a $2 tip. Just because you're a bum doesn't mean you can't have class.

6. Don't forget to check out the dirty dish hamper that's usually in the back of the room. Usually I go back there anyway looking for the newspapers they leave there. So that provides a cover as you poke around for leftovers.

7. And for godsake, if you happen to get caught by the management, don't make a scene. Just leave.

One time I was discreetly eating a table-scored salad at this restaurant and this obnoxious street woman came in with her little kid. She's making a lot of noise, and she's reaching over customers' plates — "Excuse me, are you going to eat that?" — and appealing to guilt — "Could you spare any leftovers for my *hungry child?!!*" — and generally making an ass of herself.

When the owner came over to kick her out, she started making an indignant, self-righteous speech about what a greedy, selfish bastard he was who was making all this money and throwing away all this good food while poor, innocent, homeless people *like her* were starving on the streets! Why, she was going to write an exposé for a local homeless paper and expose his worthless ass to the world!

For crissakes, people, show some sense. The owner knows all about the DOZENS of free food programs, as well as the welfare checks, the food stamps, the food banks, etc., some of which come out of his profits every week, and he might *already* be pissed about that. So why compound the situation with your bullshit speeches. All you do is mess it up for the next poor slob who tries to table-score in there. Just leave.

Another time, I was sitting in the same restaurant eating a table-scored salad when this punk kid came in and started circling around the place looking for food. I happened to have two plates of food in front of me, and he seemed pretty discreet, so I silently gestured him that he could have one. He gratefully took a plate and walked out the door with it. Then he sat down on the sidewalk across the street, in clear view of everyone in the restaurant (mistake #1) and started happily munching down his meal.

Then, he realized he forgot to get a fork, so he marched back into the restaurant and grabbed one from the silverware tray at the counter (mistake #2) and went back outside to finish his meal.

A few minutes later, two cops came in and conferred with the owner in the back. Then they went outside and confronted the kid and started writing him up a $120 ticket for stealing food.

I'm watching this scene unfolding from my window seat eating my own table-scored meal, when I notice, to my horror, that the punk kid is pointing to me and saying something to the cops. He's trying to get out of it by snitching me off (mistake #3).

The cops came back in and said to me, "That kid says that the plate of food was yours and that you said he could take it."

"I don't know anything about that," I said. "I'm just sitting here eating my lunch."

The cops went back out and wrote up the kid a ticket, which was a drag. But the weirdest thing was, the whole time this was going down, I'm sitting there gobbling down my own stolen meal, right in front of the cops, the owner and the whole world.

There's a postscript to this story that may be instructive of something: (Then again, I'm starting to wonder if this whole thing is just bullshit, writing a whole chapter about grabbing food from the garbage and shit, for crissakes. Geez. Maybe I'm just nuts.)

This radical homeless activist who sold bumper stickers at his vending table across the street from this restaurant got all indignant when he heard about this great example of police oppression.

"Fucking greedy capitalist pigs calling the pigs to arrest a poor, innocent homeless kid for taking food that they were just going to throw in the garbage, etc., etc.!!!"

To which I said: "Hey, if these poor, innocent homeless kids had been grabbing bumper stickers off of *your* vending table and walking down the street with them, I'm sure you'd be pissed too. I see plates and silverware from restaurants lying in the gutter all up and down the Ave. Half of these kids can't even bother to bring the damn plates back. I don't blame the owner for being pissed."

If there's one thing I'd like to see street people quit doing, it's the knee-jerk reaction of making saints out of the homeless and demonizing "the oppressors." Because once you start doing that, it can just as easily be flipped around the other way, my friend.

Some of these gigs I've been milking for years. There was this one guy who came into this coffee shop every morning and every night at the same time, ordered a cup of black coffee, and sat at a table in the back reading his newspaper. Never even drank his coffee, just used it to buy the table. I had it down like clockwork coming in just as he was leaving, and helping myself to the coffee. This went on for years until the guy had the nerve to cramp my style by switching to tea.

Another friend of mine buys a cup of coffee at Noah's Bagels every morning, keeps the to-go cup, and sneaks back in regularly during the course of the day to discreetly pour himself cups full of milk from the creamer containers.

I admit that grabbing food off of restaurant tables is a quasi-illegal act, and maybe, at the least, in poor taste. But I still feel ultimately, the real crime is all the great food that goes to waste.

5. Restaurants at Closing Time

This is another righteous gig. It's 100% ecologically sound, saves waste, and helps people at the expense of no one. Plus it's good karma.

Restaurants throw out an ungodly amount of food at closing time. And many of them will be happy to give it to you if you approach them nicely at closing time, and don't unduly inconvenience them or try and guilt-trip them.

Generally, most nights, the various members of my street crew will hit a bunch of joints at closing time. It's typical on any given night to round up:

1. A big bag of hot, leftover pizza from a local pizza joint (Hi, Greg!);
2. Several jugs of hot coffee, chocolate syrup, and steamed milk from a local café;
3. A box full of day-old pastries and donuts from a local donut shop;
4. A bag of hot baked potatoes, yams, broccoli, and other fixings from a local potato stand;
5. A big, garbage-sized bag full of buttered popcorn from a local movie theatre;

Plus, whatever specialties we've happened to have scrounged up that day.

I encourage restaurants to do more of these kinds of gigs. The food you don't throw out is money you won't have to shell out for food stamps and charity food programs. Everyday, restaurants throw out enough food to feed every homeless person in America. Salvaging some of it is a righteous deal that requires very little effort.

Surviving On The Streets

There's also something righteous about getting together with all your street friends at the end of the day for spontaneous, communal street feasts. Everybody contributes a little something, and everybody benefits. It's the closest I've ever come to communal living.

Compare that to my years of isolated, anonymous apartment living where I didn't even know any of my next-door neighbors' names, let alone borrow the proverbial cup of sugar from any of them.

Well, all this writing about food has got me hungry. Excuse me while I go and scrounge up some lunch.

(P.S. I scored a delicious half of turkey-on-whole-wheat-with-horseradish sandwich, four chunks of fresh pineapple, two slices of pizza, and a half-a-cup of coffee. Bon appétit.)

Chapter Thirteen
Money
or... Get a Job You Bum!

As I write this book, I realize how difficult it is to make any generalizations about street people. And yet, one general truth is that most street people are alienated from the normal, mainstream 9-to-5-work-world. It's one of the great defining lines that separate street people from the rest of society.

(And yet even here there are many exceptions. A friend of mine is working two jobs, as a waitress and cashier for Tower Records, and her boyfriend is working full-time as a dishwasher. And yet they both find themselves homeless and living in their car thanks to the insane Bay Area housing market.)

In my own case, I've never been able to adjust to working at mainstream jobs, primarily due to my inability to relate comfortably with other people. Plus, I'm lazy, I guess. This has been one of the main factors that relentlessly pushed me towards the streets. For ten years I managed to scratch out a meager living as a freelance cartoonist. But then one morning I woke up and sat at the drawing board and nothing was funny. The next thing I knew, I was sitting in the dirt under a tree, wrapped in a ratty sleeping bag, wondering how the hell I got there and where I was going next.

There are a variety of ways to make money and support yourself on the streets. Let's explore a few of them:

1. Panhandling

The classic. For many street people, panhandling is their primary source of income. On the downside, more than any gig, it inspires the "Get-a-job-you-bum!" routine from indignant passersby, whereas many street people CONSIDER panhandling their job.

Panhandling has a noble lineage going all the way back to the beginning of time and has been practiced by some of the great saints and spiritual pilgrims from time immemorial, as well as plenty of outright bums, too.

How much money you make from panhandling is a subject of considerable conjecture. Like all businesses, it depends on such factors as location and the product you're selling, namely, yourself. It's not unusual for a cute young chick with an innately sympathetic appeal (Nature has equipped waifs with a built-in advantage here) to reel in $10, $20, or even $30 in an hour. Whereas, less sympathetic types might sit at the same spot for an hour and take in only a couple of bucks. Or less.

Obnoxious or pushy panhandlers are a disaster for all concerned, ruining the climate for all beggars. You can see the victim of aggressive panhandling silently vowing to never fork over another nickel to those god damn bums ever again.

On the other hand, a mild-mannered friend of mine would sit at the same spot every night for about two hours, just quietly sitting there with a cup out while he read a book. He considered it "putting in his time," just like a job. And he sat there until he collected $2.50 for his evening bottle of wine, and another buck to cover his morning coffee. Then he'd retire to his campsite for the evening.

I'm not a big fan of "clever" panhandling lines. Let's face it; there's nothing particularly clever about sitting on your ass asking to be given something for nothing. And the standard "clever" lines, like: *"Spare a million dollars for a mansion and a yacht?"* or *"Spare change for marijuana research?"* gets less clever after the thousandth time you've heard them.

But I like the hippie chick who partially spells out the word "LOVE" on her blanket with coins, and then urges passersby to *"Help me make love on my blanket."* That gets their attention!

A less successful act is the one performed by this 250-pound street woman with an ass the size of a barn, who comes waddling up to you with a beseeching look on her face and implores you: *"Spare any change... FOR SOME FOOD!"* It's hardly a winning appeal. Now *"Spare change for some Slim Fast?"*, that one might go over.

Another guy I know who doesn't quite grasp the concept is this Black guy who angrily sneers at each passing pedestrian: *"Spare change, ya' red-assed snake!"* Even odder, occasionally people would actually give him some spare change. To which he'd say: *"Thanks! Ya' red-assed snake!"*

Another guy I know did quite well with the line: *"You can spit on me for a dollar,"* making himself some money while at the same time providing a harmless, though disgusting, outlet for society's ever-growing hostilities.

Some guys put a lot into their panhandling routine, almost like a stand-up comedian or performance artist, giving the customer their money's worth. The legendary Gypsy Catano used to stand on his hands for hours while his partner would intone, *"Help this man get back on his feet!"*

One line I particularly loathe is the *"Spare change — spare smile"* routine. Like I'm supposed to please you by smiling on command. It's bad enough that you're asking a stranger for money, but now you want to hit off of my personal emotions as well? If you really want to see people smiling why don't you do something that inspires genuine happiness. Begging people for their money rarely inspires those feelings of unmitigated joy.

Overall, I can't recommend panhandling, simply because the world is not going to beat a path to your door, and it's even less likely to beat a path to your spot in the gutter. Get off your ass and do something.

2. Drug-Dealing

Every year, I'll see a new crop of street kids hit the scene and take a shot at this venerable favorite. Most of them are just trying to sling $20 sacks of pot with enough left over to pay for their own weed, and maybe a few bucks on the side.

But there will always be those eternally optimistic few who hit the streets with big-time fantasies of being The Big Dope Dealer. It is their dream, their life's goal. And they invariably play the whole fantasy out to its bitter conclusion, namely, jail. Or did you really think you'd be that one-in-a-thousand exception?

At first it seems almost too good to be true. (Hint: it is.) It's one of those few areas of the street economy — with the exception of those perennial favorites, pimpin' and whorin' — where the general principles of Capitalist Economics 101 actually work. You can make big bucks relatively quickly.

It can suck you in, because the money can seem seductively easy and alluring. At first. Plus, you get to enjoy that heart-pumping, gut-wrenching, adrenaline-rush of excitement that comes from the thrilling possibility of being jumped or busted (or worse) at any moment. And face it; most of street life is deadeningly dull, so you gotta take your kicks where you find 'em.

But sooner or later, the law of averages catches up with you. Your nerves start to get frayed from the constant stress and constant paranoia, and from the constant over-doping you do to combat the stress. Eventually, you'll get sloppy, or just get caught in the wrong place at the wrong time, and get busted or badly burned.

And no, it will do you little good to stand in front of The Judge and try to explain how you're merely trying to raise the consciousness of the human race, your Honor, and save the Planet Earth, our Divine Mother, by spreading ten million hits of LSD to the multitudes at a fair and reasonable retail rate. Oh no. Even Jerry Himself cannot save you.

And if the judge don't get you, there are plenty of violent thugs that will. Needless to say, the drug scene is fraught with rip-offs, burn-artists, and violence, as well as plenty of nutty people who are loose in the head from too many years of too much dope. Any combination of which can take you down, and take you down badly. Oh yes. Surviving on the streets, indeed. One mishap and your life might become permanently derailed. I'm just saying, consider that now, not later.

3. Selling Your Ass

This is a perennial option for the cute, young boys and girls of the streets, as well as a source of endless confusion: If you're homeless, you're always looking for a place to sleep. And if you're young and cute, there will always be people offering you a place to sleep.

Like the drug scene, the sex-for-money scene is one of the more volatile scenes on the streets. It's a regular mini-tornado leaving a trail of havoc in its wake. I've read studies that maintained that over half of the street prostitutes working San Francisco's Tenderloin district were seventeen or under, most of whom are teenage runaways.

I put out a fairly sexless vibe (not always by choice) so I've pretty much been immune to this whole scene. Even when I was a teenage male on the streets of San Francisco in the late 70s — that great period of sexual smorgasbord, post-Sexual Revolution, pre-AIDS, where the homos were jumping on anything that moved in big, huge piles of throbbing flesh — I rarely got hit on. There was one old gay guy who'd troll around Market Street on his bike and try to entice me into coming back to his apartment to, like, get really, really high. Offers, for the record, I politely declined. But fortunately, I never experienced the constant sexual pressure that some of the street kids get.

Like with drugs, the sex scene is one of the few ways that you can make decent money on the streets. Plus, if you're so inclined, you'll have plenty of outrageous and disgusting stories to shock your grandchildren with in your sunset years. And you'll also be able to write a much more entertaining chapter than I'm capable of doing here.

On the downside, the short-term benefits rarely out-weigh the long-term effects. It's a fairly bitter, unhappy ending.

4. Attendant for the Handicapped

This gig is tailor-made for the responsible homeless person. Quadriplegics often need someone to turn them over several times a night while they're sleeping (so they don't get bed sores). So a homeless person gets a place to sleep indoors, as well as making a couple of bucks.

5. Scrounging

This is one of my favorite gigs: Walking around looking for cool stuff. Scrounging, ground-scoring, and Dumpster diving. All that's required is a love of walking and a sharp eye.

Scrounging gave a semblance of purpose to my somewhat aimless wanderings. The image of me, walking back-and-forth, back-and-forth, down the streets of Berkeley, will probably remain etched in hundreds of people's memories for decades to come. "There he is, Mom! AGAIN!"

There are many street people who don't get welfare checks or use the charity agencies, and yet manage to survive almost exclusively from scrounging. As the ever-resourceful and supremely self-sufficient Hate Man put it: "I prefer just digging in the trash to find what I need. I feel a lot of the social agencies are a parent/child set-up. I prefer the trash. It's floating down the river. I don't owe anybody anything."

I'm constantly amazed that you can find virtually anything you're looking for — no matter how obscure — just by scrounging around. Once I was looking for a display rack to sell calendars at our vending tables. A few days later I happened to find exactly what I was looking for lying by a dumpster behind a department store. It even had "CALENDARS FOR SALE" in big, fancy letters on the side. This is not untypical of the great truth of scrounging: You will find what you're looking for (so be careful what you look for).

Plus, it's fun. Every discarded box and bag on the sidewalk becomes a potential treasure waiting to be unwrapped. And a surprising number of them are actual treasures. You know what they say: *"There's a goldmine in every garbage can."* Well, that's not quite true. Mostly there's just garbage. But you will find enough cool stuff to make it more than worth your while to poke around.

Most scroungers have their field of expertise. I'm pretty good at finding books and records that I can turn into cash by reselling at the local used book and record stores. On the other hand, I don't have much

Chapter Thirteen
Money
or... Get a Job You Bum!

luck selling used clothes (my knowledge of fashion doesn't go much beyond finding shirts and pants that sort of fit me).

If you have some mechanical ability, you can make good cash fixing up and selling the endless supplies of junked out stereos, Walkman's, and bicycles.

As a warning, though, if you happen to end up as the middleman in these transactions, be wary of hot merchandise. If some street bro' comes up to you with a big box full of brand new CDs, or a big stack of hundred-dollar coffee table books that he "found" somewhere, and now wants you to sell them for him at the local used book store, you could end up with some serious explaining to do.

Most of my regular scrounging gigs range from the trivial to the even-more-trivial. But if you string enough of these gigs together they can add up to, well, slightly-above-trivial.

For instance, the Hate Man collects coupons from Marlboro and Camel cigarette packs, which he sells for ten cents each to a guy who collects them. In the course of my daily wanderings, I can easily find twenty coupons a day, so that's $2. Or, I can trade them with Hate Man for ten cigarettes. I've created this out of nothing, because I'm just walking around anyway. As an added bonus, as I'm picking up the discarded cigarette packs, I'll regularly come across an almost full pack of cigarettes — often with an expensive lighter left inside the pack (I've got a collection of about twenty of 'em).

I used to wonder why I kept finding so many almost-full packs of cigarettes discarded on the sidewalk. The only thing I could figure was that smokers were regularly trying to kick the habit with a dramatic gesture of tossing their packs into the garbage. (You often find yourself in a philosophical mood, wondering what it all means and what it says about the state of humanity in general, as you sift through society's garbage. For instance, did somebody really think that the world needed that many Dan Fogelberg and Barbra Streisand records?)

It's important that you develop these regular little scores because they keep you alert while you're waiting for your big scores. Like: the ten pairs of Levi 501s dumped outside the Goodwill that I can sell for $5 each at the Levi Outlet ($50). Or the big stack of porno DVDs and Chinese editions of *Playboy* and *Penthouse* that somebody got tired of ($75). Or the big box of brand new blank videocassettes, still in the wrapper, that some company threw out because they ordered 60-minute cassettes and got 30-minute ones instead ($50). Or the Walgreen's Dumpster that regularly contained hundreds of dollars worth of merchandise that they couldn't sell but didn't want to bother to ship back to the warehouse. Etc.

In the meantime, while I'm walking around biding my time, I know every candy machine in town that I can jiggle for free candy, every newspaper rack where I can get a free newspaper, every payphone where I can count on change in the coin-return slot. I know this all sounds ridiculous. So go ahead and laugh as I take off my shoes and wade into the fountain to pull out $1.47 in coins. Unlike a lot of street people, I've always got $5 or $10 bucks in my pocket. Plus, clean feet.

For a while I had this one payphone on my route with a jammed coin-return slot. By jiggling a plastic spoon into the slot, I could retrieve $2 or $3 a day in change. As far as I know, this is legal since the change was being returned to the customer anyway, and hey, I'm a customer, too. On the other hand, ripping the heads off parking meters with a chain saw and making off with $80 worth of quarters is definitely illegal, so be forewarned.

There was another great payphone that we discovered which, if you dialed 411 and then quickly hung up, would immediately release ALL the change in the machine. Usually at least $10 a pop. It was like owning our own personal slot machine for several weeks, until word got around and there were always ten other bums waiting in line to use that phone.

Which is an important point: Resist the temptation to blab about your personal scams. Nothing blows the goldmine quicker than hordes of homeless horning in on your fragile act. Which is why I'm not going

Surviving On The Streets

to reveal most of my choice gigs here. Plus, most of my particular gigs wouldn't be applicable to your specific environment anyway. But I will reveal one of my favorites just to illustrate some of the basic principles:

At the end of every semester the college students sell back their used textbooks at the various campus bookstores. But if the book isn't going to be part of the curriculum next semester, the campus bookstore won't buy it back, so that $75 book is now worth zero. At least that's what most of the students think, so they just dump the books in a big recycling bin to be hauled off to the trash. What the students don't realize is that many of the other used bookstores in town *will* buy those books. For a solid month I'll make $20, $30, $50, or even as much as $120 a day selling those books, as wells as hundreds of dollars in trade slips (I haven't had to actually pay for a book in years). Not bad for a half hour's work.

I also ended up with a huge surplus of great books that weren't quite good enough for the used bookstores to buy but were of value to somebody nonetheless. Boxes and boxes of them. Again, it's astounding the surplus of merchandise just lying around like ripe fruit. So I dumped them on the table at the Ave, put up a sign that said "**BOOKS 25¢**" along with a little donation cup. I didn't even have to bother to watch the table. I just cruised by and collected the coins ever hour or so, which averaged about $100 a weekend, a nice little goldmine for very little effort.

Are you starting to get the idea here? The trick is to be able to spot a potential situation first, before anyone else does. I'm not sure how much this trait can be taught. There are some people who are good at following orders, following directions. And then there are other people who can make up their own games. All I can tell you is, the opportunities are out there if you keep your eyes open.

Even a stupid little thing like picking up pennies from the sidewalk, you start doing that, and pretty soon you'll notice how many fives, tens, and twenty dollar bills you'll also start finding, simply because you're looking for them.

You just never know what's out there next, and that's part of the fun. A guy I know was going through a box of some old man's clothes that had been free-boxed outside a Goodwill. Imagine his surprise when he opened up a shoebox and found a wad of twenties adding up to $1,200 stuffed in the shoe. And then another $1,200 in the other shoe. Who knows why. (One plausible theory was that the old guy didn't trust banks so he kept his cash stashed in his closet, and after he died, they free-boxed his junk without realizing it.)

Another time I spotted an expensive-looking briefcase sticking out of a garbage can. I opened it up and there was a shiny, almost brand-new revolver and pistol in it. I'm sure that there was a story behind that one. I decided not to find out what it was. I closed the briefcase and put it back in the garbage can.

Remember the Cardinal Rule of street life: **If you're not sure, *don't*.** I didn't have any connections for selling the guns, and I didn't want the complications of stashing potentially hot items. So I passed. On the other hand, if I wanted to be legit, I could've taken the guns down to the police station and filed a claim in the event the original owner didn't claim them. But that would violate a basic agreement I have with the police, namely: I ignore the police and the police ignore me. It's a fine agreement, and I'm more than willing to continue to hold up my end of the bargain.

Promotional give-aways are another favorite gig. Keep in mind, when you're out on the streets 24 hours a day, you're privy to everything that's going on all over town. And you're usually first in line when opportunity knocks. Every semester they give out these promotional boxes full of sample merchandise to the new students. Most people take out one or two items and discard the rest of the box. By combing the outlying trash cans you can easily pick up twenty or thirty boxes. I now have enough shaving cream, razors, shampoos, soap, toothpaste, etc., to last me the next two years (and enough condoms to last me the next two lifetimes at the rate I'm going).

Another campus gig is, I'll scrounge through the aisles of the big lecture halls at the end of the day and stock up on discarded pens, markers, notebooks, etc., that were just headed for the janitor's dustbroom anyway.

What I'm doing is no different than a real job. Except that *you* go to work, get a paycheck, and then buy the stuff you want, whereas I go directly to the source. It's just like shopping, except you don't have to pay for it. The streets are your supermarket.

Are you starting to get the idea how you can supply most of your basic needs without resorting to welfare or charity or even money? It's almost a form of magic — pulling valuable items out of thin air.

In truth, there's a very mystical feel to scrounging. As the man said, "Seek and ye shall find." These treasures keep appearing in your path, as if put there by God, which in fact they are. Scrounging embodies the two great tenets of all spiritual disciplines, namely: **Faith** (that what you seek will appear by the grace of God), and **Personal Effort** (you've got to get off your ass to earn these gifts, ironically enough).

I find so much good stuff that half of it I end up giving away to my friends, which engenders goodwill, so they in turn kick down to me some of the cool stuff they find.

If I had to come up with one formula for dealing with street life, it would be: **The more you give, the more you get back. (Though don't cast your pearls before bums.)**

The Indians had a "superstition" that dramatized this concept: After eating a fish they would throw the bones back into the ocean where they caught it, "to grow another fish." In order for the gods of ground-scoring to smile upon you it's important that you give back as much as you take. Make sure you leave that ground-scored newspaper neatly folded for the next person in line when you're done with it. And those dumpster dived toys you found but have no use for, make sure to leave them for some Mom who can.

And don't forget: There can be a fine line between ground-scoring and stealing. I like to keep a surplus supply of blankets, sleeping bags, and backpacks, because these items are always in hot demand on the streets. But if you happen to find these items laying around somewhere, be damn sure that they're truly abandoned and up for grabs before you grab them. Nothing is worse than stealing from another homeless person's stash. If you're not sure, don't. It's better to err on the side of caution. I've held back on grabbing a nice down sleeping bag lying on the sidewalk, only to watch as the garbage man picked it up and dumped it in the back of his garbage truck. Oh well. There'll be another score down the street.

6. Vending

Street vending is another job that's compatible with the homeless lifestyle, providing what you're selling doesn't require a lot of stuff to carry around and store. There are the traditional street vending gigs, such as tarot reading, jewelry making, and doing henna tattoos, as well as many other unique and ingenious vending gigs.

One friend of mine makes $10 to $20 a day twisting palm branches into neat, little green roses. It's a form of magic, to be able to take a useless branch that's just lying there, and pull dollar bills out of thin air.

Another friend of mine with a guitar and a repertoire of '60s rock songs, can walk into virtually any town in America and drink for free all day long. And wouldn't YOU like to have that skill?

My partner B.N. Duncan and I were famous for running one of the worst-selling vending tables in the history of Berkeley vending tables (though around Christmas we made big bucks).

Mostly we sold street-related artwork and publications. Anyone who has tried to sell self-published art knows what a tough gig this is. But occasionally we'd hit on products that would make good money, such as our annual **Telegraph Street Calendar**, a classic photo-documentary of the local street scene, disguised as a souvenir item. Another good-selling item was as compilation CD we recorded featuring local street musicians. And another year we put our beautiful sets of Christmas cards done by different homeless artists on a linoleum press.

But even when we weren't making money, the vending table was a valuable asset functioning as a living room or clubhouse for us to hang out in. During the police sweeps of '98, when cops were running all the other street people out of town, the table and vending license provided a semblance of legitimacy that spared us from police harassment. (Which is another important tip: If you at least *look* like you're productive, you're much less likely to get hassled by the cops.)

One year the Dan Rather *CBS News* did a national feature on our **Street Calendar**, which inspired an unexpected windfall in big sales. (People will buy anything if it's *"as seen on TV!,"* I guess.) One of the unexpected consequences of this was that we began to hear grumblings from certain quarters about how we were "exploiting the homeless." *"You're making thousands of dollars off of our photos, man!"* There's a certain segment of the street population that never tires about bitching about "poverty pimps," etc. Nothing infuriates a bum more than the idea that somebody might be bumming off of *them!* So we got guilt-tripped into kicking down lots of the money. But it was funny, because a few years later when we put out an issue of the calendar that bombed and ended up *losing* thousands of dollars, not one of those people offered to kick down money to us because we had *lost* money on their photos.

7. Recycling

Bottle and can recyclers are the true heroes of the street scene. This is good, hard, honest work that provides a valuable service to society and the ecology. Some of these guys are lugging from 100 to 500 pounds in their shopping carts. Most of them make about $10 to $20 a day, but you can make up to $50 if you develop good, regular accounts. As an added bonus, recyclers are first in line to discover all the great Dumpster treasures.

Recycling is one of the few legitimate jobs that is compatible with the homeless lifestyle and personality. Society is putting a lot of effort into coming up with programs that help the homeless find gainful employment — as well they should. But in coming up with these job programs, they rarely take into account the limiting factor of the oddball/outlaw/cowboy personality of the average homeless person, or the difficulties of the homeless environment. Because, face it: you can't exactly pull yourself out of your sleeping bag in the morning, comb the dirt and leaves out of your hair, and report to work as a teller at Bank of America.

Recycling is a good model for the types of work that the homeless are capable of adapting to, and the hard labor that many of them are willing to do. Hopefully, more jobs can be developed along these lines.

8. Welfare

In the '60s, Abbie Hoffman wrote a book called *Steal This Book,* in which he listed all the different scams that the hippies could hit on to freeload off of society. One aspect Hoffman was keen on was all the different ways you could leech off of the welfare system. One of the quaint notions of the times was that

Chapter Thirteen
Money
or... Get a Job You Bum!

if everybody got on welfare we could bankrupt The System, man. And then this grand, new, revolutionary society would arise from the ashes.

Well, Hoffman and his ilk were pretty specific when it came to their plans for trashing society — and we've come a long way towards that end. But not nearly so specific when it came to exactly how this great new society was magically going to rise from the ashes. And I'm here to report that, as of this writing, that new society has not yet emerged.

Now I want to be clear about the premise of this book. I'm in no way advocating "the homeless lifestyle" as a way for bums to comfortably leech off the rest of society. This book is designed for people who, due to circumstances mostly beyond their control, find themselves out on the streets. And it offers tips to keep from sinking into the quagmire of the streets, to stabilize your situation so you don't sink any deeper. Or, if homelessness ends up becoming a long-term situation, I recommend ways of doing it that are as self-sufficient as possible.

For that reason alone, I don't recommend welfare as a first option, though I don't wish to sound like I'm making value judgments against it. Many of my friends have received government checks for decades, and it's quite possible they couldn't have survived without them.

In my own case, when my life completely fell apart in 1995 I got on General Assistance for a year. I was so fucked up, I could barely stand to be alive, let alone function as a productive member of society. So being on welfare probably saved my ass, for which I'm grateful.

There are many obvious drawbacks to welfare. I'll just mention a few of them here.

1. When you're given money for doing nothing you often lose the sense of the value of money. It becomes "easy come, easy go." And I'm amazed at the cavalier way that many life-long welfare recipients blow their dough every month. Believe me, when you've had to sweat your balls off to make twenty bucks, you'll be much more careful how you spend it, whereas I know a homeless Mother/Son combo who take in combined SSI checks of $1,400 every month, and yet they're usually broke after the first week.

2. You can get lulled into a false sense of security. Instead of hustling and developing the connections and self-sufficient survival skills that you might need later on, you're just sitting on your ass collecting a check. And if that check suddenly gets cut off, you might end up with nothing to fall back on when hard times come. As they so often do.

We're already seeing this. Twenty five years ago, one could live fairly comfortably on welfare. You rarely saw panhandlers on our city streets until near the very end of the month when their checks started running out, whereas today, hordes of panhandlers are out there every day of the month. The squeeze is on, and it's going to get tighter and tighter.

Another problem that the welfare system has never successfully grappled with is: How do you differentiate the truly needy from those who just want to live off the dole? There's no question that these welfare and charity agencies "enable" many able-bodied people into living the life of bums. On the other hand, if we set up a more ruthless sink-or-swim situation, half of these people would probably get jobs, but the other half would probably sink like a stone. It's also true that some of the craziest street people can't get on SSI in the first place, simply because they're too nutty to be able to jump through the hoops and elaborate red-tape of the SSI bureaucracy.

A large percentage of today's street people were inadvertently spawned from the well-meaning Great Society welfare program of Lyndon Johnson in the '60s. I'm talking about second and third generation

Surviving On The Streets

welfare recipients. This underclass has come to depend on these programs, and, in many cases, this is all they've known.

Tinkering with these "safety nets" is going to require the most delicate form of surgery. But it's a surgery that's coming, so we might as well face the ramifications. Society is simply unable, or unwilling, to continue funding such massive outlays for welfare programs. And yes, I've heard all the righteous speeches condemning the money wasted on the military as compared to social programs, and I'm down with that argument.

But the fact remains that, since the '60s, we've spent more money on these anti-poverty programs than at any time in human history. And yet the net result is that, 40 years later, there are *more* poor people in America than ever. Obviously, merely throwing money at the problem isn't enough. And in all likelihood there's going to be less and less money thrown at it. I'm just saying, if welfare is your primary option, you might want to be prepared for that eventuality.

By my own unscientific estimate, I'd say that probably about half the street people I know aren't getting any kind of government checks. And the percentage is probably even higher among today's street kids who hit the streets after the gravy train was over.

One of the weird and rarely talked about after-effects of Clinton's massive cuts in welfare programs in 1996 was that it was mostly white, young people who got kicked off. In California, Latinos now make up over 40% of the welfare recipients, and Blacks make up another 30%.

Well, there you go. Hopefully, this overview will give you a few ideas regarding some of the fabulous employment opportunities that await today's homeless street person on the go.

If I could give one all-important piece of advice: **Find Some Kind of Work to Do.** Even if it's just picking up trash from the sidewalk, which anyone can do. For without work, what else is there, aside from endlessly hanging out, and getting high? Which gets old real fast.

And remember: The important thing isn't how much money you make at a job, but what you become from doing that job. Now get to work.

Chapter Fourteen
Washing Up

One of the first things mainstream people ask me when I tell them I live on the streets is: *"Where do you go to the bathroom?"*

Well, public restrooms, that's where. I've spent several years washing up almost exclusively in public restrooms. I once went an entire year without taking a real shower or a bath. I wash up mostly in sinks. It's called "bird-bathing." And as far as I know, I do a good job at it, because nobody's complained that I smelled.

This was actually another pleasant discovery from street living. Because I had previously been indoctrinated with decades of anti-perspirant commercials on TV, and I lived in mortal terror of "offending" people by leaving my apartment without first taking a thorough hot shower, and putting on clean socks and shirts. It was nice to discover I could kick back for weeks at a time living in the same clothes and actually smelling a little bit like a human being instead of like soap.

The trick to "bird-bathing" is finding out-of-the-way public restrooms, and using them during off-hours when almost nobody is around. Because face it, nobody wants to come into the men's room to see some street freak with their dirty feet in the sink. It's also important — as always — THAT YOU CLEAN UP AFTER YOURSELF AND LEAVE NO TRACE! Clean your hairs out of the sink, and mop up the water on the floor, etc.

Surviving On The Streets

One year, I discovered an entire wing of a building that was under construction and generally off-limits. So I had my own personal bathroom for a year. Again, it's the art of finding "tweener" space. (I even had an entire hall of vacant classrooms where I'd lock the door, cover up the door window with my jacket, and kick back with my shoes off, plug my tape recorder into the wall and jam on my guitar. It was a great refuge, especially during the rainy season.)

For several years I shampooed my hair exclusively with the little lemon-scented, liquid-soap dispensers by the sinks. The only drawback was that the combination of the lemon chemicals and being out in the sun all day bleached my hair into a slightly yellowish/green blond tint.

When I was on the road, I'd often sneak into the gymnasium of the local campus during off-hours and take a nice, hot, steaming shower in the locker room. Boy did that feel good!

And once a week I did a radio show in this office building in the evenings when almost nobody was around. So I had the luxury of locking myself into a bathroom and scrubbing up in peace. Which is another point I can't repeat enough: GET INVOLVED IN THINGS. It will expand your horizons in all sorts of ways.

I only had two complaints regarding my years of public restroom usage. One: Like I said, I would go to a lot of trouble to find a men's room way the hell out of the way, in the deepest, darkest, most-deserted section of a building, where not another creature was stirring for miles in either direction. But inevitably, sooner or later, I'd be in there minding my own business, enjoying a little peace and quiet (and keep in mind, when you're on the streets, those four walls of the stall may be the only privacy you get inside all day long, and I came to cherish those little havens, setting out my books and newspapers and working on my journal and organizing my backpack, etc.) and SOME OTHER GUY would come in! Even worse, with ten stalls at his disposal, he'd pick the stall directly next to mine!

So I'd pack up all my stuff, and troop off down to the basement to an even MORE deserted men's room. And set up my stuff down there. Only to have the guy come trooping down to that bathroom and again take the stall right next to mine (I always knew it was the same guy, because I'd recognized his shoes). Now I have no problem with guys trying to make new friends. JUST NOT WHILE I'M TRYING TO TAKE A SHIT!!!!

My other complaint was the guys who come in and take a piss, and then spend ten minutes surgically washing their hands in the sink. I always felt like asking them: What exactly do you think is on your penis?

I also became an aficionado of bathroom graffiti. And I became such an accomplished practitioner of art, that several of my anonymous gems got written up in local newspaper articles. I guess I can't help but get published, even when I'm not trying.

Chapter Fifteen
Stashing Your Stuff
and Other Complications

    There's a whole art of stashing your stuff. Some street people get around this problem by whittling their stuff down to whatever they can carry on their back. For a packrat like myself, I had to come up with other solutions. For one thing, I had no visible income and survived almost completely off of the stuff that I scrounged, either to use myself or to sell to somebody else. So finding safe places to store all this junk was of paramount concern.
    I came up with dozens of relatively safe stash spots, sprinkled all over town. And I developed an elaborate system of descending hierarchies regarding what I would stash and where, based on such factors as the value of the item, the importance of not having it ripped off, and the distance and inconvenience I was willing to endure to get it.
    For instance, I kept a dozen or so boxes of cheap books that I used for my 25-cent-book vending gig stashed in the bushes on campus. Every six months or so, the campus maintenance people would be cleaning up the bushes and they'd throw all my books away. But I was willing to put up with this inconvenience (I could always scrounge up more books, after all) for the convenience of stashing the books only a few blocks from where I set up my vending stand.
    On the other hand, I had a nice guitar that I kept stashed in the deep woods in an out-of-the-way stash spot, and heavily camouflaged with leaves and shrubs. It was a pain in the ass to get to it. But it was always there when I went for it.

It can get complicated. I remember one time when I wanted to do my laundry, and it took me all day just to round up all my dirty clothes from the six or seven different stash spots where I stashed them.

Getting your stuff ripped off, or just losing it, is a constant hassle on the streets. One street waif forlornly conceded to me: "I've gotten used to the idea of losing everything that I've ever owned, everything that I've ever loved. Before, I would have thrown a fit or wanted to die if I had lost a prized possession. Now it just rolls off my back."

Can some of you apartment dwellers imagine what it's like to not be able to hold onto anything, to be prepared to lose everything you own, to only be able to hold onto that which will fit on your back or in your pockets?

An annoying trick that some street people play is the old "Will-you-watch-my-stuff-I'll-be-right-back" routine. OLLEY-OLLEY-OTSEN-FREE! Now you're anchored down for the next six hours keeping watch over his three backpacks, four blankets, five bags, two radios, plus his dog. And if anything gets ripped off, of course, you're responsible.

I developed this one great, convenient stash spot right in the heart of downtown Berkeley that I used for several years. How I got that spot demonstrates several key points that I'm going to keep repeating until I've bored you into submission.

It started when I got involved with a mural-painting project with the local Homeless Chaplaincy. The city of Berkeley let us store our paints and equipment in the shed of a nearby city building. I got into the habit of also stashing some of my own stuff alongside the paint stuff. After a couple of months the mural project ended, but I kept stashing my stuff there. By that time, the city workers were all familiar with me coming in and out, so they all just assumed that somebody else had given me permission to leave my stuff there. One city worker even offered to drill a hole in the bin that I stashed my stuff in so I could slap a lock on it for safekeeping.

Which highlights three points of street survival:

1. Get involved with things. There are often unexpected benefits.

2. Learn to spot "tweener" spaces that nobody is using and claim them for your own.

3. Act like you belong, and most people will assume that you do.

One Other Thing to Consider Regarding Stuff

There's a whole underground economy on the streets: buying, selling, trading, bartering, etc. This can cause some complications that you might want to be aware of.

One afternoon I bought an almost-brand-new, down sleeping bag from this street person — let's call him **X** — for only $50. It was too good a deal to pass up. Then **Y** showed up, angrily complaining to me that it was *his* sleeping bag that **Z** had stolen from him. But then **Z** showed up and angrily maintained that **Y** had ripped him off for $50 worth of heroin so he had taken the bag as payback for that, fair-and-square, and not only that but **Y** still owed him $25. But **Y** maintained he had originally stolen the bag fair-and-square from a sporting good store in a separate deal, so *he* was the one entitled to the $50. And at that point I maintained that I wanted my $50 back and to be out of the whole deal in the first place.

Which is often easier said than done. Because, like so much of the street life, it can be so *easy* to get into these situations, and so *difficult* to get out of them.

Part Three

LSAT
What LSAT course did students at the top 25 law schools take?
JAN. 15
BLAKE'S
LIVE SIMPLY THAT OTHERS MAY SIMPLY LIVE

Chapter Sixteen
The People

"The worst thing about being homeless is other homeless people." — Paul "Blue" Nicoloff

Well, that's true. But it's also the best thing. If you're a connoisseur of human oddities, the street can't be beat when it comes to people-watching and surreal street theatre.

The streets attract the most extreme human characters, both the best and the worst of the human family. And then, the constant pressure of the street environment stretches these characters like silly-putty into even more exaggerated caricatures. You will meet some of the coolest people anywhere, as well as some complete fucking assholes. But mostly they are bizarre, like the heavily symbolic characters that walk out of your dreams.

There's a Peter Pan quality to much of the street scene, this sense of children who never grew up. Many street people suffer from arrested development. They are like a tribe of lost children without adult supervision, endlessly playing hooky. You can stay up as late as you like and eat as much candy (or drugs) as you want.

The street scene is largely a scene of orphans, both literally and figuratively. They are the children of broken homes, and no homes, or families they are totally alienated from.

Surviving On The Streets

Many of them remind me of the 17-year-old stoners I used to hang out with in the parking lot of my high school. Their concerns are mostly that of boys, not mature adults: the latest rock 'n' roll bands, getting drunk or high, smoking cigarettes, and endlessly goofing off.

Street people live lives largely devoid of adult concerns such as jobs, career, and family. What's left? Well, the great bedrock of the homeless experience: *Endless, pointless socializing.* I'm not proud to say I've wasted years of my life doing little more than endlessly "hanging out."

Street people most remind me of the characters from *The Wizard of Oz*. As you stumble down the Yellow Brick Road of the streets you will meet up with many modern versions of the Cowardly Lion, the Tin Man, and the Scarecrow, as well as many would-be Wizards of the Streets who will offer you their ineffectual advice on how you can find your way back home. You are a long way from Kansas.

Unlike mainstream people who define themselves as Doctors, Lawyers, and Plumbers, street people define themselves largely by their inherent nature. Or by who they *wish* to be. And I've met countless *Gypsies, Cowboys, Pirate Petes, Ghosts, and Hobo Jims*. Having rejected — or been rejected by — society, the street person feels more free to define himself by how he feels from the inside-looking-out, as opposed to the definition that society has imposed on him from the outside.

These colorful, self-created characters give a sense of fantasy to the street milieu. Every day is Halloween.

Many street people live far outside the world of Social Security numbers and birth certificates. The vast majority of the street people I hang out with, I rarely find out their real names, aside from on those occasions when I come across their names in the police blotter section of the local newspaper.

Street people can often seem like children play-acting in their self-created dreamscapes. And yet, in another sense, street people are often more real — more true to their basics natures — than many other people. Often harshly so. Unconstrained by the need to conform to social conventions, they are free to indulge their true weirdness. Many of them get very far out, indeed. And quite a few never come back.

I've met countless *Wolfs, Coyotes, Bears, and Jaguars*, animal names which reflect the street person's wild, untamed nature, and their sense of roaming outside the confines of human civilization.

For pure street theatre it cannot be beat, for you have these extreme characters, often in the middle of desperate situations, rubbing against each other in the harshness of the street environment. In public. It is a combustible situation. And it is constantly exploding in countless ways. I haven't been to a movie in ten years, simply because none of them comes close to matching the surreal dramas enacted every day on the streets. (For what it's worth, the only movie that I've ever seen that comes close to capturing the reality of these street characters is *Midnight Cowboy*.)

It's true that you don't really know a person until you've lived with them. And, on the streets, you are truly alongside each other; sleeping, eating, shitting, fighting, and fucking right out in public view. You get to know each other in ways that you never get to know the guy who lived next door to you for ten years in your apartment building. When I lived indoors most of my relations with people were superficial. I'd put on my facade in public and only reveal my real face behind closed doors. But when you're on the streets, you *live* in public, 24-hours-a-day. Very quickly your carefully constructed mask crumbles, and your true self comes tumbling out, in all its glory and hideousness, simply because it's just too much effort to maintain the act all the time.

Which isn't to say that street people don't at least *try* to construct masks, and these masks are often designed to *conceal* more than to *reveal*. The Kind Rainbow Hippie Bro' who's standing in front of you smiling in your face, he might have the whole act down, but for all you know, he might have just got out of San Quentin for doing ten years for slicing and dicing somebody with a butcher knife. You don't know. But sooner or later you will find out. The non-stop pressure of the street suddenly rips his mask off and he

Chapter Sixteen
The People

reveals himself. Such is the ongoing drama of street life, where nothing is ever what it seems at first... but it often gets real all too fast.

Most street people exist without *Pasts* or *Futures*. They just show up one day on the scene and there they are, with an incredibly dramatic *Present*. You rarely know where they've come from, aside from what they choose to tell you (and who knows if it's bullshit or not). It's almost rude to ask about their background. Simply because where they're coming from is so often bad. And where they're going to is so often nowhere.

The streets are like one big, brawling, dysfunctional family. But a family nonetheless. Many people find a sense of community and belonging on the streets that they've found nowhere else.

Generally, street people are surprisingly generous when it comes to forgiving and forgetting the foibles and fuck-ups of their fellow street people. The scene is just too small for long simmering grudges. Street people often pound the shit out of each other one day, and shrug it off the next.

Many of us know what it's like to be run out of town. So we rarely wish to run somebody off the street scene. Simply because we know that there's often nowhere to go after the streets, for we're usually on the streets in the first place because we've got nowhere else to go. There's a precarious sense of "last stand" to many of our lives. So we realize the seriousness of pushing someone over the edge. The streets are an all-inclusive club that anyone can join. Not that we're particularly proud of all of our members.

One of the great pieces of practical advice I got from my great guru, Swami Muktananda, was: *"Avoid bad associations."* It only takes one spoiled curd to ruin an entire vat of milk.

This is often easier said then done on the streets, for bad associations come launching at you, one after another, like deranged torpedoes. Most street people aren't *bad* people. In fact, a surprising percentage of them are among the nicest, most soulful people I've met anywhere. But all too many of them are on serious downers, and they will take you down with them if you are not very careful. The effect is rarely dramatic. Like most of what you endure on the streets, it's a subtle, cumulative effect. One downer after another, slowly grinding you down, down, down and out.

Without a doubt, one of the things you definitely will have to survive on the streets is the other street people. So it might be instructive to take a look at some of the characters you will come across:

1. Hippies and Punks

Ten years ago, there was a certain amount of antagonism between these two countercultural groups. They were almost like competing cults proselytizing for prospective members. The Punks would mock the Hippies for their phony baloney idealism, and the Hippies would mock the Punks for their defeatist, negative attitude.

But then the Punks realized that, beneath their facade, the Hippies were just as lost and bitter as they were. And the Hippies realized that the Punks liked to smoke pot. So nowadays, the two groups have kind of cross-pollinated into all-purpose Street Freaks.

Many young street people find a sense of family and community within these counterculture subgroups. On the downside, the counterculture tends to romanticize one's sense of alienation from mainstream society, which can lead them down a dead-end path that gets narrower and narrower.

Sadly, very little that is new seems to be coming out of these countercultural trends these days. Punk may not be dead, but, in the year 2001, it might very well be a spent force.

2. The Classic Bum

Truly, the never-ending mantra of the streets is: "Spare a cigarette, bro'?"

We talked about walking around scrounging to fulfill your needs in the last chapter. Well, there's a breed of specimens lurking everywhere on the streets who walk around scrounging YOU. Jiggle change in your pocket and you will see their heads suddenly turn towards you with that unmistakable look on their face that says: HMMM… MAYBE THAT GUY HAS SOMETHING THAT I CAN *GET!*

I hit the streets as Classic Bum meat. I had this pathological character defect that all Bums instantly recognize; I was a "nice" guy who wanted everybody to like me. Actually, I really wasn't particularly nice; it was more a defense mechanism that I employed to please everyone in the hopes that they wouldn't hurt me. And it wasn't long before I was surrounded by an endless swarm of Bums, offering me endless opportunities to please them.

The problem is: To give to a Bum merely results in him coming back to you for more. And more. And, finally, *MORE!!!* There is no end to their bumhood, for it is their basic nature and prime survival skill. The only way to deal with the Bum is to say "NO!," loudly and firmly and occasionally with a boot heel wedged up their bum ass.

I am making no moral judgment here. The parasitic leech is as much a noble part of the splendor of Nature as any other creature on God's Green Earth. It was just with personal chagrin that I began to look down and see that several of these types had attached themselves to my side and were beginning to insert their probes and feelers into my very guts. They always look up to you with a big, cheerful, beaming smile and say: **"HEY THERE, *BRO'*! DON'T MIND ME! I'M JUST SUCKING THE LIFE BLOOD OUT OF YOUR BODILY ORGANS! HOWZ'IT GOIN', BRO'?"**

Smile, smile…

A weird form of Darwinism-in-reverse takes place on the streets. You find the less-resourceful feeding off the more resourceful. And the even-less-resourceful feeding on the less resourceful. And so on. Until you find the poor sap at the bottom of the food chain gnawing on the most chewed-up piece of gristle. Try to avoid having them chew on you.

Remember: The Classic Bum knows no limits other than *What He Can Get Away With*. It's up to you to draw the line. You generally have only two choices when dealing with the Classic Bum:

- Have an ugly scene immediately and get rid of the Bum, or
- Put up with it, put up with it, put up with it, etc., and have the ugly scene anyway eventually. It's better to just cut to the chase and get it over with quick.

3. Con-Man/Hustler

Related to the Classic Bum is the Con-Man/Hustler. Most of these guys are almost comically inept and transparently easy to spot. Usually you can spot these W.C. Fields types from a mile away. If they were any good at their cons, after all, they wouldn't be on the streets. They'd be in the Senate attaching their parasitic tentacles to the public trough.

There's sort of a noble myth about the non-materialistic poverty of the street people. Salt of the earth. Sure. Fact is, most of us street people are just as greedy as your average Wall Street junk bond crook. We're just not as good at it.

Most of these street hustlers come from a long line of two-bit chicken thieves and card sharks. A hundred years ago they would've been hung for trying to steal your horse, for they always get caught. They would be laughable except that, sooner or later, you get careless and they burn you.

For awhile I was in the habit of stashing a case of Henry's Red under my vending table, and cracking them open with my friends after a hard day of sitting around doing nothing. Now nothing attracts the Bums and Hustlers of the streets more than a case of Henry's sitting there under a table (with the exception of "Hey, anybody wanna smoke some of this here crack?"). And I'd always notice two or three of them angling towards the seat closest to the beer stash.

Now these Hustler types usually reveal themselves quickly if you're looking for it. I remember this one big, fat, blonde dude, let's call him Hippie Swede. He just showed up one day with an expensive backpack and a fancy coal-miner's helmet-with-flashlight-attached-to-it, that he had "found" somewhere and was looking to sell for a mere $20.

Hippie Swede was one of these guys who just naturally blends in with the party — smile, smile. That is, until it's time to buy the next round and then his fat ass is gone. I remember this one Christmas Eve; the Henry's Red got me going, and the Barcardi-and-eggnog finished me off. And it was then that Hippie Swede made his move. For the Hustler is always poised to strike when he senses your weakness (which is why it's important to spot 'em and rid yourself of 'em *before* they strike, because who wants to be on guard all the time?).

He'd watched me drunkenly throwing my cash around on booze all night, so he hit me up with this big spiel about this great pot deal he had lined up. Twenty bucks and I'm in. Not being of sound mind, I forked over the dough to him, and that was the last we saw of Hippie Swede, or my $20, that night. He probably figured I wouldn't even remember it the next morning. He figured wrong. I've got a very nasty temper, and a bad hangover does little to help it along.

Now there are two ways to play this. Sometimes — if, say the Hustler happens to be big and crazy and violent — it's best to just write off your losses and not let the guy near you next time. On the other hand, if you sense the guy is a coward, or if you think you can beat his ass, it might be worth it to put the *Fear of God in Him*, if only to make him think twice about the next guy he tries to burn. I made it quite clear to Hippie Swede that if he didn't give me my money back I had better not see his fat ass back on the Avenue. And a few days later he did, if fact, reimburse me (probably by burning somebody else).

As an epilogue to this story, a couple of weeks later, Hippie Swede had ingratiated himself with another vendor. When the vendor's back was turned, he made off with up to $500 worth of tie-dyed shirts. And that was the last we saw of Hippie Swede. Which is the only good news: his type rarely stays around very long. But it highlights the damage they can do if you don't spot them quickly and draw the line.

4. The Perpetually Helpless

One of the heart-rending aspects of the streets is that you're surrounded by helpless people in constant need. And you, yourself, will probably be one of them at some point.

The streets are a family, after all, and it's very important that you help out your fellow street brothers and sisters. Even if it's only out of the simple, selfish motive that you, yourself, will need help from them at some point. And what goes around, indeed comes around. And ouch! If you never kick down, if you're just a Bum or Hustler, you end up getting the boot everywhere you go. And that's a lonely way to live.

The Perpetually Helpless, on the other hand, would often give you their last dollar. Problem is, they rarely have one.

Surviving On The Streets

It's also part of the great on-going tragedy of the streets that some of those that are the *least* capable of dealing with life are precisely the ones that end up on the streets dealing with the most EXTREME difficulties of the street life.

But it can be exasperating. There's always the guy who's out there in the cold and rain with no sleeping bag. So you hike a mile to your stash spot and get him an extra one you've got. Then, two days later, he's out there again. *Somebody stole my sleeping bag, man!* Bummer! So you give him some extra blankets you got. Three days: *My blankets got ruined in the rain, man!* Bummer. On and on it goes. What can you do?

I'm reminded of a cartoon by Tuli Kupferberg in regards to Reagonomics:

"FEED A MAN A FISH AND YOU'VE FED HIM FOR ONE DAY... FEED A MAN *TO* THE FISHES AND YOU'RE RID OF HIM FOREVER!" (drawing on Reagan throwing perpetually helpless bum to the sharks).

There are just some people on the streets who genuinely need your help, and it's a constant struggle to find that line where you decide how much you're willing to help. It's one of the on-going complex moral and karmic issues that you must grapple with: How to give without being sucked dry.

Further complicating the issue is the fact that the Classic Bum and the Con-man/Hustler will regularly mimic the Genuinely Helpless in order to get you to serve them (and they are masters of every manner of guilt-trip). The difference is, The Bum wants you to wipe his ass for him simply because he doesn't want to bother doing it himself, whereas the Genuinely Helpless really *can't* do it himself.

Unfortunately, it's not as black-and-white as I'm making it out here. And I've erred in both directions. There were times when I should have helped out a Genuinely Helpless person, but I didn't want to be bothered. And there were other times when I *did* help out a Classic Bum and only ended up feeling used.

Worst of all is the Hustler who mimics the Genuinely Helpless to take advantage of your Good Samaritan impulses. One night, this middle-aged, housewife-looking woman came rushing up as I walked down the street:

"MISTER!! MY DAUGHTER JUST GOT HIT BY A CAR AND TAKEN OFF IN THE AMBULANCE!! I NEED $5 IMMEDIATELY TO CATCH A CAB TO THE HOSPITAL!!"

"Oh man, sure thing," I said, forking over the dough.

"Thanks!" And she was gone.

A week later, I was walking down the same block and she came rushing up to me again: "MISTER!! MY DAUGHTER JUST GOT HIT BY A CAR AND TAKEN OFF IN THE AMBULANCE!! I NEED $5 IMMEDIATELY TO CATCH A CAB TO THE HOSPITAL!!"

There may be a special room in Hell for people like this. I'm certainly no authority on the Laws of Karma, but I wouldn't be surprised if people like her ended up reincarnated as a Perpetually Helpless. And when they call out for help, no one heeds their call.

5. LOST SOULS

You will run into many Lost Souls wandering around on the streets. They come from Nowhere. They are going Nowhere. They are doing Nothing. And, meanwhile, there they are in front of you, trying to get a hit off of your Somethingness. If only they can find it. You can very easily suffer from serious soul-drain if too many Lost Souls begin swarming around your space. If you're strong enough, you can elevate them a bit to your level. But if you're weak, they will drag you down to theirs.

*Chapter Sixteen
The People*

You ever read accounts in the newspaper about some terrible tragedy that nailed somebody: The mother who committed suicide right in front of the son, or the 7-year-old kid who was regularly fucked in the ass by his uncle. And you wonder: How do they go on after something like that?

Well, many of them don't. Many of them end up flopped out on the sidewalk for a year or twenty, staring into space in a daze. Consider that the next time you see a seemingly healthy person sitting there begging money. You have no idea where that person is coming from and what's happened to them. People get crippled in all sorts of ways that aren't visible.

Now I don't mean to imply that the average street person suffers any more than the average suburban guy going off to a job he hates to support his family. The main difference is that the suffering on the streets is in fast-forward. You see intense cosmic dramas played out right before your eyes. It is not a scene of hanging-on-in-quiet-desperation. You are force-fed enough heavy karmic issues in a very short time to fry the strongest soul. If you don't start out as a Lost Soul, you can very easily become one.

6. The Flaming Asshole

These types exist at all levels of society, of course. But on the streets you get a particularly virulent brand of dysfunctional Asshole. Their basic attitude is: "I'm not okay — you're not okay." And they inflict that on you in every possible way. They can't elevate themselves so they endeavor to endlessly drag you *down* to their miserable level.

As always, it's important to learn to differentiate the Merely Annoying Asshole from the Truly Dangerous Asshole. In either case, there is no easy way to deal with the Asshole, for *any* dealings with them diminish you. All you can do is strive to give them no hooks into you, and get away as soon as possible.

Ultimately, I concluded: *Water seeks its own level.* And the people that surround you are a direct reflection of the level *you're* operating on. So if you find yourself surrounded by Assholes, the only way to really deal with them is to look into the mirror and start working on elevating your own character to the point where you, yourself, are not one.

(And if anyone thinks I'm being unduly harsh in my critiques of these street types, I should add that, at one time or another, I've fit into just about every category in this chapter myself. So maybe you should watch out for me, fucker.)

7. Trust-fund Babies

Trust-fund Babies often end up on the street scene by default. Lacking the normal social scene revolving around work or family, they gravitate towards the endless party of the streets. William Burroughs is the classic example of the genre, the low-rent leisure-class.

Usually, they start out skimming and gliding across the surface of the streets like a dilettante. But soon enough they find themselves entangled in all the same shit-trips that the average street person gets mucked up in. With a crucial difference: When the going gets tough, the Trust-fund Baby can get going. Usually by rushing back to Mom's house, or by hiring an expensive lawyer, or by checking into a high-class detox center.

I remember one Trust-fund Baby bitterly complaining to me that his Dad had just cut off his Gold Card and he couldn't even afford to eat dinner at an expensive restaurant (I, myself, had just finished eating dinner out of a garbage can).

"But you don't understand, Ace!" he explained. "If my dad cuts me off, I could end up... ON THE STREETS!"

Imagine my chagrin.

On the positive side, since the Trust-fund Baby usually has connections beyond the street scene, they often provide valuable connections for street people who wish to pull themselves back into the mainstream. Or, at the least, an occasional couch to crash on.

8. The Wingnut

There are street people who are just gone. As a friend put it: There's "out there" and then there's "OUT THERE!"

I like Lily Tomlin's line: "We should take all the Wingnuts who are walking around talking to themselves and pair them up, so at least it would *look* like they're talking to someone."

A friend of mine once asked a Wingnut why he talks to himself all day. He answered: "Because nobody else will listen to me." Makes sense to me.

I hang out with a lot of people who would be written off as "crazy." But what does that even mean? My own feeling is that what most people accept as Consensus Reality is nothing more than the commonly accepted delusion. The crazy person just happens to come up with his own unique delusions. Life is an illusion after all, say the Buddhists. And I wish you luck stumbling through your own hall of mirrors.

Hanging out with the highly individualistic and idiosyncratic street people gives you an appreciation of just how subjective "reality" is, and how we each filter the world differently through our own unique nervous systems. There's a fine line between genius and madman. And on the streets you meet plenty of both.

9. Teenage Runaways

Among the more poignant and tragic of the street population are the Teenage Runaways. They often find themselves forced to deal with heavy, heavy adult situations long before they have the maturity to deal with the consequences. Many of them are forced to grow up early. And many of them never succeed at growing up at all.

The Teenage Runaway exists in a weird, in-between netherworld: Too young to function as legal adults, but with nowhere for them to exist as children.

They can often tug at your heart with this weird juxtaposition of breath-taking innocence existing side-by-side with premature hardness. I remember one adorable little waif up in Arcata. She looked just like she stepped off the set of *The Brady Bunch*, aside from the word "FUCK" crudely tattooed across her knuckles. I once asked her if she ever regretted the tattoo. She said: "Yeah. I started to regret it after the 5,000[th] person asked me about it."

Like the kids who were institutionalized at an early age in reform schools and end up permanently entrenched in the prison system, the kids who hit the streets at an early age make up a large percentage of the *permanently* homeless.

Many of them never dropped out. They were never *in* in the first place. Usually they are running from seriously fucked up "homes" (in the loosest sense of the word). It's a sad commentary that the state of homelessness they find on the street is often an improvement over where they've come from.

I'm not a sociologist, and I certainly don't go around taking a survey on the subject, but I certainly suspect a high degree of sexual abuse in their backgrounds.

I remember these two little Punkette Twins who were part of the first wave of squatter street punks back in 1982. Probably 15 years old. They proudly showed me the scars on their arms from suicide attempts. I published their photos and poetry in the very first issue of *Twisted Image #1*, a punk tabloid I was putting out at the time.

With street people, you rarely find out the true story of what actually happened to them. You see the damage, but you can only make educated guesses at the cause. But in the case of the Punkettes, I happened to come across an article about them ten years later in an issue of *People* magazine, of all places. Turns out, when they were three years old they were discovered by authorities living alone in an abandoned building in Oakland, crawling with rats and shit and seriously malnourished. Their parents were both drug addicts. They ended up being adopted by a "respectable" UC Berkeley professor in the suburbs, who fucked them the whole time they were stuck living with him. The *People* article detailed their lawsuit against the Professor. He ended up in jail, and they ended up with his house. Good for them. A victory for the street people, for a change.

And it shows you how fluid these categories can be, so don't give up hope if you happen to be stuck right now in a category you don't like. The Punkettes started out as *Teenage Runaways* and *Lost Souls*. And the Professor ended up as an *In-the-Joint* and *Homeless*.

10. Hermits

There are some street people who live more like wild animals than human beings. Their daily existence is more akin to that of mangy alley cats, scurrying gutter rats, and wild raccoons.

There's one guy I know who always sits off by himself. Never talks to anyone, aside from occasionally bleating out these weird animal noises. He scrounges all his food eating scraps from garbage cans. He sleeps in a hole he's burrowed in the bushes. He's been around for years. One day he'll be dead, and it'll be as if he had never even been here. Strange, isn't it? The range of human experiences.

In a way, it's reassuring to me that you can *completely* drop out of society and yet still exist. These Hermits can function and survive without being dependent on any other humans. Can you say that?

And I take solace in that. For there have been times when I've felt like thumbing my nose at the whole lot of you, myself. Or when I felt like a pariah who was on the verge of being driven out of the human tribe. It gives me a little leverage to know that that could yet happen and I'd still be able to survive. For I am pretty far out there myself.

11. Vietnam Vets

For a while I kept reading that a large percentage of the homeless population was made up of Vietnam vets. Lately, I've been reading that a lot of these so-called homeless vets are actually Con-men/Hustlers using the vet angle as a sympathy ploy.

Who knows. I *have* met some homeless vets on the streets, of course, but not a lot. It could just be that I'm on a different circuit. Again, I'm hardly a sociologist, and this book is hardly intended as a scientific overview of the streets.

I do remember one homeless Vietnam vet who talked about killing so many people that his entire body would be drenched in blood as if he had taken a shower in blood. And I believed him.

There was another guy in Arcata, this clean-cut, blonde guy. He described his experiences to me this way:

"I loved Vietnam. It was like a great party, with killing. We got the best drugs. The best whores. The best weapons. I know some guys who suffered serious post-trauma stress from what they experienced. But as far as I can tell, I haven't experienced any serious psychological damage."

It would have been a more convincing disclaimer if he hadn't been standing in front of me with his pant leg drenched from having pissed himself.

12. Blacks

I'm certainly not qualified to write much about the unique challenges that face the average Black street person. Or Latino or Asian street people, for that matter. (Actually, there are very few Asian street people. I guess they just haven't been Americanized yet. But give 'em a couple of generations of good ole American drugs and they'll be flopped out on the sidewalks with the rest of us.)

I would imagine that Blacks face all the difficulties that White street people face, only more so, due to such factors as, an even greater degree of shattered family structures, the fear and suspicion that greets many Black street people (especially those of the "Crazy Street Nigger" variety), and the fact that they can't blend in as easily in the more affluent, non-black neighborhoods.

One of the cool things about Berkeley is, if a Black street kid gets a Mohawk and listens to hardcore, he's accepted as just another punker. Or if a White kid wears baggy pants and listens to rap, he can hang with the gangbangers.

On the other hand, because there is more intermingling between the races in a town such as Berkeley than in other, more segregated areas, there are probably more outbreaks of racial antagonisms between us.

From a personal point of view, one of my beefs with a lot of Black street people is the constant "You-Owe-Me-Whitey!" attitude they keep throwing in my face, and the obsequious appeasement that they require of me. Some of these Black guys, they've seen me eating out of the garbage cans and sleeping in the dirt for YEARS, and yet they still act like I've got some secret Swiss bank account or something.

And I find the level of serious street violence that I've consistently experienced from Blacks over the years to be sickening and abhorrent.

Those of us who were out on the streets during the Rodney King years absorbed the full brunt of the undeclared race war that raged during those years. And those in the joint were on the front lines of that war even more so.

Everyone on the streets can tell you DOZENS of stories of Being Attacked By Black Guys, just within their own small circle of acquaintances. Horror stories. It's sickening. And I'm even sicker to death of you fat-ass White Liberals who get bent out of shape at the mere mention of this, of the subject of Black Crime. When YOUR adjustment is to just White Flight it out of the Black neighborhoods at the first hint of this. And then you give your Liberal white-guilt sermons to those of us on the streets who weren't afforded the luxury of fleeing.

I remember a Black newspaper columnist addressing the subject of what he called "the Black community's dirty little secret, Black Crime." And I thought: "Secret from WHO? Certainly not anybody on the street level."

I vividly remember how this one Black friend of mine described the payback that was running rampant during those Dark Days of Reginald Denny:

"It was like sharks in a feeding frenzy," he said. "I'd look over and know that that White Boy was going to get it. And there was nothing I could do about it."

Lest anybody take my comments out of context, I'm well aware of Vietnam, Hiroshima, World War I, World War II, and countless other European wars, as well as the 100,000 Iraqis we recently buried in the sand for the sake of oil.

In truth, I don't think ANY race has much in the way of bragging rights when it comes to being non-violent. My comments are only intended in the context of this book, which deals with *street* violence, of which Blacks commit a grossly disproportionate amount. And, unlike the average White Liberal who makes with his platitudes from the safety of suburbia, if you're on the streets you had better be ready to deal with it.

13. The Sexually Damaged

Sex is difficult for most people. On the streets it's even more so. There's no question that there are a lot of victims of childhood sexual abuse on the streets. Some of them get over it. Others embark on a string of fucked up sexual relationships, leaving a trail of havoc in their wake.

Mostly, street people treat sex like a game, a form of self-entertainment, a way of hot-wiring their nervous systems for kicks. This approach tends to work at cross-purposes when we try to use sex as the basis for a stable relationship. When we try to do both at the same time, we fail at both. As Bukowski put it: "We don't know what to do with sex. We try to treat it as a toy. A toy that destroys people."

One night, this street kid with a sleeping bag rolled under his arm, was crying and wailing about his girlfriend: "SHE *CHEATED* ON ME!" he cried.

One of her friends chimed in to her defense: "Everyone knows that *oral sex* doesn't count as *cheating!*"

Ahhh, the Bill Clinton Generation.

There's a lot of sex-charged people on the streets, simply because many of them are young, they have too much free time on their hands, and a surprising number of them are extremely good looking. All these beautiful, damaged Sirens vamping up and down the streets. SHEESH.

I've never been able to figure that out, why there are so many beautiful looking people on the streets. Part of it, I guess, is that I'm getting older and more decrepit so their youth looks more impressive to me by contrast. And part of it is the dash and élan of their natural street style. When you live in your clothes, you tend to develop a style that is both functional and highly reflective of your personal nature. Plus, the sun and wind and rain in your face can bring out a natural beauty that artificial creams and make-up can never simulate. Plus, if some chick is sitting there in her pile-of-laundry, free-boxed-clothes look, with her hair matted with mud, and she's STILL beautiful, well, you KNOW she's beautiful.

But I have this other theory (I have theories on virtually everything). It's the Beautiful Ones who are constantly having sex thrust at them, therefore, they're more prone to casual, accidental affairs. And the unintended consequences. Namely, unplanned children. Years later, you find the beautiful children of these haphazard affairs wandering lost among the city streets.

If you're around long enough on the street scene, you actually see this cycle come full circle. You see those lost beautiful children, hook up with other lost, beautiful children in these half-assed sexual relationships, produce a baby, struggle to keep it together, fail, the relationship falls apart, give up the baby for adoption, go off and shoot some smack, what the hell.

Surviving On The Streets

And then, fifteen years later, that beautiful orphan in turn hits the streets, and the whole damn cycle starts up anew.

The breakdown of the Traditional American Family Structure is certainly a complex subject. We've gone through a period of great experimentation and so-called innovation during this era of so-called Sexual Liberation. Let's just say, on the street level you meet very few people who seem to have been liberated by all this.

On the streets, you will occasionally see a couple that keeps it together, that holds onto their baby, and succeeds at making a real family for themselves. And when they do — when they manage to break out of this dysfunctional cycle of "the sins of the Father are revisited on the Son" — it's a cause for celebration. For it is so fucking difficult with all the forces of the streets working against you.

Remember: Few things will send a person careening over the edge quicker than a bad sexual love affair. And on the streets you're tiptoeing through a veritable minefield of sexual damage. You very well may meet some beautiful, alluring siren and wonder to yourself what this beautiful person is doing on the streets. Sooner or later you will find out.

14. In-and-Out-of-the-Joint

These guys are the true wild cards of the street deck. I'm talking about the ones in and out of prison all the time, struck in the revolving door of our prison system.

Most of them are pretty nice guys, actually. And I have a number of friends who are regularly in and out of San Quentin and other hardcore joints. Most of them are not violent people, and most of their crimes are non-violent. They're more *wild-and-out-of-control* than *psychopathic*. They're more "outlaw" than "criminal." They're more Fuck-ups than Fuckers.

Indeed, there's a definite Outlaw Mystique to the streets. Hanging out after midnight at your quasi-illegal campsites with your crew of whacky street renegades, you can get this weird sense of déjà vu, like you're Robin Hood and his Merry Men, illegally poaching venison off the King's land... as the Sheriff of Nottingham drifts by ever-so-slowly in his squad car... and he's eyeing you and nobody but you.

I've got one friend, he's in and out of the joint so much, we no longer talk about how long he was in for, but how long he managed to stay out this time. The other night he was regaling us around the campsite with *Tales From His Latest Stint* — always a popular pastime on the streets — giving us the gossip on some of the people he was locked up with, like the actor Robert Downey, Jr., and the guy who kept a woman locked up in a box for ten years as his sex-slave.

Unfortunately, his story telling was abruptly interrupted when eight cops suddenly surrounded him and hauled him back off to the joint, evidently for some kind of parole-violation bullshit. Or maybe he killed somebody. Who knows? But he'll be back on the streets eventually with new stories.

One thing that seems to separate the guy who keeps going in and out of the joint from the guy who does his time and never returns is that the habitual inmate was usually institutionalized in reform school as a kid. You sense the joint is almost their natural milieu, and that they adjust better to the imposed discipline of "three hots and a cot" than to the freeform, swirling chaos of the streets. They often look better when they just get *released* from the joint — new haircut, well-fed, good shape — than the bedraggled street person who slinks back to the joint.

You meet some sad, weird cases among them. I knew one guy in Eureka who had been locked up in reform school as a kid, and some of the other inmates held him down and tattooed "SHIT" and "HEAD" across his fingers. Later, he took a hot butter knife and scarred the words off his hands.

When I met him, he lived in a little flophouse hotel room crammed from floor to ceiling with animal cages filled with birds, snakes, frogs, mice, you name it. And he'd march back and forth amongst the cages, rapping on the sides of them, and saying stuff like: *"Hmmm... I see you've been a BAD birdie today! NO food for you today!"* Now *he* was the warden, and he decided who got punished.

Again, it's very important that you develop an inner sensor that can differentiate the Merely Weird from the Truly Fucking Dangerous. For every now and then you will stumble into a character who can turn your world upside down in a blink of an eye.

Last month a friend of mine got into a trivial little disagreement with this Black guy in People's Park while they were waiting in line for a bag lunch. What was nothing became something very quickly. Next thing he knew, my friend was lying in a pool of blood, gutted open like a fish. Oh yes.

Occasionally you may have the misfortune to stumble across someone who is just plain evil.

Back in the late '80s an idealistic friend of mine came up with the idea of starting a community of "mobile dwellers," people living in their cars, trucks, and school buses. He talked the city of Berkeley into fencing off a parking lot down by the marina where they could legally park and live. The city even installed running water and porta-potties. It was an experiment. They dubbed it Rainbow Village and, for a while, it was pretty cool. But then it started turning into a dumping ground for people just out of the joint. And things started heating up real quick.

Every now and then I'll hear these idealistic types with their big plans about mobilizing "the homeless community" into some kind of fighting force, into some kind of progressive, constructive mode. They always underestimate the destructive and dysfunctional segment of the street population that is always there and ever-ready to sabotage the best laid plans.

Anyway, one night there were these two little Deadheads who happened to be in town with the Dead tour, and they parked their hippie school bus down at Rainbow Village. They were just seventeen and eighteen years old, boyfriend and girlfriend. You can imagine how little they understood of the milieu they had walked into.

Around midnight they were confronted by this dreadlocked Black guy who lived at Rainbow Village, one of those guys just out of the joint, with a rap sheet longer than your arm. First he tried to rape the chick. And when the boyfriend tried to intervene, this piece of shit put bullets in both of their heads and dumped their bodies in the Berkeley bay. And that was the end of fucking Rainbow Village.

I remember going to the trial and seeing the parents of the two kids sitting there in the courtroom day after day. I'm sure the whole scene was a parent's worst nightmare. I don't want to scare anyone. But I would be amiss in my role as a writer of this cautionary tale, if I didn't pass on what is hardly a secret: There are some human beings walking amongst us in this world of ours who would make your skin crawl. And you very well may have a higher chance of getting acquainted with them on the streets than in other, more genteel walks of life. So be on guard, my friend. Be on guard. They are out there.

15. The Secret Homeless

Mainstream people have a completely distorted impression of who the homeless are. They base their impression on the bag ladies, the panhandlers, and the raving wingnuts, simply because these obvious street stereotypes are the only ones they happen to notice.

In fact, these obvious types make up only a small percentage of the homeless population. Most of the homeless you wouldn't even notice if they walked right by you. *Can you spot The Secret Homeless amongst us?*

The fact is, homelessness is such a quasi-illegal situation that most of us go to great lengths to disguise our state of homelessness. Even after you've been on the homeless scene for quite some time, it's hard to peg precisely who is or isn't homeless. Most street people are eminently cagey about their specific sleeping arrangements after all. And for good reason.

I'm just saying: Don't be too quick to think you've got us pegged. Just tonight at the old campsite I was hanging out with a crew that included:

a.) a guy who used to write for the *New York Times*;

b.) a Jewish guy who graduated from Yale and did post-graduate rabbinical studies; and

c.) a guy who spends all day in the computer library designing web sites.

Do you still think you know who the homeless are?

16. Skid Row Types, Bag Ladies, Shopping Cart Pushers, Hobos, Tramps, Road Dogs, Gypsies, Winos, and Street Bro's

There are some street people, of course, who are right out of central casting. There's a certain segment of the human family that's been on the streets since time immemorial; the Road Dogs huddled around campfires on the outskirts of town; the Winos drinking cheap wine in an alley on Skid Row; the Hobos tramping from town to town begging for a sandwich.

Their numbers may fluctuate with the whims of the economy (and the streets are as much a barometer of the state of the economy as any Wall Street indicator). But they've always been out there. And they always will be. This strange, movable, underground subsociety of Gypsies, Tramps, and Thieves, and bad Cher songs. You would almost feel part of an ancient, noble tradition except for the fact that we're so fucked up.

Oddly, these Classic Types are among the more stable denizens of the streets, for most of them have made peace with their situation. Unlike many people trapped on the streets, they aren't struggling and straining to get off the streets. In fact, the street is their natural milieu. Many derive their sense of identity from being a Street Person.

When I think of the archetypal street person, I often think of this old guy who used to live in a doorway in the Tenderloin district of San Francisco. He looked like he was about 100 years old. Just ancient. He was so grizzled and wizened and hunchbacked, his head looked like it was growing out of his bellybutton. He mostly slept all day in his doorway a half a block from the St. Anthony's Dining Hall, bundled up in five overcoats and three pairs of pants. You could hardly see his face, except for his pale blue eyes staring out from this little slit between his hat and overcoat.

At lunchtime, he'd push his shopping cart the half-block to St. Anthony's, creaking along, inch-by-inch. Then he'd sit down at a table and put his face a few inches from his plate and shovel the food in his mouth until his plate was clean. Then he'd creak back to this doorway, inch-by-inch, and huddle there until the next day, when he'd start the pattern all over again. He'd been living like that for years. And for all I know, he's still there.

In the heart of the sick and dying American cities, you will find the most gnarled and twisted human characters.

I remember this other guy on the St. Anthony's circuit. He looked like a big rat. He even gnawed at his lower lip like a rat. His entire body was covered with UFO tattoos. I once asked him what was up with the tattoos. He said: "I used to get robbed of my SSI check every month. So now, on the first, I spend the whole thing on tattoos. Because it's the one thing on these streets that they can't steal from me." (Well, on some of these streets you can get skinned alive.)

He once confided to me that he was from the planet Venus. And I can't say I completely disbelieved him.

You realize on the streets, the wide spectrum of adjustments that a human being is capable of making to survive in this world. And what may seem tragic or horrifying to you, may in fact feel perfectly natural, and even comfortable, to the person who has made that unique adjustment. All most of us ask is that you don't pity us. Which may even be reassuring for you to hear. You often hear Liberals beating their breasts about "compassion fatigue." But what we mostly want is to be left alone.

17. Art Boys/Bohemians

Mostly it is circumstances beyond their control that force people onto the streets. An exception to that rule is the Art Boys.

Many of them are drawn to the streets by the great blessing (and curse) of street life: Free Time. They are willing to endure the poverty of the streets in exchange for the opportunity to dedicate themselves to their artwork. And I have met some brilliant artists, writers, and musicians on the streets.

There's a certain authenticity to street life that has always attracted creative types. It's funny, I know all these street people who wish they were famous celebrities. And then there are all the famous celebrities who wish they were "from the streets." They could be millionaire actors in Beverly Hills, or rock stars ordering room service from a five-star hotel, but to have "street cred" is still an issue with them. And I'm sure Keith Richards will be telling the story for the rest of his life about how when the Stones were first starting he was so poor he had to eat potatoes for two months cuz he couldn't afford lobster, man.

In fact, much that is new does comes out of the streets. Many of the great cultural, artistic, and fashion trends of our times came from the street first.

One reason the streets are such a fertile ground for spawning the new is because there's a greater freedom to experiment. We're already fucked, so what difference does it make if we gamble on something new.

It's also true that there's a whole different feel — and impact — to these organically grown, street-level trends, as opposed to the ones that are artificially manufactured from the top of the corporate media food chain. Artists of the streets: I salute you!

18. Spiritual Seekers

Similar to the Art Boys are the Spiritual Seekers, who take advantage of the endless expanse of free time to develop their spiritual practices.

In America, the spiritual drop out is unlikely to find much of a support group. Perhaps because, spiritually, we're still in our infancy when compared to ancient traditions like in India. The best you can hope to find on the wandering American holy man circuit, is a bunch of hippies flopped out in the town square,

Surviving On The Streets

smoking a bunch of pot and beating on hand drums. But something of substance could yet develop out of this.

Bhagavan Das — a Southern California boy who embarked on a spiritual pilgrimage to India in 1964 and later became the inspiration for Ram Dass' bestseller *Be Here Now* — described how in India, people would support the wandering street yogis with free food so that they could concentrate completely on their spiritual practices:

"If you meditated a lot, people felt you were doing good work that benefits everyone. You purified the psychic airwaves, so they took care of you. It's not like in America where, when people hear you're focusing on a spiritual life, they roll their eyes and tell you to get a job. In India, being a full-time meditator is a job, which comes with a great benefits package."

In my own case, my latest collapse onto the streets was inspired by a major spiritual crisis.

I vividly remember when it started. It was 1994 and I was still living in my apartment and entrenched in my so-called career as a cartoonist. One night I was in the middle of a bad acid trip. And when it's bad, it's *bad*. I grabbed my address book and began leafing through the phone numbers looking for someone to talk me down from my bummer. And I realized, amidst the hundreds of business names and numbers, there wasn't a single real friend I could talk to. It was at that point that I realized there was something seriously wrong with the way I was living my life.

Shortly after that, a friend of mine jumped in front of a train. And I realized I wanted to, too.

Instead, like countless fools before me, I packed away all my stuff and hit the Open Road. I had no idea where I was going, I only knew that I couldn't stand where I was at. I remember one typical day in the middle of nowhere. I was hitchhiking up Highway 101 North headed towards Portland. I couldn't get a ride so I just crossed the road and hitchhiked down south. It didn't seem to matter. Whichever way the wind blew, I went. For I was completely adrift in my pointless Hell. I looked north, south, east, and west. Something was missing and whatever it was, I couldn't find it anywhere. For two years, every day was more hideous than the last. As I sunk down, down, down.

Then one day I met the kind of magical character you sometimes meet on the streets. He had a droopy mustache and he sold rainbow-colored magic wands that he made himself on the street corner for $2 each. He quoted extensively from Kerouac, Bukowski, and Henry Miller. He was about 50 years old, but he had such translucent blue eyes that total strangers, 17-year-old girls, would exclaim: "You have the most beautiful eyes I have ever seen!" "Why thank you, my dear," he would answer. For Christmas '96 he gave me a copy of a book by Swami Muktananda, *Where Are You Going?* "He's great good fun," he said.

I spent the next two years sitting in the woods in the Berkeley hills meditating and chanting my mantra to the deer, the raccoons, the blue jays, and the blood-sucking ticks. And I can tell you: Not only did I survive the streets. The streets unequivocally saved my fucking ass.

Swami Muktananda himself was part of that great lineage of wandering street holy men, including Jesus and Buddha and countless other Great Beings from the beginning of time and back again. At age fifteen, Muktananda left his home and spent the next 30 years wandering on foot, covering the length and breadth of India, as he searched for the Truth, experiencing all the hardships of the streets. At one point, he was so hungry he strained mud in order to get something to eat. Ultimately, Muktananda found his own Guru, as well as the answer to all of his questions. By the end of his life, ironically, the former homeless wanderer was the head of an international corporation controlling hundreds of ashrams and millions of dollars worth of real estate. Strange are the ways of our personal karma.

But let me add a cautionary disclaimer here, just in case anyone gets all excited reading this and decides to throw all their possessions into a Dumpster and hit the Open Road: It is very easy to drop out, but very difficult to drop back in. Consider that carefully.

19. The Martyr

Some street people use their patheticness as their primary survival skill. Again, I don't wish to disparage the Genuinely Needy who genuinely need our help. But there are some others who milk this routine for all they can get. And it's a very dangerous game to play, for you get locked into Pavlov's Dog reflex: *The more pathetic I become, the more treats I get.*

The Martyr needs to continually be upping the ante of his public demonstrations of wretchedness, in order to continue to be fed, which often sends him on a downward course from which he never recovers. Be careful what you pretend to be, my friend, for it's often what you become.

I know Martyrs who are getting SSI checks for mental and physical disabilities, and one of their biggest fears is that they might get healthy or sane. That's one of the biggest threats to their source of income.

20. Acid Casualties

To deal with your fellow street people you almost need to be a child psychologist. Problem is, most of us are more child than psychologist. With many of these weird ones that come to you, you have to ask yourself that basic question: *"What is wrong with HIM???"*

Is it drugs? Or is it family conditioning? Is it a psychological quirk? Or is it physical brain damage? Is it trauma from a personal tragedy? Or is he just an asshole? Or is it some combination of all of these?

One particular Acid Casualty is a local legend on the Ave. The story I got, from typically unreliable street sources, was that he had raped a 15-year-old chick on the Dead tour. So, in revenge, they dosed him with about a thousand hits of acid. Permanently scrambled his brains, now he hangs out on the Ave all day in his tie-dye t-shirt, endlessly raving about "Jerry Garcia! Grateful Dead!" Somehow, he became convinced — in what's left of his brains — that one of my cartoon characters (which I developed ten years before I met him) was based on him. Therefore, I now owed him "thousands of dollars in royalties," which he assured me he would give "to Jerry and the kids."

Every time he would see me, he would pester me and harangue me. Finally one day, I had had enough. As he approached me, I let him have it before he could even open his mouth:

"LET ME GUESS! YOU **WANT** SOMETHING FROM ME, **RIGHT**?! YOU WANT ME TO GIVE YOU SOME **MONEY**, RIGHT?! YOU WANT ME TO GIVE YOU SOME **CIGARETTES**, RIGHT?! YOU WANT ME TO **KICK DOWN TO THE BRO'**, RIGHT?!"

He looked up at me and said: "**YES!**" smiling happily as if I had finally come to my senses and was finally going to kick down to a bro'.

21. Natural Leaders

Most normal social scenes revolve around specific places like churches, clubs, bars, homes, etc., whereas the street scene tends to revolve around Natural Leaders. We usually get run off of any *place* we start hanging out at, after all. So the ever-fluid, ever-transitory street scene tends to revolve around charismatic *individuals* instead. Wherever one of these Natural Leaders sits down, a crowd of street people usually starts congregating around them. They are the social equivalent of a movable living-room couch.

When one of these Natural Leaders suddenly moves out of town, you'll see his former street crew drifting around listlessly, like lost puppies or satellites thrown out of their orbit. Until they find another Natural Leader to revolve around.

Aside from the social aspects, these Natural Leaders sometimes function as something akin to Tribal Elders. They offer advice, lay down the rules, mediate conflicts, help negotiate the ever-tenuous terrain between the street world and the mainstream world, and instill a sense of order and group consensus to the street crew — no small accomplishment given the generally oddball, rebellious, and anarchy-minded tendencies of the street denizens.

After a few months on the streets, I was surprised to discover that a pack of hangers-on were beginning to congregate around *me*. This was more a testimony to the lost nature of most street people, than to any particular charisma on my part. I quickly solved this problem by allowing my naturally unpleasant personality to come to the surface. That got rid of most of them real quick.

22. Just-Can't-Pay-The-Fucking-Rent

The newest addition to the street scene are those who Just-Can't-Pay-The-Fucking-Rent. There is nothing particularly "street" about any of these people. They defy every category I've laid out in this book. They don't identify with being "street" in any way. And most of them, it probably never even occurred to them that they could end up on the streets until it happened. Usually with a resounding shock. It's an on-going tragedy playing itself out in slow-motion in most cities in America on a daily basis.

They could be your mother, your sister, your uncle, the guy you went to school with. Anybody. It's the old "one paycheck from the streets" routine.

When I first hit the streets in '76, you had to be seriously dysfunctional to be on the streets. It wasn't a matter of there not being enough housing — there was plenty of that back then — but that the street people were largely incapable of being *housebroken*.

No more. Especially in the urban centers. Our supply of housing is shrinking, shrinking, shrinking. And the squeeze is on. And it's going to get worse and worse. So you had better prepare yourself for this.

And spare me your lame-brained "solutions" to our housing shortage/homeless crisis. I've heard them all... rent control initiatives... Section 8 housing proposals... "affordable housing" plans... anti-gentrification protests... righteous sermons condemning landlord greed... etc., etc. It's all so much hot air.

As long as our population keeps EXPLODING at the rate it is now growing, there is NO solution to our housing shortage. None. It's simply going to get worse and worse. Period. But we'll be getting to that later.

What can I say about all the amazing people I've met on the streets? And the thousands of weird movies we've lived out together. Living and dying. Going through every possible mind-fuck and wrenching tragedy. As well as soaring joy. Jesus fucking Christ, what can I possibly say to all of you? Except that I was mostly glad you were there along side of me. On our respective soul journeys. From here to wherever the hell we're going to next.

Chapter Seventeen
Drugs and Alcohol

If you have any inclination towards drugs and alcohol, they will be waiting for you on the streets, like a poised trap.

Drugs are so prevalent in all facets of society, it's hard to say if there's more drug use on the streets. Probably out of all the different groups I've been involved in, I'd say that musicians have the highest rate of drug and alcohol use of any of them. And I wouldn't be surprised if doctors are even more whacked out.

But there's no question there's a lot of drug use on the street scene. I remember the year I was on welfare, we'd all ride back and forth on the way to our work crew assignments. And the one conversational subject that all of us welfare recipients seemed to have in common was comparing notes on all the different ways we got high and drunk.

On the streets you meet countless people trying to live out the romanticized, media drug myths of their youth. You got the Keith Richards junkie-wannabes; the Jerry Garcia acidhead-wannabes; the Sly Stone crackhead-wannabes; the Charles Bukowski alcoholic-wannabes; the Hunter S. Thompson gobble-down-everything-you-can-get-your-fool-hands-on-wannabes. On and on it goes.

Now the whole issue of whether the media *affects* reality, or merely *reflects* reality, is a complex one. I will say, I'm not blaming these media figures for my own drug abuse. The fact is, we probably create these media figures more than they create us.

On the other hand: I doubt very much I would have gotten into LSD to the extent that I did, if John Lennon — this eminently "successful" man that I sought to emulate — hadn't glorified acid as one of the great, enhancing experiences of his life.

I also believe the Laws of Karma when they state "what goes around comes around," and that every soul we affect in this lifetime, for good or ill, will boomerang back at us in equal proportion. And John Lennon did in fact meet up with some of the acid-addled souls he affected in this lifetime — people like Charles Manson and David Chapman. And he very well may meet up with a few more in the next lifetime.

But that's probably neither here nor there, as I've got more than enough to worry about regarding my own soul. Speaking of which:

My Own Personal Drug History

I got stoned on pot for the first time in 1973 at age sixteen, at a huge, free Carole King concert in Central Park. It was an extremely exciting experience. I spent the rest of my miserable senior year of high school getting stoned in the parking lot with other stoners. At seventeen, I hitchhiked cross-country from New Jersey to California with a pocketful of acid in search of the psychedelic hippie dream. At nineteen, camping in Humboldt redwoods with a head full of acid, I had a premature satori experience, which was probably just bullshit, but at least I didn't realize that Charles Manson was my personal savior. I spent much of the next 25 years getting stoned on various substances.

I had this quaint notion regarding drugs similar to the concept of crop-rotation, only I rotated my organs: I'd smoke *pot* for a year, and then when my lungs started bothering me I'd switch to acid. I'd drop *acid* for a year, and then when my brain cells started burning out I'd switch to alcohol. I'd drink *alcohol* for a year, and then when my liver started going I'd switch to speed. I'd snort *speed* for a year, and then when my central nervous system started frazzling I'd switch to smoking crack. I'd smoke *crack* for a year, and then... well, by then I'd ended up on the fucking streets.

In retrospect, I guess my Organ Rotation idea wasn't one of my more brilliant notions. But if you take enough drugs, I guess *anything* can start to make a certain sense.

Now there are some people who think you're some kind of party pooper if you're critical of drug use. Well, I guess I'm just not cool. Still, if you happen to think drugs are great and that they've enhanced your life in all these different ways, and that marijuana is the magic plant that is going to, like, save the fucking planet, man, more power to you. I'm not trying to invalidate your reality.

At the same time, I've got a fucking laundry list of people I've known *personally* who have been severely damaged, and in some cases ruined, by their drug use. So I ask that you don't invalidate my reality either.

I remember this one radio show where I called Jerry Garcia, among other things, "a fat, stupid junkie." After the show, a hippie friend of mine got wildly indignant. How could I say that ABOUT JERRY?! THE GREAT MAN?! Halfway through his tirade, he paused for a moment and considered his own situation — his own body was almost completely wrecked from his own drug-related strokes — and conceded: "I guess the truth hurts."

Of course, one thing that many anti-drug zealot/idiots are loathe to admit is the fact that the reason we take drugs in the first place is because, sometimes, they work. At least in the short term. They do give you some semblance of a "high." They will in fact alter the state of your brain. And, considering how miserable so many of our brains are, that counts for something.

*Chapter Seventeen
Drugs and Alcohol*

The problem is, in the long-term they work less and less, and you end up doing more and more drugs to get less and less high until you're a big ole mess. Drugs are the classic case of "diminishing returns."

That said, I think all drugs should be decriminalized and regulated. Considering the horrific level of murder, rape and assault in this society, the last thing we need to be doing is wasting the cops' time with all this Drug War bullshit.

The cops claim that these drugs lead to these other crimes. Fine. If a junkie is breaking into your apartment to support his junk habit, bust him for the burglary. But if he's just shooting up his junk, leave him the fuck alone. But the cops are lazy like the rest of us; they know it's easier to bust somebody for drugs than to catch them committing an actual crime. So there it goes. Cops figure we're all just guilty anyway, so they'll use whatever is the simplest way to nail us.

The "legal" aspect of drugs is such historic bullshit anyways. One generation prescribes heroin and cocaine as medicine, and the next generation declares them illegal. One generation declares marijuana illegal, and the next generation prescribes it as medicine. Can't we get off that crap?

Considering the ambiguous attitude society has towards drugs; considering how the media has distorted, demonized, and romanticized what these drugs are; perhaps it would be worthwhile to take a closer look at what these drugs actually do, or don't do.

1. Pot

One of the beguiling things about drugs is how different people react differently to the same drug: One person smokes pot and feels relaxed and mellow, while another gets tense and paranoid. One person drinks beer and gets sloppy happy, while another gets in barroom brawls.

So, needless to say, my reflections on these drugs are going to be highly subjective and individual, of course.

But take pot, for example, which I smoked for twenty years. Most pot smokers can probably relate to this: I used to get stoned all the time and scribble down all these incredibly meaningful thoughts in my journal. But then the next day I'd read it back when I was straight and be disappointed at how banal the entries were. You realize that on pot, you may be *feeling* things more profoundly, but what you're *thinking* is not necessarily more profound. It's fool's gold, really.

I'm reminded of the old Grateful Dead joke: What did the Deadhead say when he ran out of drugs? "The Dead *SUCK!*"

From the perspective of the streets, you already have all these lethargic street people who are having problems sustaining any kind of motivation. Lying around getting stoned all day is hardly a recipe for kick-starting your life into gear. For many street people, pot is like a banana peel they keep slipping on. Apply for the job? Sure. But first that hit off the ole bong... So much for that day.

2. Alcohol

Some of the best times of my life have been spent sitting across from a good friend with a pitcher of beer, and slowly getting schnockered together. For most of my life I was a social drinker — go out with the boys on a Friday night and tie on a good one, that kind of deal.

But on the streets, *every* night is Friday night. One of the biggest dangers of the streets is the endless expanse of free time. And drugs and alcohol are an easy way to kill it.

Surviving On The Streets

Pretty soon I was hanging with some of the hardest drinkers on the scene, the kind of guys who start drinking for breakfast and drink all day long until they pass out. I thought there was something almost mythic about hanging out in an alleyway getting drunk with a bunch of winos. It was like a scene out of a movie, or a dream. And I'd look at myself going down, and I'd see the people I was with going down, and well, what else can you do at that point but have another fucking drink?

It's like Bukowski put it: "When something good happens, I drink to celebrate. When something bad happens, I drink to commiserate. And when nothing happens, I drink to make something happen."

I spent a year drinking the cheapest of the cheap beer, 40-ouncers of Hamm's Ice at $1.40 a pop. That was the magic figure: a buck-forty. It's funny how we were all so unmotivated we couldn't even motivate ourselves to keep a roof over our heads. And yet we always had motivation to hustle up the next $1.40. I have no idea how we did it. We always came up with the next $1.40 somehow. We'd always find a way to drink all day long.

And that was part of the appeal, maybe even more so than the effect of the booze on our brains. It was *Something To Do*. Even if our purpose was hardly noble, at least we had *some* kind of purpose. And that was something. Scrounging up the next 40-ouncer was like men going on a group hunting-and-foraging expedition. And then after yet another successful expedition: the group celebration. With, you guessed it, another 40-ouncer of delicious, nutritious Hamm's Ice!

And the truly beguiling thing was: Sometimes, it actually worked!

I don't wish to make light of the incredible suffering the average street person often endures. But a surprising — and rarely mentioned — facet of the street experience is: When it works, it can be as good as it gets.

The sun is out, the sky is blue, the weather is perfect, and you're just at the beginning of that creamy buzz. You don't have a care in the world, and the conversation is soulful, and the jokes are all good, and you've been smiling so hard you can feel your face getting shiny. And then the guitars come up and they're all perfectly in tune for once, and we're all singing "Tangled Up and Blue," and "Hey Joe" and "I been to the desert on a horse with no name, it felt good to be up on the reins..." And this 16-year-old street chick is dancing along, and she's the most beautiful thing you've ever seen in your life, just unbelievable, you keep looking at her to make sure she actually exists in front of you and it's not just an alcoholic delusion, in her skimpy, little backless gypsy halter and her little tits are flopping around in there. And the whole crew piles into buses and station wagons and we're off to the beach, and there are a couple cases of beer, and someone passes the whiskey around, and everybody is buzzing on 'shrooms, and we build a big bonfire in the sand and roast up some fresh fish, and the moon is full, and the hippie boys are all beating wildly on drums, and the hippie girls are all dancing in the sand around the crackling fire, and the waves are crashing to the beach for the rest of eternity and everybody is happy and beautiful and content and nobody is even beating the crap out of anybody for a change. And even the gangbanger white kid from Richmond with the bullet-hole scars in his legs and the bitter Steve McQueen face, is shouting with a big, beaming smile: "We're all Beautiful!" and he's decided to turn over a new leaf starting right now and he flings his Frisbee as high as he can into the black sky and it disappears into the silvery black ocean of eternity.

And it all works. This is what you had been looking for the whole damn time and never finding. Until now. And suddenly, there it is in front of you. And you sit back and take another pull off your beer and think: "What did I do RIGHT this time for a change?"

Of course, the next morning it's 90 degrees and muggy and the school bus has broken down on the side of the road and we're all stranded there on a cliff overlooking the ocean and our hands and face are grimy with oil and dirt, and everybody is cursing under their breath. And we're all scratching our heads because

Chapter Seventeen
Drugs and Alcohol

everybody on the bus has bugs in their dreadlocks and we're probably gonna have to shave our heads or douse them with kerosene. And the hippie goddess from last night is no longer dancing, dancing, dancing; her face looks haggard and she's pissed, why?, because you're an asshole and a loser and she hates you.

It's hard to describe the endless socializing of the streets. It was like we were partying, only "party" isn't quite the right word to describe it. Because all too often the scenes were like scenes out of a nightmare. For there was this underlying unhappiness to so much of our lives. There was often this sense of: The Party's Over But The Guests Won't Go Home. For we had nowhere to go.

We'd be sitting on a bench in the middle of the town square passing a bottle around, and everything is starting to speed up as night comes, and the weird gay guy that nobody likes is laughing hysterically, he can't stop laughing even though nothing is funny, and everybody is saying "SHUT THE FUCK UP!" but he just keeps on laughing and laughing, and some idiot is pissing all over the sidewalk, and then the gay guy is suddenly puking and he's on all fours wretching into the grass. And this father walks by us with his little daughter as we're all sitting there on the bench, and he looks at us with this piercing expression of disgust and disapproval, and then hurries off away from us. And in that moment I realize where I'm at and what I've become.

And always, these heavy dramatic scenes. Because we were all seriously damaged and hurting in some way that we couldn't deal with; couldn't figure out a solution to; because maybe there *was* no solution, maybe life just sucks, it just gets worse and worse until you die; so the only thing to do was take another fucking drink. That's why we were all drinking after all.

And your best friends' skin is turning a mottled yellow color because his liver is going from twenty years of non-stop boozing. He's dying right in front of you. He's *ready* to die. He looks you in the eye and tells you about his mother and father who died when he was twelve. And it's a heavy moment. Maybe we should head up to Seattle or Eugene. Maybe it would be better up there than this goddamn town. And did I tell you about the time I blah, blah, blah. And the cops are coming, let's get the fuck out of here. We stagger through backyards in the darkness. Find someplace else to sit and drink.

Or even worse, when there is NO drama, no catharsis. When it was just boring. And we were killing our hours and pissing our lives away for nothing. For our lives had amounted to nothing. Less than nothing.

One afternoon, we got the word that a kid we all knew on the scene, a 17-year-old homeless boy with a broken arm, had O.D.ed on heroin. I had sat right next to him on the ledge just yesterday during Food Not Bombs. And now he was gone.

We drank vodka that night, for it was his favorite drink. A toast to a fallen comrade. It was sad, and for just a moment we would pause in silence with our private thoughts. We wouldn't so much think about the kid who died, but that we were barely alive ourselves. To be trapped in this weird zombieville of the walking dead. How did this happen? Why were we here? How did we end up like this? And where were we going? Well, we were going to the same place that the 17-year-old kid had just gone to. Which seemed a closer destination at this moment than anywhere else in this strange, strange world of life and death. "My father used to own massage parlors in San Francisco when I was a kid," said the cute, little homeless redhead sitting next to me on the ledge, as she took a big hit on the vodka directly from the bottle. Passed it to me. Somehow, that seemed to explain it, how she ended up sitting on this ledge in this strange, accidental circle of lost souls getting drunk at midnight.

But was there really an explanation to any of this? What was it all for? Could this be all there is? And was there any way out of this trap? Well, no answer. Never any answers. But after a couple more drinks, the questions won't even matter.

3. Acid

Probably nothing has done more to give drug use an aura of legitimacy than the quaint notion that psychedelic drugs could enhance one's spiritual development. This rather dubious premise was at the very heart of the '60s counterculture, and it's still widely accepted on today's street scene, as well as on many other levels of society.

Now, regardless of whether one can actually attain mystical insights by scrambling one's brain with powerful chemicals, the fact remains that once you swallow this premise, you have opened a whole 'nother can of worms. For if one can attain the ultimate — spiritual wisdom — from taking one drug, then what's to stop you from thinking you could also attain more mundane benefits from other drugs? One drug to make you happy. Another drug to calm your nerves. Another drug to give you energy. Another drug to help you sleep. And so on.

The hippies were known to vociferously squawk at the idea that pot and acid could lead to harder drugs. But that's exactly what happened in my own case, as well as with numerous other druggies I've met over the years.

Jerry Garcia himself — who did in fact embody the '60s in all its glory and hideousness — was a classic example of this genre. Garcia would be up on stage nodding out, and all the little hippie buds in the audience would be thinking: "Wow! Jerry must be experiencing all kinds of cosmic bliss on acid!" When in fact he was just experiencing oblivion on smack. And yet, the whole bullshit LSD myth that he perpetuated lives on.

I'm not proud to say I've done acid hundreds of times. Probably the only benefit I derived from it (if that's even the word) was the first couple of times I took it, when I realized that what I had assumed was Reality (with a capital R), was merely a construct of my mind, and one of innumerable possible constructs. But after that, all I really experienced on all my other acid trips was a chemically distorted construct, so big deal.

I will say, in one way acid did expand my consciousness. But not "expand" in the sense of "growth," but more like how you expand a rubber band. And every time I stretched the rubber band of my mind, it ended up snapping back a little less pliant than the time before.

Now I don't want to come across like a Fundamentalist Christian condemning other people's vices, because Lord knows I have enough vices of my own. What I am saying is, you can get locked into a particularly vicious cycle when you *mistake* a vice for a virtue (and, for the record, I consider Fundamentalist Christianity a vice disguised as a virtue). In my own case, acid turned out to be a sickness I mistook for a cure. The sicker I got spiritually, the more I reached for the acid-cure, which only made me sicker, etc.

I was greatly influenced at the time by 60s guru Alan Watts, one of the prime popularizers of psychedelic spirituality. Unfortunately, Watts was a guru who hadn't really practiced any form of spiritual discipline himself (he just gave lectures about them). So, as I drifted more and more off course spiritually, I found myself with little to fall back on, aside from taking more acid. With disastrous results.

On the other hand, as Hunter S. Thompson put it: "Anyone who thinks they can get pre-digested wisdom for $5 a pop, got what they deserved."

4. Speed

When you're homeless, and sleep is the enemy, speed can seem like a godsend. Just get wired and stay up for days and days and that pesky problem of finding a place to crash is magically solved. Or at least postponed. Until you finally end up collapsing in the gutter for 16 hours like a burned-out zombie. But it was fun while it lasted.

I used to enjoy the seemingly endless energy I'd get from speed, this tingling sense that my life was this exhilirating, Technicolor movie, with me as the star, and the sense of extroversion that helped me keep on top of the endless wave of socializing on the streets. For once I was never at a loss for words. And did I tell you about the great, INCREDIBLE idea I just had. On the downside, one night I was trapped in a rainy doorway with a tweeker chick who talked at me non-stop for three straight hours, only several minutes of which actually made sense (that was the part when she kept repeating *"Poo-poo butt-fuck!! Poo-poo butt-fuck!!"* Over and over). And the come-down from speed is particularly brutal. For a week I'd sit on the sidewalk in a blanked-out daze with a head made out of cement. Ugh.

Certainly no drugs inspire more useless energy than speed.

I remember this one night wired on speed when I realized I had lost a twenty-dollar bill somewhere. I spent the next four hours obsessively searching through every thing I owned, looking for it. Then I thought: Maybe it had fallen out of my pocket on the walk back to my place. So I spent all night retracing my steps through the deserted city streets looking everywhere for that twenty-dollar bill. Of course, the next morning I remembered I had spent the twenty on speed.

One of the last really good ideas I got for my daily comic strip *Twisted Image* was when I decided to do a series of strips under the influence of different drugs. Each day I'd do a different drug. I'd start out the first panel of each strip with: "IT'S MONDAY, 11:30 AM, AND I JUST DROPPED THAT ACID..." or "IT'S TUESDAY, 2 PM, AND I JUST SNORTED THAT SPEED..." and so on. And I'd document not only my thoughts on these drugs, but the effects that they had on my motor skills as I drew the strips. A great idea. Except I ended up doing the drugs but never got around to doing the strips.

No question, the central nervous system drugs such as speed can really tear you up. Whatever benefits you get in the short term is hardly worth the long term damage. And hopefully you'll realize that sooner rather than later.

5. Crack

Crack is the one drug that really physically damaged me. I spent a summer seriously smoking that garbage, and for several years afterwards I noticed myself slurring my words. And there was a certain fractured disjointed quality to how the sentences jumbled out of my mouth, which seemed to imply some kind of brain damage.

On the positive side, there were a couple of times where I got the hit just right and it was like bells going off and floating up to heaven. It was about the most purely euphoric two minutes of my life. It was the feeling you'd *always* been looking for, of contentment and bliss and pure, sensual pleasure. Even the *air* tastes delicious. And you hand the crack pipe back to the guy in front of you, some guy you just met, but you realize he's one of the best, most wonderful human beings you've ever known and he very well could be your best friend in the whole world. I have no idea how the cocaine molecules chemically interact with the cells of one's brain to produce this heavily drugged state, but as I started drifting downwards I remember thinking: "Now I can understand why people are willing to die and go to jail for this shit!"

But it's useless, because the fleeting high is over so quick it merely accentuates how *un-high* you are now, when you come down, which is most of the time.

So, of course, you want to get back up there, so you take another big hit of crack, only you get *less* this time. You keep wanting more and more and, finally, *MORE!!!* But yet you keep getting less and less. No drug inspires more pure, naked greed for *MORE!!* than crack. It's horrible. Crack is truly the cock-teaser of all drugs, because it promises so much and delivers so little.

You spend the rest of the time chasing after that first high, which you never get back. Fools gold. Eventually you realize that the high is nothing more than a crude way of jacking around with your body's thermostat. And you feel incredibly stupid about the whole affair.

6. Intravenous Drugs

If a person is shooting up drugs, they're on a self-destructive death trip and they're going down. And there's probably not a lot you can do about it.

I had one friend, he couldn't stop shooting heroin; he got so sick of the whole scene he jumped in front of a train.

Another friend of mine, a beautiful young woman, was shooting up speed balls, a combination of heroin and cocaine. She fell down right in front of me with a stroke. Half of her body is paralyzed now for the rest of her life. She calls herself "Quasimodo" because of how she feels dragging her half-dead body all over town. What "high" could possibly be worth that risk? In truth, you don't get high from drugs, you just get lower and lower.

You really wonder what life means to some people. One morning I was having a casual conversation with one of my druggie friends, talking about the weather and where to get some breakfast.

"Oh, by the way," he said, off-handedly, "I almost died last night."

"Oh, really," I said.

"Yeah. I shot up this dope and it was a little too pure. I O.D.ed. If the paramedics hadn't come and taken me to the hospital I woulda died right there with the spike in my arm. But the weird thing was, as I was drifting off, I knew I was dying, and it didn't feel bad or nothing. It was painless, like disappearing into nothingness. In a way, it was reassuring because now I know that if I have to die, it doesn't necessarily have to be an unpleasant experience."

"Hmmm…," I said.

"Hey, do you know if they're serving donuts at the Drop-In?" he said.

And off we went, with what passes for our lives on the street.

In a way, it reminded me of the old junkie joke: These two junkies came across this junkie who had just O.D.ed.

"Holy shit," said one of the junkies. "That stuff was too pure. He's dead."

"Damn," said the other junkie. "Do you know where I can get some of that?"

If you really want to know what drugs are all about, just take a good look at the people who are doing them all the time. They're all miserable. Do you need to know anything more about drugs than that?

That's one of the devastating things about these famous celebrities who glamorized their drug use, because they gave a totally unwarranted aura of success and coolness to these drugs. But behind the media myth of success, they're all miserable, too.

Chapter Seventeen
Drugs and Alcohol

I have one friend who specializes in falling in love with junkie whores. Then he tries to save them from themselves. It never works. All you end up doing is standing too close to their suffering. And it really hurts.

Against my better judgment, I ended up falling for this drugged-out street waif. She was adorable, this lost, little girl with these big, sad, puppy dog eyes that called out "HELP ME!" even as she was giving the world a big fuck-you. It was weird. I'd be walking down the Ave at 2 a.m. and the doorways would be filled with grizzled old homeless bums. And her. This beautiful teenage waif.

She was another one who started on the drug circuit via acid and its "myriad of spiritual possibilities" as she put it, but soon graduated to the harder stuff. She was half-crazy to begin with, and the drugs pushed her all the way out there. She got less and less coherent, and more and more whacked out into this witchy, incomprehensible, spiritual netherworld.

I'd see her sitting in a doorway in a big puddle in the middle of a rainstorm, her blankets and stuff completely soaked and ruined. One night she asked me to watch her stuff while she took off to score, these three big bags of stuff she'd been lugging around with her everywhere. When I realized she wasn't coming back, I rummaged through the stuff. Three bags crammed full of complete junk: broken hairdryers, metal candelabras, worthless office paperwork, totally tweaked-out shit. And at the bottom of one bag, a big 20-inch butcher knife.

Generally, people start shooting drugs because they have some deep psychological wound that they can't deal with. The drugs block out the problem. But it's a form of spiritual checkmate, for it prevents them from resolving the problem. In a sense, the junkie sublimates all of life's complex, little problems into one big, simple problem: Junk.

In the case of my tweeker friend, it got to the point where I couldn't tell if her craziness was a result of her mental problems, her personality problems, her traumatic life experiences, or the drugs. Or maybe she was just an asshole. Or maybe I was just an asshole. But at some point, it's just a hopeless mess, a hopelessly snarled knot in your soul that only gets tighter and tighter the more you tug at it.

Junk also appeals to the narcissism of certain people. There's a kind of person whose whole life revolves around nothing more than a never-ending series of self-indulgent desires. They want a cigarette. They want a cup of coffee. They want a jelly donut. They want a hamburger. They want a new CD. But, unfortunately, there are just not enough of these desires to string together to fill the day. But the junk addiction gives them an All-Consuming Desire to chase after forever.

I've always suspected the addictive aspect is one of the key attractions to shooting up drugs. Many street people have difficulty coming up with *any* kind of motivation. So the addiction supplies an all-encompassing motivation that gets them off their ass, and in and out of all sorts of different rooms, and misadventures.

But the whole concept of drugs is flawed: this idea that if we just get $5 or $10 we could buy something that would make us feel happy. If only it were that simple. I'd be out there buying $5 or $10 worth of happiness right now, rather than writing this crap.

And while I'm on the subject of shooting up drugs, probably one of the most stupid things I've ever heard are these so-called "clean-needle" programs. Making it easy for junkies to shoot up drugs is just completely wrong-headed. I happen to agree with UC Berkeley microbiologist Prof. Peter Duesburg that AIDS doesn't have anything to do with HIV. It's not the *needles* that are killing people, but the *garbage* that they're shooting up into their bodies.

The "clean-needle" program is so stupid. Sure, clean needles are better than dirty needles. But it's like somebody eating poison off of dirty plates. Sure, it's better to have clean plates than dirty plates, but what's the point of making a big deal about the clean plates when they're going ahead and eating the fucking poison?

I'm saying this in black and white: **AIDS has nothing to do with HIV**. You can call me a fool and a crackpot but just make sure you check back with me in twenty years so you can tell me you were wrong.

The idea that AIDS is a sexually transmitted disease is one of the biggest hoaxes ever perpetrated on us by the scientific community. I happen to have lived in the San Francisco Bay Area for the last twenty years — the very epicenter for this so-called contagious plague. And yet — contrary to what almost every one of these brainy scientists predicted — I don't know one single, non-hard-drug-using heterosexual who has died from AIDS. Not one. How do you explain this? Why, this must be the strangest, most peculiar contagious disease in the history of contagious diseases.

Who *is* dying of AIDS in the Bay Area? The same people who *always* die. People who are shooting poison into their veins. And it's no mystery to me WHY they're dying. It's called "drug burn-out."

When you look at the people who *are* dying from AIDS they all just happen to be so-called "high-risk" people who just happen to be doing something *else,* aside from the HIV, that could have killed them, also. What a coincidence.

And the gays who died? There were countless people in the gay community who were so irresponsibly promiscuous that they ended up getting VD dozens of times to the point where their bodies built up an immunity to the antibiotics, and that was all for them. And all the "poppers" — i.e., amyl nitrates — that they were popping like M&Ms didn't help either. I repeat: The central nervous system drugs will just tear you up. And AZT finished off the rest of them. What a "cure." It wiped out the HIV virus, along with one's bone marrow.

And the moral is: If you don't want to die, don't blast your body apart by repeatedly shooting garbage into it. And don't make a habit of getting fucked in the ass by 950 men, either. A public service message brought to you by me, Ace Backwords.

7. Prescription Meds

When it first began to sink into my addled brain that I was taking way too many drugs and that I needed to clean up my act, I made an appointment to see a psychiatrist. The first thing the doc recommended was that I start taking medication. Ironic, no?

Actually, the psychiatrist was a young German woman intern; when you're poor they sort of practice on you. After about three or four sessions I realized she wasn't making me feel any better, but I was making her feel worse. She started saying stuff like, "Gee, maybe life does suck after all." I figured I better stop seeing her before she was as nutty as me.

Now there was a period where I was so miserable, I was drinking beer every night for the express purpose of medicating myself. I figured, fuck, if I was going to medicate myself, at least beer is time-tested; it's been around for centuries and we know what it does and doesn't do, and what its side effects are.

But all these brand new meds they're coming out with every week, God only knows what the long-term effects are. *You* are the guinea pig. And the results of the experiment, at present, are hardly encouraging.

I know so many people on the street scene staggering around doing the thorazine shuffle. They have that horrible, glazed-over dullness, like their minds have been slathered with molasses.

I had one chronically depressed friend; they hooked him up with all the latest, new miracle drugs — from Valium to Prozac to Zoloft. None of them worked. For two years he saved up one of his meds each day, and when he got up to 500 he swallowed them all. But they didn't even work for *that*. Finally, he ended up hanging himself on his fire escape.

If you happen to benefit from your meds, more power to you. But I happen to think 90% of the people are being poisoned by these quacks.

8. Coffee and Cigarettes

The one drug I ended up getting addicted to was coffee. I remember when I first tried to quit coffee for 30 days. I exhibited all the classic withdrawal symptoms: splitting headaches, the sweats, wild mood swings. I figured I better go back to the coffee before I killed somebody.

Cigarettes? I started smoking on the streets because it gave me something to do while I sat there doing nothing. Cops look at you doubly funny when you're just sitting there. And it was a social thing, too. In the free-form, here-one-moment-gone-the-next flux of the streets, sitting down and sharing a smoke with a pal was a way of committing to being there with the person for the next five or ten minutes. This might sound trivial. But you might not understand the effect of not having homes to visit with your friends.

I concluded that drugs are basically just poison. So, finally, I pretty much quit drinking and drugging entirely. I realized that if I wanted to reach the higher states of consciousness, I would need a subtle, highly refined mind to get there. And I certainly wasn't going to get there by blasting my brain with powerful chemicals.

And oddly, being straight felt like being on drugs. Because it was such an unusual experience after decades of drugging. Being straight for a change felt like an altered state.

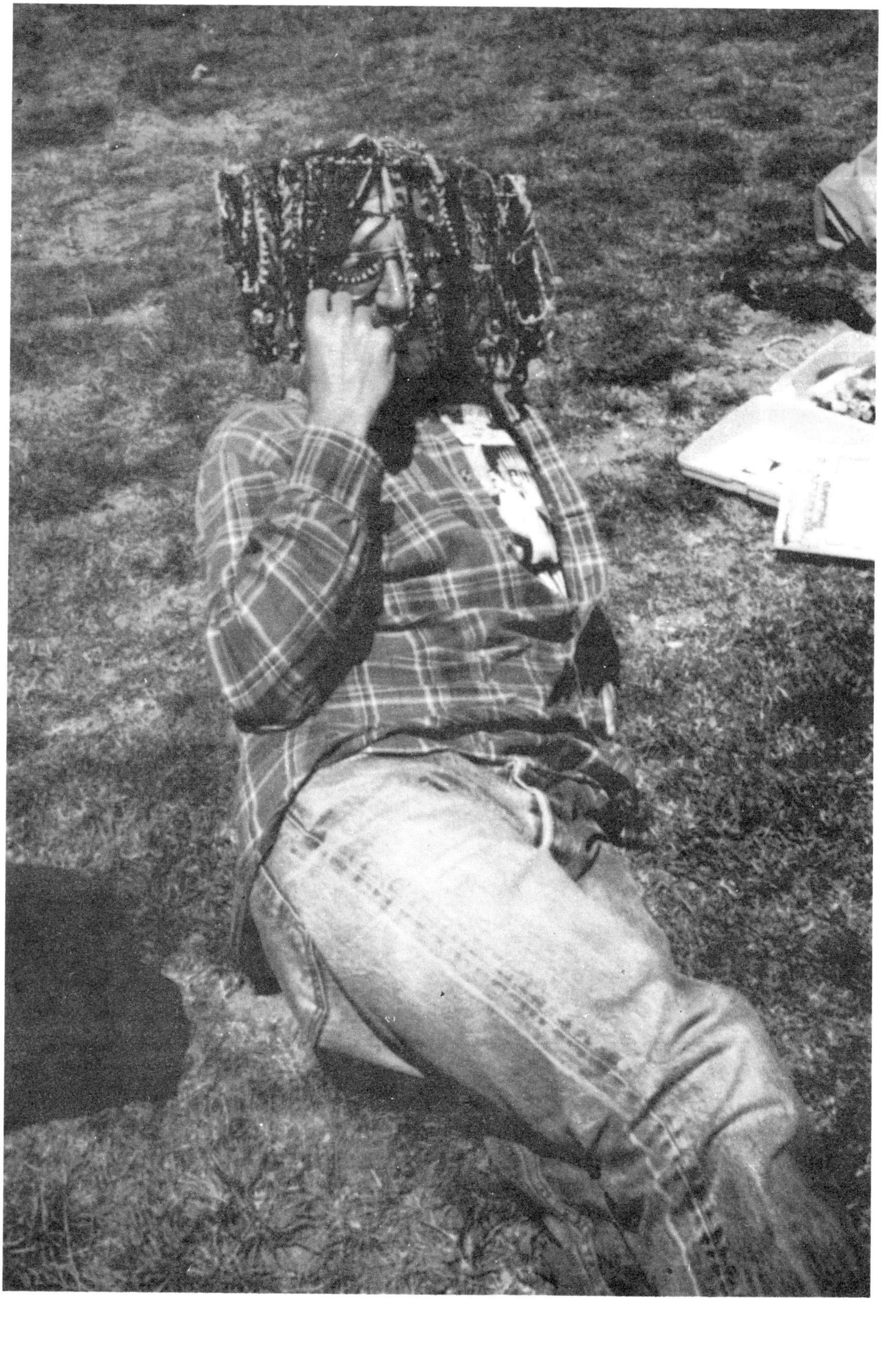

Chapter Eighteen
Violence

There's a lot of fighting on the streets. Needless to say, many street people are dysfunctional, bitter, crazy, and/or assholes. So if you cram them all together in the same place, violent sparks are inevitable.

Most of the violence on the streets is just sort of bitch fights: Pushing, shoving, slapping, brawling, yelling, cursing, maybe a couple of punches thrown, usually one guy wrestles the other to the ground and pins him. Most of the time, there's little actual damage aside from the occasional black eye or bruised ego. And these skirmishes often serve the purpose of resolving long-festering disputes and establish a pecking order among the street denizens.

On the other hand, you never know when one of these minor spats is suddenly going to escalate into The Real Thing, into real violence where lives are forever changed in its wake. With dreary regularity, street people do in fact get shot, or stabbed, or beaten to a pulp. So people tend to get tense whenever street people are facing off yelling at each other. Because it can get serious in the blink of an eye. With you in the middle of it.

As a general rule: "If they're talking, they're not fighting." But, unfortunately, not always. Most of it is just chest thumping and hot air. If someone really wants to beat your ass, he usually won't make a big speech about it beforehand; he'll just do it.

When I was a teenager on the streets, I was so stupid and naïve, it's a wonder I have a head attached to my shoulders. I've had loaded guns cocked up to my fool head, and razor sharp knives pressed up to my Adam's apple. But I wised up real quick. You don't get me twice, fuckers.

Well, that's not exactly true. The fact is, if you *really* want to get somebody, it's not hard to arrange (or if I want to get you, fucker). I reference everything back to Ronald Reagan, "The most powerful man in the world," surrounded by heavily armed bodyguards. And yet some twerp who barely knew how to shoot a gun came within inches of offing him. If someone really wants to get you, they will. I'm not saying you shouldn't take precautions to minimize your chances of being victimized. But don't waste too much energy trying to defend yourself against every possibility. Relax. In any case, your karma awaits you.

Deal With This: 101

Probably the best defense is cultivating the ability to recognize these Violent Assholes BEFORE they spot you. And it's good to develop some basic strategies for dealing with The Asshole when they DO spot you. Consider the following scenario from which countless violent street episodes have sprung:

You're sitting on a bench late at night smoking a cigarette, minding your own business, when suddenly Some Asshole is standing in front of you.

"Got a smoke?!" he demands, not asks.

"Sorry, I bummed this one," you respond.

"Well, then give me that one!" he demands, pushing his face inches away from yours.

How would you react at this point?

Now quite often, what you *really* want to do is kick the bastard a hard one in the nuts and then grind your butt out on his forehead. But this approach can sometimes prove counterproductive.

The second impulse is to just give in and give him your cigarette. But that rarely works either, for you've given The Asshole an opening into your world — the one thing you want to avoid at all costs. Plus, if he senses you're weak, the true Asshole will rarely stop at a cigarette.

Instead, I'll simple grit my teeth and say, firmly:

"No. I'm smoking this one."

I've become a master of putting out a surface politeness, with a firm subconscious message that says: *"Don't push me, boy. Go away."* In my tone of voice, I strive to get across the dual message: *"I am not fucking with you,"* along with the corresponding message: *"You had better not be fucking with me."*

It's important too, not to let your macho bullshit side kick in. If you want to turn every slight into a fight to the death, you'll never survive a year on the streets. And yet, it's important to fend off these Violent Assholes with just a hint of menace. But not so much that he takes it as a challenge, or an excuse to take offense. Because The Asshole is always looking for an excuse to take offense. His game, often, is to be obnoxious, be obnoxious, be obnoxious. Then, finally, when you retaliate by being obnoxious back to him, he responds: "What? How dare you disrespect me!" as if YOU are fucking with HIM. And then it's on. I guess that's why they call them Assholes.

If our Cigarette-Grubbing Asshole still persists at this point — after "no," "no," and finally *"NO!!!!!"* — well then, you KNOW you have a grade-A Asshole on your hands. Generally, I have a code: I'll get up and walk away. *Once.* It's a big world after all, and the whole point is to occupy a part of it that doesn't include The Asshole. On the rare occasion when The Asshole follows me, I'll make my stand, if need be. And, usually — but not always — I'll succeed at driving The Asshole out of my space. Generally, I'll go to a lot of trouble to avoid violence. At the same time, I'm not going to spend my street career bobbing and weaving and running from bullies. It's up to you to decide where you draw that line, depending on what you're willing to back up.

Sometimes there's just no way out; the ugly scene is coming anyway, so there's no point postponing it; just cut to the chase and get it over with. I've taken guys by the collar of their shirts and pushed them backwards twenty feet and slammed their backs against the wall and told them, "ENOUGH!" But only because I sensed in that particular situation that that was the quickest way to end that particular bad scene.

What you DON'T want to do is allow the potentially violent scene to escalate. This requires a certain amount of delicacy and finesse. Just the right tone. In these situations I often make the demeanor of the Bomb Squad defusing a potential bomb. Mishandling these minor hassles can turn them into major problems.

One night at the Hate Man's drum circle, a hippie friend of mine got into an argument with three black high school kids over precisely who was throwing off the rhythm of the drum circle:

"Hey man, you're fucking up the beat!"

Accusations were thrown around. Challenges were made. Lines were drawn. And a minor situation suddenly escalated to the point where my friend ended up getting his head bashed in with a big stick and spitting out a couple of teeth. A situation that could have been avoided, perhaps. Nobody likes having to deal with these Assholes with kid gloves. But people like spitting out teeth even less.

Remember: An ounce of prevention can save you a pound of getting pounded.

Them Whacky City Kids

Avoiding drawing the line, unless you're willing to back it up. And, if at all possible, avoid threatening or challenging, for that's a sure-fire recipe to escalate the situation.

One night I noticed this group of black and white kids — 15-, 16-, 17-year-olds — shoplifting a piece of jewelry from my vending table.

"Man, that's not cool, stealing from a homeless person," I said. "Put that back."

"Oh yeah?" said one of the kids. "Check this out." He pulled open his jacket revealing a pistol jammed into the waistband of his pants.

"Man, you city kids are tough nowadays," I said evenly. "Back when I was kid, if we had a beef with someone we just put up our fists and beat on each other. But you kids nowadays take out guns and shoot each other. Man, you kids are tough."

"Nah, we're not so tough," said the kid with this strange air of resignation. Since I didn't challenge him, he didn't feel the need to back it up. And I was being straight with him.

One of the kids turned out to be a friend of mine — this baby-faced Black kid who I had given a jacket to one night when he was stuck out in the cold. We talked for a bit about mutual friends. Finally, the other kid returned the piece of jewelry to my table.

Right on cue this white woman rushed up to the table screaming: "WHAT THE HELL'S WRONG WITH YOU KIDS?! I SAW YOU SMASHING MY CAR WITH YOUR METAL CHAINS!"

The kids quickly ran off into the night. No different, really, than the mischief me and my friends used to cook up as kids egging cars and shit. Only, the level of violence has certainly escalated these days. You have these kids walking around with very little brains and very big guns. A very bad combination.

It also helps if you can develop your psychic abilities. Trust your intuition. Learn to spot the omens before shit happens.

Surviving On The Streets

I remember this one afternoon, a vendor named Jim with emotional problems had been missing for several days and we feared he had committed suicide. Another vendor callously took his table and took over his spot. I warned a friend of mine: "That's bad karma, disrespecting the dead. If Jim is really dead his spirit will come out of the grave like an EC Horror Comic and smash their table."

Even I was surprised when, a few hours later, their table did indeed get smashed. Unexpectedly a gang fight broke out all around us. Real vicious stuff. White kids. Black kids. Hispanic kids. This mad blur of bodies, smashing each other over the heads with metal chairs and shit. When you see these vicious little gangbangers in action, it's like your worst urban nightmare coming to life.

Even stranger, later that night I found out that some of the 'bangers were actually friends of mine. It had all happened so fast that I didn't recognize them in the blur of bodies. And most of them are actually pretty nice, soft-spoken kids, for the most part.

"What was the fight all about?" I asked them.

"Tagging," they said.

"Why are you fighting over tagging?"

"We got to fight about something," they said.

Sometimes it can feel like you're trapped in a bad James Dean Movie.

Spotting Them First

Again, the one thing that will save you the most problems is developing the ability to spot the Violent Asshole and the Potentially Violent Scene *before* it happens. You must learn to trust your intuition, and develop the ability to separate useless *paranoia* from legitimate *concern*.

The other night this drunken, pushy, obnoxious white street guy approached me selling *Street Spirit* — that crusading homeless newspaper — on a street corner.

"CHECK IT OUT, DUDE! *STREET SPIRIT!* ONE DOLLAR!" — blared Street Guy.

Within ten seconds of talking with him I had him pegged:

Asshole.

The data processor in my mind immediately starts picking up the signals and churning out the data: *"in-and-out-of-the-joint all the time... angry... belligerent... a bomb waiting to go off... give him no hooks to attach himself to you... be blandly polite and get away as soon as possible... he'll probably kick the shit out of somebody before the night is over (preferably not you) and he'll be back in the joint and out of your hair for the next six months...."*

Unfortunately, there happened to be this big, soft, Middle-Class Dude standing on the next block who lacked this data in his mental processor. He was standing outside the movie theatre chatting with three friends, when Street Guy approached him on the lookout for fresh meat:

"CHECK IT OUT, DUDE! *STREET SPIRIT!* ONE DOLLAR!"

"Excuse me, you are *bothering* us," said Middle-Class Dude. "We're trying to have a private conversation here. Please leave us alone. Go peddle your newspaper *elsewhere.*"

Middle-Class Dude was a big guy — 6'4", 250 pounds — wearing an expensive tan overcoat, and he had a little black ponytail. He had the air of a hip lawyer, or maybe a college professor. A *professional*. A guy no doubt used to snapping his fingers and having people follow his orders. He dismissed the obnoxious street pest with the imperial wave of the back of his hand, the classic *begone-you-peasant* gesture. Then he turned his back on the guy and went back to talking to his friends, probably thinking: *That got rid of that asshole.* Well, not quite.

Chapter Eighteen
Violence

"NO! **YOU'RE** LEAVING PAL!" announced Street Guy.

He gave Middle-Class Dude a hard shove in the chest, sending him reeling backwards. Then he pushed his chest right into Middle-Class Dude's chest and waved his fist in his face.

"C'MON, YOU BIG SUNV'BITCH!, LET'S GO!! **YOU'RE** LEAVING, NOT ME!" He pushed him again, sending him reeling.

Middle-Class Dude stood there frozen. He was about a half-foot taller and a hundred pounds bigger than scrappy, little Street Guy. But there was something soft about his bulk. He looked like one of those guys who hadn't been in a fistfight since the second grade. He was probably used to getting away with pushing people around thanks to his size and his status. But all of that counts for nothing on the streets. The obnoxious little Street Guy was calling Middle-Class Dude on his shit, seeing if he had any heart to back up his act.

You could see the gears whizzing in Middle-Class Dude's head as he realized — too late — what he was up against:

"Well... if I try to hit him, he will probably kick the living shit out of me and I will be rolling around in the gutter in my expensive, new, tan overcoat in severe pain, embarrassed and humiliated in front of my woman and my friends... On the other hand, if I flee like a sissy-boy, I'll still end up being embarrassed and humiliated in front of my friends, but, on the upside, I will have avoided physical pain as well as soiling and tearing my expensive new overcoat..."

Middle-Class Dude quickly saw the wisdom of the latter position and fled into the safety of a nearby diner. Only it wasn't so safe. The vicious little Street Guy rushed into the diner after him and started to attack the big blob right inside the diner. Several waitresses managed to wedge themselves in between the combatants and forced the little Street Guy back outside, screaming and wailing all the way. He stood there outside the doorway of the diner, waving his fist at Middle-Class Dude.

"COME ON OUT HERE! I'LL KICK YOUR FAT ASS, YOU BIG PIECE OF SHIT!!"

Now the poor guy is trapped inside the diner. He sat there meekly in the lobby, his hands folded in his lap, pretending he wasn't there, while every eye in the restaurant was trained on him. A most unfortunate predicament to be in.

I'm outside on the corner — voyeuristic bastard that I am — watching the whole scene unfolding, which I could see coming a mile away. With these vicious little time bombs, it's never a matter of *if*, but *when*.

Finally, Middle-Class Dude's woman walks over to the raging, little Street Guy, and, though I couldn't overhear the conversation, I imagine it went along the lines of: "Please don't kick the shit out of my cowardly weasel of a boyfriend." Eventually they reached some kind of agreement; they laughed and smiled and shook hands, and she even bought several copies of that crusading homeless newspaper — *Street Spirit*. And finally Street Guy stalked off down the street in search of further victims, giving Middle-Class Dude the chance to escape from the diner and go off and nurse his bruised ego.

Now I relate this story to you, for cheap kicks, but also to give you an idea of some of the volatile characters you're forced to deal with on the streets, and to impress upon you the wisdom of being able to spot them *before*, not *after*, they unleash their volatility on you.

But what was more interesting was my own reaction to the scene. On the one hand, the street person was a total asshole and I disliked him on sight. On the other hand, I've been looked down on by plenty of these middle-class snobs, too. I couldn't resist a perverse pleasure at seeing this privileged guy stripped of his façade of power and forced to stand his ground, man-to-man. For, on the streets, you're often forced into exactly these kinds of situations where there's nowhere to hide. You can't go running for a cop or a

Surviving On The Streets

lawyer or write an indignant letter-to-the-editor. You are on your own. And when someone calls you on your shit, you find out what you're really made of.

That can be highly unpleasant. But it can also be very revealing and educational. If the streets can be said to be anything, they can be said to be quite real. And that can be a good thing in the long run. On the streets, you've been stripped down to nothing but yourself. You finally get down to that. The so-called nitty-gritty. After years of dodging and avoiding it. As I said before: You can learn more from losing than winning. And on the streets you'll be given ample opportunities for those lessons.

Street Justice

One night this gutter punk — a pretty nice guy actually, aside from the satanic Pentagram tattooed on his forehead — got in a fight with his ex-girlfriend and slammed her head against the window of a local bookstore. Her head was okay, but the glass cracked. Nonetheless when the chick's friends heard about this attack the whole gutter punk crew confronted Pentagram and said:

"Meet us in the Park tomorrow at 10 o'clock for a beating or else you're 86ed from the scene."

Dutifully, Pentagram showed up the next morning, and about five gutter punks jumped him and pounded on him for about five minutes. ("He took his beating like a man," said one, respectfully, later, "and he fought back like a warrior.")

After the beating was over, Pentagram hobbled across the street, and sat there nursing his black-and-blue bruises, and went back to his panhandling. And that was considered the end of it.

Now this kind of vigilantism might seem crude and brutal to some of you. And I'm not necessarily advocating it. But, when compared to the brand of justice doled out by some of these high-priced lawyers in their perfumed suits, who's to say which is more just? At least in this particular case, the dispute was resolved — closure if you will — and the parties went on with their lives.

Another night, this old black guy raped this 14-year-old runaway chick at her crash spot. I can't say for a fact that this is related, but a few months later, I saw the black guy being chased across the park by five guys, one of whom El-Kabonged him over the head with a metal trash can. I happened to come upon the scene right as the ambulance crew was strapping his unconscious bulk onto a stretcher. Street justice.

I still see that black guy, to this day, hanging out in the park, perhaps slightly dizzier for the experience. And I assume the parties involved consider the case closed. Though one never really knows for sure. Street justice.

Another night, these street hippies were fighting on the campus. Now, I crack up when I see these nice, clean fights in the movies where it always looks so manly. In real life it's usually more like girls pulling at each other's hair and clawing their eyes out. Anyway, these guys are wrestling around on the concrete — you can hear every elbow and knee thudding against the hard pavement. Every now and then one of them would get the advantage and start bashing the other one's head up and down against the concrete like he was trying to bash the guy's brains out of his head.

A couple of one of the guy's friends were circling around the fight offering encouragement: "C'MON BOY! BEAT THAT LITTLE FAGGOT'S ASS!!" At one point, the guy managed to pin the other guy's hands behind his back, leaving his head exposed like a big, soft pumpkin. The friend hauled off and kicked the guy in the head, like teeing off on a football, as hard as he could with his big old boots. For a moment the guy had that stunned look on his face, that *"Am-I-about-to-go-down-and-get-gang-stomped?!!* look.

Now when one of these street fights suddenly erupts in front of you, you, as an observer, have three basic choices:

1. you can mind your own fucking business,

2. you can try to break it up, or

3. you can call the cops (rarely recommended on the streets).

This can get tricky, because generally, you have no idea what the fight is all about. For all you know, one of those guys might DESERVE a good beating.

If, for example, I see two guys fighting it out over a drug burn, I'll just let 'em pound on each other. Hell, you get into that scene, you know what you're getting into.

On the other hand, if I see a bunch of guys ganging up on one guy, I might intervene. You've got to play it by ear.

In this particular case, I happened to see a car pulling towards us so I called out, "Hey, man, the cops are coming. Cool it." Often this ploy will work, because often the combatants are looking for a way to end the fight without losing face, which is how it worked out in this case. They stopped fighting. At least for a few minutes. Until one of them stole the other one's bike and took off on it, with the other guy in hot pursuit waving a big knife in the air.

Later I asked the boot-kicker what that was all about.

"When I was in the joint, that guy ripped off my old lady for a lot of her stuff," he explained.

"Street justice," I concluded.

But who knows. Like a lot of street life, you just blunder along and hope you make the right decision every now and then. Don't kid yourself that I can lay out some kind of set of "street rules" for you here.

Take the issue of the cops. In 95% of the cases, if a cop happens to come along after a fight, I'll just say, "I didn't see anything." We take it as a given that the Criminal Justice System doesn't work for us. That's why we have to police ourselves in the first place.

On the other hand, a friend of mine was recently knifed in the park, gutted like a fish. OVER NOTHING. A minor, verbal disagreement that almost cost him his life. He ended up lying in a hospital bed, cut open from his neck all the way down to his dick. Now this attack happened in broad daylight, with at least 50 eyewitnesses. But as far as I know, not one of them "saw anything." Now in this particular case, had I been there I would have helped the cops in any way I could — complete description of the suspect, etc., for I would like to see this guy locked up and out of my world for a long, long time. But this is just my own particular code in that particular situation. And I'm in no position to tell you where you should draw your own line.

Sexual Violence

There was one barefoot hippie chick who danced into town one bright, sunny day. She was the classic free-spirited Deadhead type: a long gypsy skirt, bracelets, with bells on her bare ankles. A real blissed-out Rainbow Child. She was a bit of a space cadet, possibly even brain-damaged, but she really put out that "positive vibe" thing. She never talked much. She was one of those people who mostly communicated with her body, dancing and singing and smiling and giggling. She was always laughing and smiling. She was a real bright spot on the scene for several months, wailing on her saxophone on the street corner.

Then one afternoon I noticed her sitting on the sidewalk propped up against a tree, crying and wailing and sobbing. Her long hippie hair had been shaved off, and she kept scratching herself. She just sat there with her head in her hands, sobbing and shrieking hysterically. Then she'd start laughing hysterically. And then she'd go back to sobbing. Then she'd just sit there, staring into space. This went on for about a week, until they finally hauled her off to the nut house and that was the last I saw of her.

Like so much of what happens on the streets, you rarely find out exactly what happened. You witness these dramatic scenes — these dramatic transformations — for people are living out their actual lives right out in public view. But it's like watching disconnected jump-cuts from twenty different movies all edited together in a jumble, totally devoid of any context.

The word on the street was that she had been gang raped in the park, which seemed plausible. But who knows for sure?

A couple of street people had tried to talk to her; tried to help her get through her trauma. But, unfortunately, the street scene is not a place where you will find much in the way of a support group. When you go down, you usually go down alone. Too many street people are on too many bummers of their *own*, to have much left over to help you with *yours*. And when you see someone going down, there's a natural tendency to turn your back and just try and block it out. Simply because you can't bear one more tragedy on your already overloaded nervous system. The streets are a very Darwinian milieu.

I have no idea where the hippie street chick went, or what the whole episode was all about. But in my mind, it was sort of a dramatic reenactment of a scene that I've seen unfold in countless variations over the years: the hopeful hippie getting their idealism crushed into the dirt by the cruel realities of the streets.

Predators

The threat of rape is a constant mental grind for the women of the street. If you're new in town, I'd recommend talking with some of the other street women about places and people to avoid.

There are Wolves and Vampires lurking on the fringes of the street scene who specialize in luring naïve, young street chicks with drugs, scrambling their brains every which way, and then fucking them over in ways that would make your skin crawl. It is amazing some of the specimens you will meet in this world of humans.

Indeed, witnessing the destruction of innocence is one of the most heartbreaking aspects of street life. You see some of these gullible young street pups hit the scene like lambs being led to slaughter. Usually you can't prevent it, even when you can see it coming from a mile away. You can only hope they wise up fast before they really get damaged. In a way, the violence on the street is even worse than the violence in prison. At least in prison it's mostly hardened cons who are catching the brunt of it. On the streets, everyone catches it, the young, the old, the weak, the women.

Most people on the streets are good people, but fuck ups bumbling through their lives. But, never far from your scene, just a stone's throw away, in the shadows, are: the pimps, the Hells Angels, the gangbangers, the thugs — the veritable definition of a Bad Crowd. A *very* Bad Crowd. I've seen unsuspecting street kids stumble into the maelstrom and never be seen again. Some of the movies you see play out before your eyes are like the stuff you thought only existed in sordid dime-store paperbacks.

When I lived in the hotel room in the Tenderloin, I used to wake up to the sounds of the pimp next door beating the crap out of his teenage runaway prostitute: "GET OUTTA BED AND GET TO WORK, BITCH! YOU CAN'T RUN HOME TO YOUR MOMMA ANYMORE!"

*Chapter Eighteen
Violence*

Whattaya gonna do? Pull a Travis Bickle and save the day? When you step outside to the streets, you'll find twenty more chicks just like her.

My own bumbling entry into the world of the streets was not particularly stellar either. When I was seventeen, I hitchhiked cross-country from New Jersey to San Francisco with a pocketful of acid in search of the hippie dream. On the return trip, I got picked up by a pervert who put a gun to my head and forced me to suck him off. I'd rather not go into the details, but I'd be remiss in my job as a writer of this cautionary tale, if I didn't warn you about some of the bastards that are waiting for you out here. Certainly, nobody had warned ME. I was that naïve.

I've concluded that what ruins people isn't so much what *happens* to them — because, face it, horrible shit happens to most of us in this damn life. But how you *react* to what happens to you. It's the bitterness over your "raw deal" that will kill you quicker than the raw deal itself. This is a particularly crucial aspect of surviving on the streets. For most street people feel they have been shafted by life. If you don't find some way to put your suffering into a meaningful context, you are really going to be in the soup.

In my own case, I concluded that I had probably done something equally vile to the pervert in the last lifetime, and that this was my karmic payback.

Some of my more cynical, "hard-boiled realist" type readers will no doubt attribute this line of reasoning to a wishful thinking on my part, and a need to project a moral order onto the Universe when no such order exists.

I can only say that terrible, inexplicable shit happens to all of us in this life. When it comes to dealing with life's suffering, all of us must face the question: "Why me?" And I wish you luck in making sense of it in your own minds.

Street Crime

While there's no question that there's a lot of brawling and fighting on the streets, when it comes to *seriously* violent crime, there's no question that a hugely disproportionate amount of it is being committed by Black males. Virtually everyone on the streets can regale you with dozens of accounts of *Being Attacked By Black Guys*, just from within their own small circle of friends. I'm talking rapes, stabbings, beatings, robberies, murders, etc.

I once read a column in the *Oakland Tribune* by this fat-ass White Liberal who bemoaned the fact that he saw — with his own sensitive White Liberal eyes — this elderly Chinese woman on a bus bench in the inner city, take her purse and move it to the other side of her body when a Black man sat down next to her. He went on with his soggy little liberal sermonette about how terrible it was, that the Asians had now been infected with America's (i.e., "White people's") racist attitudes towards the Blacks. Blah blah blah.

How about this, fat-ass? Maybe that Asian woman had *already* experienced numerous criminal assaults at the hands of these Black males, so now she was understandably once-bitten-twice-shy.

How about that?

Sometimes I get accused of being "prejudiced" towards Blacks in this regard. Let me assure you I am not *prejudiced* — i.e., *prejudging*. I'm *post*-judging, after two decades of experience living alongside Black people.

I admit (unlike all of my clear-thinking critics) I do in fact have my prejudices. For example: I *immediately* distrust people who drive red cars. I also intuitively dislike *anyone* who tucks their pant legs into their boots. And I immediately assume that anyone who speaks with an English accent is *extremely* clever. I'm willing to cop to these prejudices. But my observation of black crime is not one of them.

Surviving On The Streets

Unlike the fat-ass White Liberal columnist, who makes his useless pronouncements from the safety of his locked-and-fortified suburban home, the average street person is right out in the city street actually living with these people.

Supposedly I'm "racist" if I happen to treat different races differently. Well how about this? I'll treat all races the same when they start *behaving* the same. How about that? I'd be more than willing to hold up my end of that bargain.

The fact is, Blacks make up about 12% of the U.S. population, and yet they are committing around 50% of the rapes, robberies and murders. They are committing these violent crimes at four times the rate of the rest of society. Therefore, I am going to be four times as wary in my dealings with them. You can call this "racism" if you want; I prefer to call it "common sense." And if you wish to keep your head attached to your neck, you'd be well advised to heed my words.

Some liberals accuse me of manipulating and falsifying numbers when I cite these crime stats. But these very same liberals are the first ones to White Flight it out of those black neighborhoods precisely because they *know* what I'm saying is true. Evidently I'm supposed to be very impressed with their heroic words and not notice their actual actions.

If my words sound harsh and startling, it's probably because you're so used to being fed the candy-coated bullshit of the PC media. I remember reading this black columnist writing about *"the black community's dirty little secret — Black Crime."* And I thought: *"Secret from WHO?"* Certainly not from anyone living on the streets.

It's also true that in 90% of the cases, the victim of Black Crime is another Black person. So who actually is benefiting by covering up and failing to honestly address the reality of this issue? Certainly not all the Black victims, or the overwhelming percentage of Blacks who *aren't* committing crimes but nonetheless must deal with the bad vibes that inevitably spring from their collective reputation (just as I, too, as a White person have been forced to bear the brunt of the sins of my fathers). Last year in Oakland, 85% of the murders were committed by Blacks, and 82% of the victims were Black.

I'll give you an example of the double-speak you hear constantly on this subject in the town of Berkeley. People will often tell you: "Don't go there, it's a *bad* neighborhood." And everyone knows exactly what that means: It's a *black* neighborhood. But heaven forbid you ever actually stated the obvious and said it was a bad neighborhood *because* it was a black neighborhood. That would be "racist."

Even worse: I'm continually told that, as a White person, Black crime is somehow *my* fault.

Bullshit.

Let me state the obvious for my many Black friends: Contrary to what the Liberal Mind-fuckers have been telling you for the last 40 years, YOU are responsible for your life, YOU are responsible for your behavior, and YOU are responsible for your success or failure.

If you want to blame Whitey, go ahead. You can jump me on the streets, and think you're delivering some kind of "payback." But you're the one who has to live in your rotten neighborhoods. And they will STAY rotten until you start taking responsibility for yourself. Believe me, I speak from experience here, as someone who wasted twenty years blaming my mother for all my problems, and all I succeeded in doing was fucking myself up.

What upsets the liberal the most isn't black crime, but that I actually *mention* it. There was one guy who wrote an indignant letter to a local newspaper complaining that in almost every article in the local police blotter, the suspect was described as a "black male." Apparently he wanted some form of Affirmative Action, where Blacks would only be named as criminal suspects in 12% of the crimes, in proportion to their percentage of the population. Perhaps White, Asian, and Latino suspects could be arbitrarily slotted

Chapter Eighteen
Violence

into the other crimes. If that sounds ridiculous and absurd, it's because most of the talk on this subject over the last 30 years has in fact been ridiculous and absurd.

Speaking of absurd, the *San Francisco Examiner* — one of the most vile pieces of Politically Correct garbage you could imagine — actually has made it part of their editorial policy to avoid mentioning in print the racial descriptions of the alleged perpetrators of crimes. I've never heard an editorial explanation for this peculiar form of journalistic self-censorship. One can only assume it's yet another form of PC "racial sensitivity." But it's funny how that "racial sensitivity" doesn't cut both ways with them.

Last year some White street people ran a Black guy out of the Haight Ashbury neighborhood. The next day, the *Examiner* blared headlines on the front page in a typesize worthy of World War III:

"HATE CRIME IN THE HAIGHT"

along with a sensationalized article detailing this great racial hate crime of the century!!!! It's funny (ha ha), when its Black guys attacking Whites — something that happens every other day — the racial aspect mysteriously gets censored out. But when it's the other way around…

Even more infuriating, a few weeks later, the real story came out. The reason they were chasing the Black guy out of the Haight in the first place was because he had robbed some of their friends. Of course, this little tidbit ended up getting buried in the 48th paragraph at the bottom of page 27.

These PC mind-fuckers in the media, they're just sick and demented. But that's just their karma, and I suppose it's silly of me to be worrying about it.

If I sound bitter it's because I am. When I first hit the streets as a naïve teenage, I'd pretty much been brainwashed by these worthless media bullshitters. Four Black males coming towards me on a dark Tenderloin street? Why, it would be "racist" for me to look at them differently than any other human being on God's green planet. Heaven forbid, I would be *"racist."*

The Exciting Adventures of FramptonMan!

One dark and stormy night back in 1976, when I was a 19-year-old fool, I was renting a room at the flophouse, the Empress Hotel, deep in the heart of San Francisco's Tenderloin district. And what a magnificent joint it was, the Empress Hotel. I had been living on the streets, but I thought it would be "safer" to be indoors, behind lock and key. Ha ha. Don't kid yourself. Some of those inner city flophouses are death traps. And by and large it's the Black males that make them so deadly. You got a problem with me saying that? Then go and live in one of them. Hmmm?

Anyway, as I walked down the hallway to my room on the third floor one night, I passed four young Black males loitering around in the hallway. Heaven forbid I would pay any attention to this situation. Why, to react any differently to them than I would react to, say, *four elderly Chinese women*, would not only be "racist," but "sexist" and "ageist" as well. Could anything be a greater crime than that under the PC Thought Control Regime that we all live under nowadays?

Anyway, before I could get inside my room they came running down the hallway after me and one of them managed to wedge his foot in my doorway before I could shut my door. They forced themselves in my room and one of them grabbed a razor-sharp knife from my bureau that I used to sharpen my pencils and pressed it up to my throat. He began ranting and screaming at me about how his girlfriend "had just been killed by a motherfuckin' White guy!!" In other words, it was payback time. One of the Black guys immediately stationed himself at the window as a lookout, while the other two guys rifled through my stuff grabbing anything of value. It was obvious they had done this routine many times before.

I don't know if you've ever been in this kind of situation, but the weird thing is, you don't feel any fear. I have this distinct memory of floating out of my head and up to the ceiling as I watched the scene unfold, like watching a movie of something happening to somebody else. Weird.

At the time, I had this dream of making it as a cartoonist. I had been laboring over a strip called *FramptonMan* — it was a superhero take-off featuring rock star Peter Frampton, (who was big at the time), as a superhero, fighting against the evil Mick Jagger and the heinous Stones Gang. During one scene, Mick and the boys execute Donny and Marie Osmond with heavy metal power chords, and then *FramptonMan* flies in to save the day. It was one of the first strips I ever drew. Really horrible stuff.

Anyway, the *FramptonMan* strip-in-progress happened to be sitting on top of my dresser. For some reason, I said to the Black guy terrorizing me with the knife: "Wait! I want to show you something," and I cautiously picked up the drawing pad from the dresser and held it up in front of me like a shield. "I draw cartoons," I said. "That's all I want to do, draw cartoons."

He looked at me for a second; looked at the drawing pad; looked back at me. To this day, I don't know whether I struck some kind of responsive chord of humanity in him by sharing with him my meager hopes and dreams of making it as a cartoonist. Or maybe the *FramptonMan* cartoon was so lousy that he felt sorry for me. But, for whatever reason, he decided not to slice my head off. One of his partners said, "We got the stuff. Let's get out of here!" And, after a moment's hesitation, they all fled out the door and down the hall.

I often think how easily my life could have ended right there, before I even got started. Nineteen-years-old. In a sense, everything since that point has been gravy. Or it could just be that Life was not finished with me yet. And the moral is: Fuck you, you fat-ass White Liberal columnist spewing your mind-fucking poison. Be on guard, my friend. You might not get a second chance.

An Odd Epilogue

I had another odd scene a couple of months ago. I was walking down a dark, deserted street, when I noticed four Black guys headed towards me. Of course, I immediately tensed up a little (unlike the heroic White Liberal, of course, who, in similar circumstances, would certainly be immune to such low tendencies). It was a narrow sidewalk, and I braced myself for the old "No-you-get-out-of-MY-way-boy!" routine, or whatever other trouble might be inflicted on me.

Just as they got right up to me I realized it was Hootie and some of the guys I used to play basketball with in the park. Some of the nicest, sweetest guys you could meet. We slapped hands and reminisced about those days on the b-ball courts, some of the best days of my life. I was famous for being out there every day, for years. This was in the days before Rodney King and before O.J. Those days. It was the days of Magic Johnson and Larry Bird and Chris Mullin and Manute Bol. Those days.

But after Rodney King, it was just different somehow. I stopped going to the b-ball courts and I stopped hanging out with Black guys. There was just too much racial tension and animosity — hundreds of years worth of it. And for me, *normal* human relationships are difficult enough, without this racial shit thrown on top of it. Those old carefree days were gone. Now it was the days of Latrell Sprewell and Black guys strangling White coaches. These days.

As I walked away from Hootie and the guys I felt sad. They had asked me why I didn't hoop anymore and I told them I was "on the disabled list." The mentally disabled list.

*Chapter Eighteen
Violence*

If there's any good news on the Black Crime front, it's that, after 30 years of the crime rates getting worse and worse every year, it finally peaked around the Rodney King/O.J. period in the mid-90s. And now it's finally starting to go back down.

I've heard plenty of explanations for this decline in our violent crime rate — tough-on-crime measures, three-strikes laws, more funding for police, etc. But I don't think it's a coincidence that the crime rates started going down almost exactly right after Farrakhan organized that Million Man March. Correct me if I'm wrong, but that's the first major Black demonstration in my lifetime that wasn't centered around the concept of *Blame Whitey*. Instead, the Million Man March was an appeal for Black men to reflect on their own lives and their own behavior and to seek atonement and forgiveness. My hats off to Farrakhan for organizing that thing.

A Final Note

A certain amount of the violence on the streets is unavoidable. But a lot of it *is* avoidable if you take a few precautions:

1. Avoid Black neighborhoods.

2. Avoid the drug and prostitution scenes.

3. Learn to spot and avoid Violent Assholes.

4. And above all, try not to be a Violent Asshole yourself, because what you put out will indeed come right back in your face.

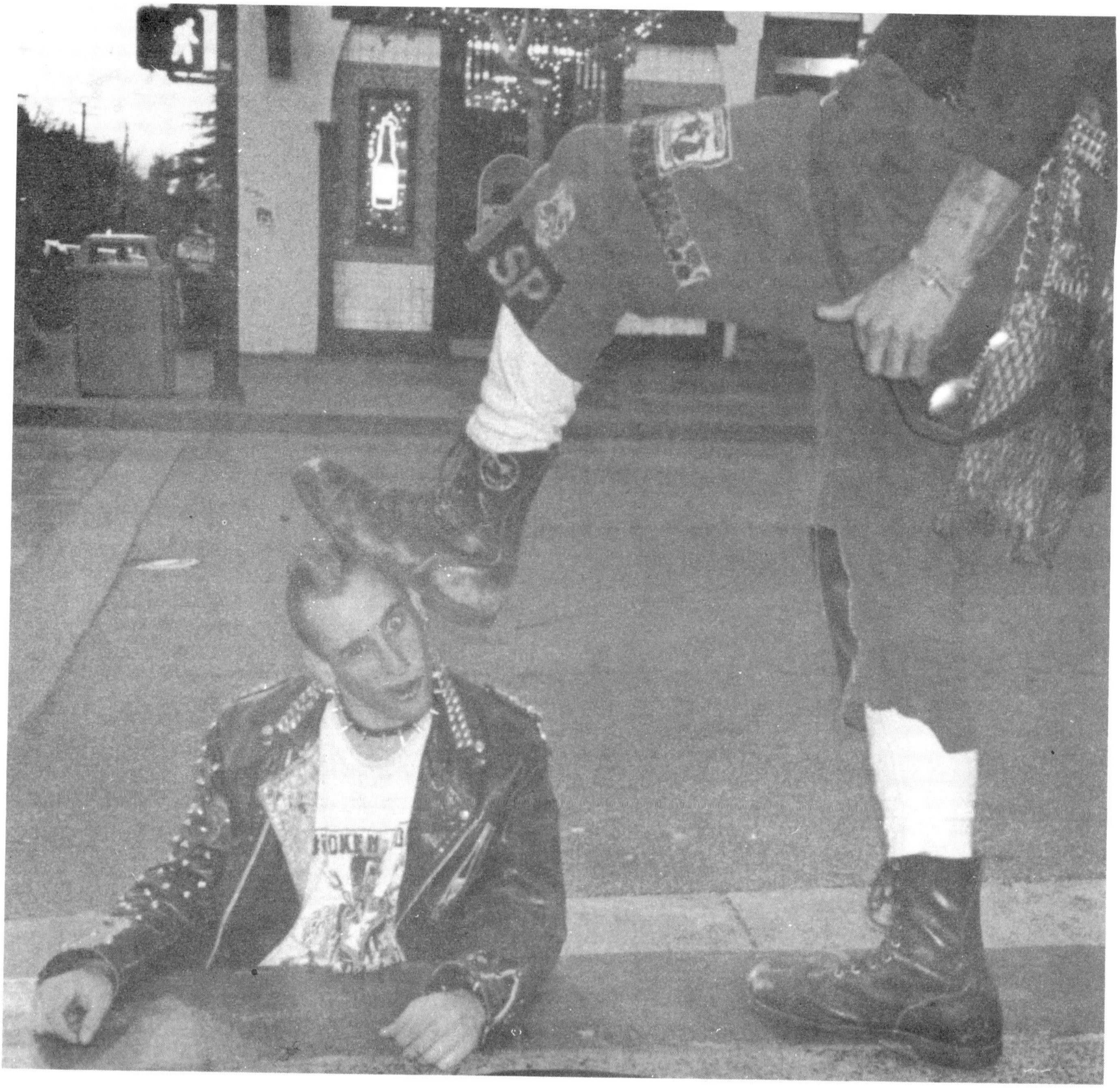

GUTTER RAT

| DOES IT SEEM LIKE... | IT'S GETTING A... | LITTLE BIT MORE... | CROWDED EVERY DAY? / WHADJA' SAY? |

Chapter Nineteen
Why Homeless?
Why Now?

For most of this book we've been dealing with the microcosm of the homeless experience: Where to sleep, what to eat, how to avoid the cops, etc. It might be instructive to step back and take a quick look at the big picture, at some of the social forces swirling around you that have created you, The Modern Homeless Person.

For most of America's 200-year history, we didn't have much of a homeless problem. What great shifts have taken place over the last 30 years to create this phenomenon? Why now, in the midst of a so-called "booming economy," do we have millions of homeless in America? And why are their numbers growing greater every year?

Now when most sociologists and brainy-type thinkers search for *The Root Cause of Homelessness*, they generally split it up into two aspects: **Behavior** and **Real Estate**.

Basically, one group mostly blames the individual *behavior* of the homeless person: they're lazy bums who don't want to work, they're alcoholics, they're nuts, etc. The other group says, No, it's primarily a *Real Estate* issue. And they blame the greedy landlords and the yuppies who are supposedly "gentrifying" the poor out of existence. Just about everything I've read about homelessness — its causes and possible solutions — has pretty much revolved around these two aspects.

And yes, there's some truth to both sides. Individual homeless people need to be encouraged to clean up their act — to work on their dysfunctional behavior — if they want to pull themselves off the street. And landlords need to temper their lust for a profit motive with a social conscience towards those who are less fortunate.

But, in my opinion, this still doesn't begin to explain the modern homeless phenomenon. Thirty years ago, we had plenty of nutty, dysfunctional people, we had plenty of skid row alcoholics, we had plenty of lazy bums. The difference was, there was still plenty of affordable housing for them to live in back then. Thirty years ago there were plenty of greedy landlords. But there was also a surplus of available housing, which, by the laws of supply and demand, kept the prices reasonably in check.

What happened to all the housing? That's the twenty million dollar question: What happened to all the housing? What great shift has taken place in the American real-estate market over the last thirty years? Well, I am going to tell you.

Chapter Twenty
Mass Immigration

A few years ago I read something in the paper that literally stunned me. According to the U.S. Census Bureau, **eighteen million new immigrants were projected to be moving to California over the next twenty years!**

Now, we *already* happen to have a severe housing shortage/homeless crisis everywhere up and down the state of California. Now, I'm told that eighteen million, mostly low-income immigrants are projected to come flooding into the state over the next twenty years. As soon as I read that, I realized the obvious: If we allow this to happen, this is the death knell for *any* solution to our housing shortage/homeless crisis in our lifetime. Period.

And then I was in for a second shock. When I began raising this issue with these so-called homeless activists, I was met with almost complete and total silence. Or, if they did say anything, it was to question my motives for even bringing up the issue in the first place. As if I had farted in the quaint little elevator of their minds. I hadn't yet realized the extent to which politically correct orthodoxy had short-circuited the brains of otherwise reasonably intelligent people.

I raise the question now that I raised then — and still haven't gotten an answer to — namely:

WHERE THE FUCK ARE THE eighteen MILLION NEW HOMES WHERE THESE PEOPLE ARE GOING TO LIVE?????

Ahem.

Like a detective hot on the trail, I began to uncover all sorts of startling facts. For instance, here in California over the last few years, *we've been building new housing at an all-time record rate* (as anyone who's witnessed the urban sprawl tearing up what's left of the natural environment in their neighborhoods can readily attest to). Why then do we have an acute housing shortage? Because the population is growing even faster than we can build new housing. Why is the population growing? According to the Sierra Club: *"80% of the U.S. population increase since 1970 is directly attributed to recent immigrants and their offspring."*

What Happened?

For most of this century America had a reasonable, sustainable, level of immigration set at about 200,000 new immigrants a year. All that changed in 1965 when good old Senator Teddy Kennedy sponsored, and Congress passed, a bill that totally changed our immigration policy.

The net results? The floodgates have been opened!!! We are now allowing well over **a million** new immigrants into the country every year. When you factor in illegal immigrants, and the various amnesty programs and other shenanigans, the number is closer to **two million new immigrants every year**. Every one of who needs a home to live in.

If that wasn't bad enough, these recent immigrants are making babies at TWICE the rate of the rest of the country, they are, in effect, DOUBLING their numbers every generation.

Now are you STILL wondering why our population is exploding out of control and why we're running out of housing?

The Horrifying Results

Does it seem like it's getting a little more crowded every day? It's not your imagination. It *is* getting more crowded every day. From 1970 to 2000 the U.S. population increased from 200 million to 280 million (with no end in sight)! Over the last ten years, we've been adding three million new people to the population every year. Do you happen to know where those three million new homes are? Well if you don't, then maybe you should listen to what I'm saying here.

Here's some more numbers to boggle your mind. The U.S. Census Bureau predicts that *a million new people* (mostly Asian and Latino immigrants) will be moving to the Bay Area in the next twenty years. Now I did the math on this. This comes out to 150 new people moving to the Bay Area, every fucking day, for the next fucking twenty years. Now do you happen to know where 150 new homes per day *are? Do you???*

The city of San Francisco has been averaging — *AVERAGING* — naturalizing a thousand new citizens (mostly Asian immigrants) every month! Again, do you happen to know where the 1,000 new homes per month are where these people are going to live?

And yet, we have all the geniuses scratching their heads wondering where all the available housing disappeared to. It didn't "disappear." Millions of recently arrived Asian and Latino immigrants are now living in it.

Is it really so hard for you Liberals to figure out? If millions of people are flooding in, other people are going to be squeezed out. That's exactly the story of our modern homeless phenomenon. Remember the game of Musical Chairs as kids? You'd have six people competing for five chairs with the slowest person left chairless. That's exactly the situation we now face regarding homelessness, with the slowest people ending up homeless. Just as I was typing this chapter the news on the radio reported that 25% of the people getting evicted from their homes in San Francisco are senior citizens. And all you have to do is look at the "shifting demographics" to see who's been replacing them. This is a slow-motion nightmare being played out in every city in California, and I'm sick to death of watching it unfold.

What I'm saying here is so obvious, that the most interesting aspect to me is the psychological aspect, the Emperor's New Clothing aspect, where reasonably intelligent people pretend not to notice something that is very obvious. I guess because it's not intellectually fashionable.

Who's Getting Caught In The Crunch?

Some of you middle-class liberals seem to be very magnanimous about this process. But the ones who are getting squeezed out of the housing market to make room for this endless horde of newcomers are the American citizens on the bottom: the young, the old, the weak, the crazy (and the lazy). Particularly taking it in the ass is this young generation, and the blacks. The young come to the cities for the ever-daunting task of kick-starting their young lives into gear, only to find hundreds of thousands of recently arrived immigrants competing with them for the same scarce housing, jobs, and social services. Being homeless is almost a rite of passage for today's youth. And the Blacks, on the bottom of the economic heap, find themselves being squeezed out of their neighborhoods by the ever-encroaching hordes of immigrants. Remember the scene from the Rodney King riots with the Korean shopkeepers atop their buildings with shotguns trying to protect their businesses from Black rioters? Well, this powder keg is still very much still in place.

The Solution

Let me state the obvious. Unless we stabilize our population, there is no solution to our housing shortage/homeless crisis. None. It's just going to get worse and worse. (Or do you really have some plan as to how and where we are going to be creating these three million new homes, every year, from now until the end of time?) And the only way to stabilize our population is to get those idiots in Congress, who opened up the immigration floodgates in the first place, to close them.

Some More Thoughts

Some people wistfully look at the Statue of Liberty and maintain this is the American way. Bullshit. No nation has *ever* allowed anywhere near the level of immigration we are now allowing. There's a *reason* why no nation in their right minds have ever allowed this level of immigration. We are going to find *out* that reason.

Since people often miss this point, let me make it clear: I'm not against *immigrants*; I'm against our *level* of immigration, which is insane. Too much too fast. It's one of the most disruptive things that could be inflicted on a society. There's no other way to put it. What we've allowed to go down over the last thirty years is totally fucking insane.

I don't wish to sidestep the complexities of this issue. My father's father was an Italian immigrant who came to America looking for a better life. My mother's father was an American Indian who I'm sure didn't want any of us bastards here.

What I'm most against is allowing millions of new people — all of whom need homes — to come flooding in here, with no plan — none! — regarding how and where we're going to house them. About the only thing we've come up with is a nice-sounding piece of horseshit called "Smart Growth" that some faceless bureaucrats thunk up in a think-tank. Let me state the obvious: "Smart Growth" hasn't worked anywhere. It certainly hasn't worked in any of the countries these immigrants are fleeing from. Ric Oberlink of the Sierra Club put it best: *"Unrestrained, never-ending growth is a sign of cancer, not of a healthy organism. 'Smart Growth' makes about as much sense as 'Smart Cancer.'"*

Homeless Activists

Instead of dealing with the *cause* of our housing shortage (our exploding population from mass immigration) these homeless activists have mostly been trying to deal with the *effects* after the fact (rent control, HUD programs, trying to shame sinners into having more "compassion" for the homeless, etc.). Could anything be more futile than dealing with the effects but not the cause?

And, thus far, our efforts have been futile. These professional homeless activists have been little more than Professional Criers of Crocodile Tears in terms of having any effect on stemming the rising tide of homelessness. (We used to do a regular feature on our homeless radio show called "Sobbing For the Plight of the Homeless." For twenty seconds each week we'd wail: *"OH, POOR HOMELESS!! BOO HOO!! SOB WEEP!!"*)

Of course, it's the PC aspect of the immigration issue that causes these liberal activists' brains to turn to mush. There's this one editor of the local *Bay Guardian*, Tim Redmond, who blamed San Francisco's housing shortage/homeless crisis on, and I quote, *"...hordes of white yuppies"* who are allegedly flooding into the city and squeezing out "minorities." Of course you'd think a journalist like Redmond could check the demographics and see that it's whites who are getting squeezed out of the city, and minorities who are flooding in. But journalists like him never let facts get in the way of their liberal proselytizing. (For the record, Asians now make up 40% of San Francisco's population, and are projected to reach 50% within the next ten years. Meanwhile, San Francisco's homeless population is mostly made up of thousands of young, white kids.)

Affordable Housing

Even more useless is all the liberal talk about "creating affordable housing." Now what creates the affordability, the price, of everything in this world? Well, supply and demand. Why is our supply of housing scarce? Because the demand has exploded along with our exploding population. Why is our population exploding? Mass immigration. It all comes back to that. We either deal with this head on, or just forget about it.

Right now, people are so desperate for housing in the Bay Area they're willing to pay $1,000 a month for a box with a bed thrown in it. How do we magically create this "affordable housing"? By making housing so shitty that people would only pay $200 a month for it?

Chapter Twenty
Mass Immigration

The Liberal Rationale

The liberal rationale for allowing this insane level of immigration seems to be that America is guilty of ruining the world via U.S. imperialism, therefore we have a responsibility to take in all these people from countries we've ruined. If this sounds like a dim-witted overstatement, it's because it is. And while there's *some* truth to this premise — for example, if we're going to be sucking in a disproportionate percentage of the world's resources, then we're going to be sucking in a lot of people along with it — I hardly go all the way with this premise.

Let's take a quick look at two of the countries where a lot of these immigrants are coming from, China and Mexico.

We all know about China's billion-plus population. Do we as Americans have a moral responsibility to take in the endless millions of Chinese that they no longer have space for? Do we? Make your case.

Or Mexico. As recently as 30 years ago, Mexican women were averaging an astounding seven babies per woman. Not surprisingly, this had a ruinous effect on Mexico. Their solution? For all the excess millions to come pouring into America and start doing the same thing here. Do we have a moral responsibility to let them? Do we? (One particularly specious argument is that the Mexicans stole California from the Indians first, therefore they have the moral high-ground here.)

Some More Sodden Thoughts

So why is this happening? Well, it's interesting, the confluence of support on this issue you get from both the Liberal *and* Conservative elites that are running this country right now (with the rest of us saps stuck in the middle paying for it).

To hear the bullshitters in the liberal media talk about it, you'd think the whole country was doing back-flips of happiness over the unmitigated joy that is "cultural diversity." Shit. We've already seen the complete mess — the apocalyptic nightmare — that Southern California has turned into over the last thirty years. Now, according to these liberals, I should be thrilled that the same process is now being inflicted on the country at large.

And these conservative corporate types, they look at millions of new people as nothing but a new market to sell their shitty products to. They look at the masses as nothing but cattle to feed on. Cheap labor and more consumers.

(If fact, I've always felt the main reason behind our so-called "booming economy" was the flood of immigration: More people buying stuff. While ironically causing our busted quality of living: More people jammed into less space.)

Or I suppose you could look at this in purely Darwinism terms. Every day in Berkeley I witness this odd tableau: All these white kids flopped on the sidewalks getting stoned and begging for spare change, while Asian kids rush off to fill the slots in the University, and Latino kids rush off to work in all the restaurants on the Ave.

I Could Go On (And On)

As long as three million new people — *(all of whom need homes, homes which, as of this writing, do not exist)* — are being added to the U.S. population every year, our homeless problem is going to get worse and worse. Period.

The bottom line is this. If we're stupid enough to allow millions of people — who are fleeing countries they've already ruined by overpopulating themselves — to come pouring into this country and do the same thing here, then we're stupid enough to get what we deserve.

I'll end this chapter with a line with which I ended many a radio show on this subject: ***"Let's find homes for the MILLIONS of American citizens who are already homeless before we keep inviting millions of foreigners to make their home here."***

Chapter Twenty One
Counterculture Casualties

Another new development over the last thirty years is the emergence of the counterculture casualty. There are lineages on the street scene that have been around since bums immemorial: the Skid Row Wino lineage, the Hobo/Tramp lineage, the Gypsy lineage, etc. But since the '60s, a relatively new and virulent strain has emerged: the Counterculture-Casualty lineage.

Much of today's modern street scene spawned out of the '60s hippie counterculture, and continued on with the '80s punk counterculture. So it might be worth it to take a quick look at some of the values and assumptions that came out of this. As well as some of the pitfalls you might want to avoid stepping into. Because one thing you will definitely have to survive on the street scene is The '60s, man!

Kerouac was the forerunner, Kesey and the Merry Pranksters created the prototype, and then the Haight-Ashbury was the explosion. And kids have been dropping out ever since in search of that elusive countercultural dream.

Every year I'll see a new crop of dazed street kids looking for it. The hippie kids looking for *Rainbow Hippie Village*. Or the punk kids looking for *Punk Scene USA*. Where *is* that cool scene they've read about in all the cool books and magazines anyway?

Surviving On The Streets

Now it's certainly a reflection of something seriously lacking in the mainstream culture, that so many people seem to be seeking an alternative in the first place. And I certainly don't have space here to do justice to the whole *Counterculture vs. Mainstream Culture* debate.

All I'm trying to point out here is what you'll most likely find, on the street level, when you come looking for the counterculture:

Very, very little.

Let's face it. This world just doesn't *need* any more hemp-jewelry makers, or hardcore punk-rock bass guitarists. So cut your hair and become a yuppie, okay?

(*And what exactly is wrong with being a yuppie, anyway? Can anyone explain the universal scorn I keep hearing being heaped on "yuppies" these days? It just means you're young, you live in the city, and you've got a fucking job. That makes more sense to me than this phony "counterculture rebel" pose I see so many kids trying to live out.*)

All I'm saying is: If you decide to drop out of straight society, BE PREPARED TO PAY THE CONSEQUENCES. *"Living in the moment"* might sound nice if you're nineteen and picking up Zen for the first time, but many of you may be unprepared for the truly tenuous nature of day-to-day existence on the street scene.

Take me for a tragic example. You want to talk drop-out? I haven't driven a car in 25 years. I haven't been to a doctor or a dentist in twenty years. I haven't had a bank account in fifteen years. I haven't watched a TV show in ten years. I haven't lived in anything that would remotely be considered a "home" in six years. (Which reminds me of the old street person joke: *"What does the street person do when he gets sick? He dies."* Ha. Ha.)

Now if you want to try and exist without the security of the corporate tit, that's fine (and it may be an illusion that such a thing as "security" even exists in this ever-changing world of ours). I'm just trying to warn you here about the *reality* that's waiting for you, as opposed to the highly romanticized counterculture *myth* that you've been fed by the media.

Now it could be I'm overreacting here with the scorn of a lover betrayed. Because, at one point, I shared most of the values of the counterculture. I was certainly one of those kids who tried to live out the whole countercultural dream. For several years in the early '90s my work appeared every month in both *High Times* (the bible of the hippies) and *Maximum Rock'N'Roll* (the bible of the punks). An accomplishment I'm still not sure if I should be proud of, or embarrassed by.

Which reminds me of something else. A lot of people seem to think there was a big difference between the hippies and the punks. But what's the difference between Sid Vicious and Jerry Garcia? That one of the dead junkies was "positive"?

Speaking of media myths: It cracks me up when I hear these so-called "'60s-icons" congratulating themselves for the greatness of the '60s (and the greatness of themselves for bringing us the '60s). This would be all well and good, aside from one niggling detail: Virtually every aspect of American life has gotten *worse* since the '60s. Much worse.

In a radio interview, cartoonist R. Crumb talked about coming to the Haight-Ashbury in '67 right before the so-called Summer of Love. He mentioned what a beautiful city San Francisco was then: the streets were clean and safe, the people were friendly, housing was cheap and plentiful, living was easy, etc. And he mentioned an idea that was very much in vogue then amongst the countercultural set: How much *more* wonderful the city (and the world) would be when the Age of Aquarius set in and all the old farts died off and all the groovy hippies took over.

Well, I'm here to tell you, all the old farts did in fact die off, and all the hippies (including me) did in fact come tramping through the city. And it was hardly improved by our presence.

Chapter Twenty One
Counterculture Casualties

But here's the funny part. These "'60s icons" seem to think it's still 1967 and that they should be judged on all the groovy, idealistic things they *intended* to do, as opposed to the actual *effect* they've had. I think it's getting a little late in the game for that.

In the '50s, Oakland was averaging about twelve murders a year. After the '60s it started averaging about 150 murders a year. What would we have done without all the "love" the hippies invented in the '60s?

I think we all could benefit from an honest appraisal of what actually went down in the '60s. Lord knows we still haven't sorted it out. Lord knows this society is schizo in its attempts to assimilate the counterculture into the mainstream. I think of the day Jerry Garcia died. The mayor of San Francisco gave a heartfelt eulogy and lowered the flags at City Hall to half-mast in honor of this Great Man. And then, after shedding a few tears, went back to his Matrix program of busting and throwing into jail any of the street freaks dumb enough to try and emulate the example of this Great Man.

Which reminds me of George Carlin's great joke about Jerry's death: *"It's a sign of the great progress we've made since the '60s that rock stars are no longer O.D.ing in hotel rooms, but they're now O.D.ing on the way to detox centers."*

My opinion? LSD is garbage, Jerry Garcia was an idiot, and the '60s was bullshit. The '60s was basically a dead-end we went staggering down.

The '60s impacted on the modern street scene in several devastating ways:

1. Drugs (need I say more?)

2. The sloppy sexual unions that came out of the so-called "sexual liberation" movements — and the shattered family structures and the generation of orphans (especially in the black community) that resulted from that.

3. The romanticized notion of being *against* the mainstream society.

Number three is probably the most devastating, because usually the street person starts out feeling alienated enough from society to begin with. Then the counterculture ethos feeds him this romanticized notion of the Hip Rebel Outsider, which locks him permanently into this state of alienation. Why try and integrate yourself into society when your alienation is your badge of honor, the very source of your identity.

Criticizing certain aspects of this world is one thing. Hating the world is another. It's one of the most damaging things for the human psyche to endure. And all too often, the counterculture encourages and justifies this sense of alienation from society.

Over and over I'll hear these Counterculture Casualties give me a big speech about how they're "against the multinational corporations, man." That's fine, except for one thing: the corporations *own* virtually *everything*. What world are you planning to live in? Well, the sidewalks, I guess.

What does it actually mean when you say you've "dropped out of the corporate system?" Most of the *food* you eat, the *clothes* you're wearing, the *beer* you're drinking, 95% of the *media* you're consuming, all the *electricity* you're using, all the *money* in your pocket... all these things were produced by big, big corporations. All you're saying is: you'll *consume*, but you won't *produce*. Does that somehow make you more noble?

The '60s was a noble experiment, perhaps. All I'm saying is, the time has come to clearly assess the *results* of that experiment. I'm not looking to go back to the '50s. Maybe what I'm looking for is a *counter*-counterculture. In the meantime, beware of the pitfalls of the generation that preceded you.

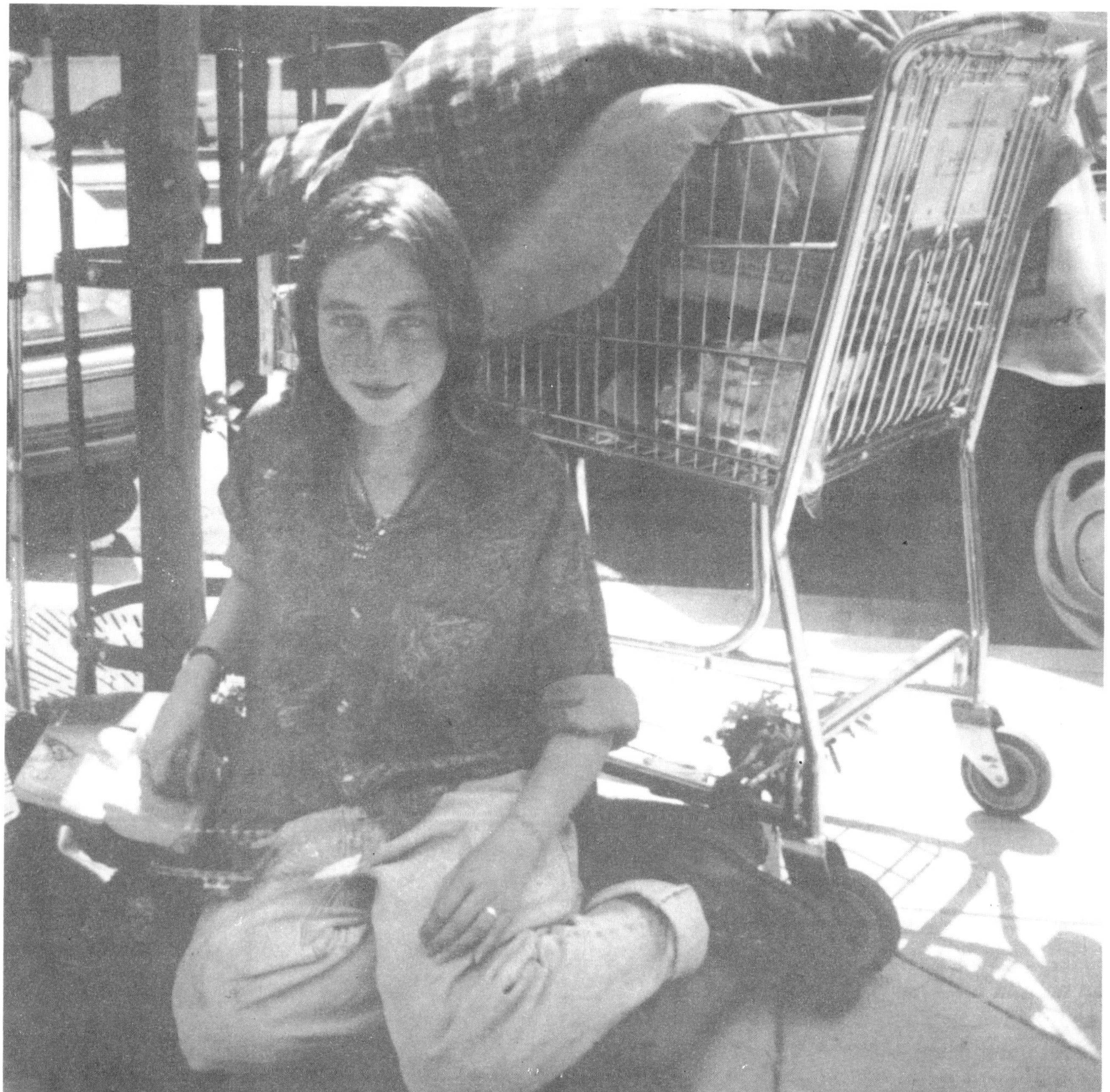

Part Four

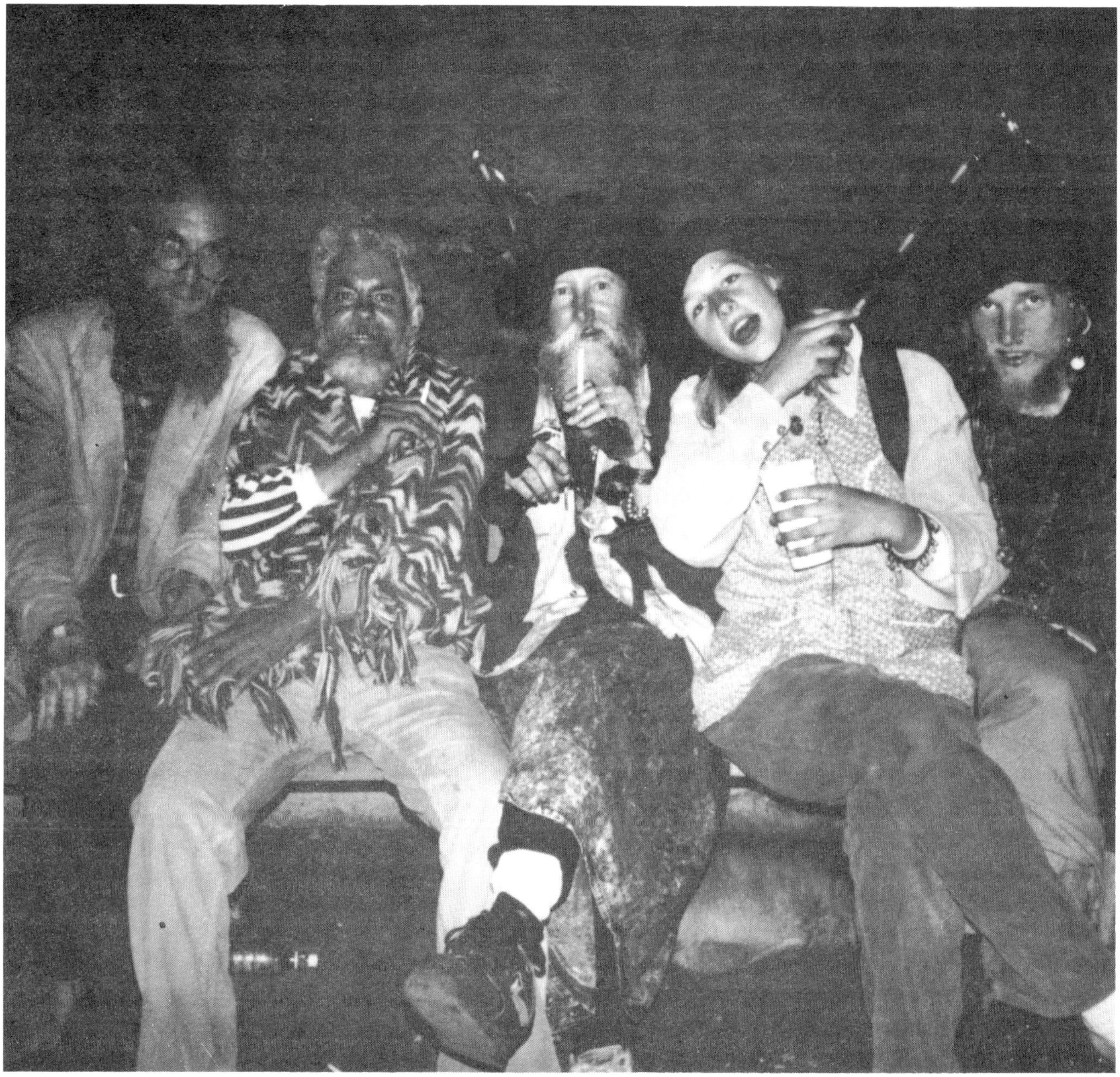

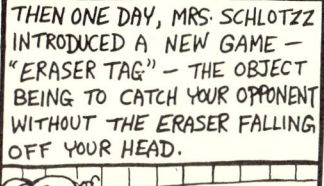

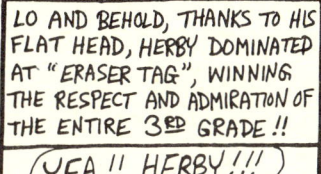

Chapter Twenty Two
Four Street People:
Profiles in Weirdness

Nothing can prepare you for the people and the situations you'll have thrown at you when you're on the streets. I'll give you four peculiar examples of individual street people I've stumbled into over the years, which gives sort of an overview of the three different street scenes I've been a part of.

Fearless Frank
San Francisco 1976

One of the first friends I made on the streets was Fearless Frank. I'm not sure why I hooked up with him, for we had nothing in common. I was young, heterosexual, and just getting started with my life. He was middle-aged, homosexual, and just about finished. Maybe it was because he was a gentle soul. I was completely shattered at the time and I couldn't deal with anyone harsh. I met him one day at St. Anthony's Dining Hall. I was on the soup kitchen circuit. And I just hooked up with Frank.

"Some people are hunters who grab for the meat," explained Fearless Frank. "Me, I'll wait until everyone else is done and eat any scraps left over. Thank you very much."

Surviving On The Streets

Fearless Frank was one of those guys who just had bad luck — or whatever you call it — from the word go. As a kid Frank was raised among Mormons in Utah. Frank's family tried to cure him of the "disease" of homosexuality by sending him to one psychiatrist after another. He was not cured.

When he was thirteen, he got drunk and took his Daddy's Cadillac out for a joyride. Ended up getting in a car crash and fucking another person up. His Dad got sued, because Frank didn't have a license, let alone insurance. His father was financially wiped out in the settlement. Imagine you're thirteen and you've just wiped out your Father. That was the kind of luck Frank had. Fearless Frank.

When he was eighteen, he came to San Francisco with a couple thousand bucks in his pocket. He rented out a room at the Fairmont, one of the most expensive hotels in town. For three days he ordered room service for champagne and caviar until his money ran out. And he'd been on the streets ever since. "And if I ever come into some more money, I'll do the same thing all over again," he would say with a smile.

When I met him he was about 35. He was the swishiest queen you could imagine. You could tell he was a fag from two blocks away as he swivel-hipped and limp-wristed it down Market Street. He vamped it up for all it was worth.

His drink of choice was Thunderbird wine. Little green bottles of green death. He sort of reminded me of Andy Warhol, mixed with a slightly cracked Toy Maker. He was always smiling behind his glasses. And whenever anything bad happened to him — which was often — he would say, "Oh, dear," and giggle nervously to himself. He was falling apart and going down. And he didn't give a shit. He was always sort of laughing at himself, at his predicament, at the whole weird goof of life.

Once, when I was renting out a flophouse, we got a bunch of Thunderbird and went up there and drank and listened to the radio. Frank sort of danced around to the music. At one point, he kept saying, "I love you I love you I love you..." But he was saying it in such a silly, ridiculous, campy way, that I didn't take it seriously.

Every afternoon, after eating at St. Anthony's, he would walk across the city to the Golden Gate Bridge. "I'd think of jumping off," he told me once, "but then I'd look out to the Pacific at the sky and the water, and it all looked so beautiful that I'd always come back."

One day, he walked to the bridge and didn't come back. Fearless Frank.

Two Guys Camping in the Woods Humboldt 1995

On the streets, things are rarely as they seem on the surface.

When I hit Humboldt I camped for a while in the Redwood forest. Until it got a little too weird. Sleeping alone in a sleeping bag in the deep dark woods *can* get a little spooky, especially if you're smoking a lot of pot and reading a lot of Castaneda books. Suddenly that gnarled tree branch hanging over your head metamorphoses into an ancient spirit of some long-lost netherworld creature returning to earth to reclaim what's left of your clammy soul. And then you hear a faint, rustling sound coming from behind the tree. You think:

"Hmmm... What was that noise? Was that a twig blowing in the breeze? ...Or was that... *SOME KIND OF PSYCHOPATHIC MASS-MURDERING MANIAC LIKE THE DUDE IN FRIDAY THE 13TH WHO'S ABOUT TO JUMP ON TOP OF ME AND CHOP MY HEAD OFF AND DISEMBOWEL MY VERY GUTS AT ANY MOMENT, MAN??!!"*

*Chapter Twenty Two
Four Street People:
Profiles in Weirdness*

Well, no. Actually it was just a squirrel jumping from a tree branch. But meanwhile, your heart is now pumping 90 miles an hour and you won't be getting back to sleep any time soon.

And you hear just enough grim reports on the Bum Grapevine — like the serial killer during this period who was preying on hobos and tramps in the train yards, bashing their heads in while they were sleeping — to give a dose of legitimate fear to your most paranoid imaginings.

Anyway, one night I was sleeping in my tent in the Redwoods and I start hearing these strange noises. Some guy was outside my tent. I could see the shadow of his body silhouetted against the side of my tent. He was circling around my tent making these weird guttural sounds, like he was chanting satanic gibberish or something. For a second I thought I was being surrounded by the Manson Family and they were going to perform some weird ritual on me in the deep, dark woods. I jumped out of my tent and said: "WHAT ARE YOU DOING OUT THERE!" and the guy ran off into the woods. I could see him off in the distance, crouching under a tree, making these weird noises. I didn't sleep particularly well that night.

The next morning, in the light of day, I spotted him sleeping in the grass and wild flowers about 50 yards from my tent. He looked like an aging blond surfer boy with crazed Rasputin eyes. He was barefoot and had his arms wrapped around a big jug of tea. When he came to he told me, "I've been tripping for three days on datura root tea. The flowers grow all over the place in these woods. The stuff makes you go crazy. You hallucinate like crazy. Half the people that take it end up in the psych ward." I was so miserable in my own state of consciousness I was willing to try anything. I asked him if I could try some tea, but he said: "No, I don't want to be responsible."

A couple of nights later, I camped in the same spot with some guys I'd been drinking beer with on Arcata Plaza. They slept in sleeping bags outside my tent. In the middle of the night, Datura Tripper showed up again. First he started talking to the foot of the guy's sleeping bag, having a very animated conversation with the bag. Then he sat on the guy's head. The guy jumped up and screamed, "WHAT ARE YOU DOING TOUCHING ME WHILE I'M SLEEPING!" and punched Tripper right in the face, knocked him on his ass into the bushes. Tripper jumped up and said, "I never fucked your wife!" was his explanation, and ran off into the woods. And that was the last I saw of him.

So I decided to find another crash spot. Found an awesome spot on this cliff overlooking Baker's Beach. It was a powerful spot. The waves crashing on the rocks. The whole cliff vibrated with power. It was like sleeping on top of an engine.

Baker's Beach was a nude beach in the middle of nowhere. You had to climb down the cliff to get to this isolated little beach. I was heartbroken at the time. Going through my Mid-Life Crisis. Looking for a beautiful young hippie chick with flowers in her hair, preferably topless and barefoot. Mostly Baker's Beach got gays trolling for action. But hippies, too. A hippie school bus would pull up and the freaks would hit the beach.

And one afternoon, there she was, just off the bus, topless and barefoot, and a big flower on one side of her curly brown hair. I watched her from my tent site on the cliff, as she strolled dreamily up and down the sand and surf.

There was another guy who camped in a tent up from my campsite. He looked like a younger, softer Jim Morrison, only cuter. Straight-looking. Collegiate. A nice guy. The kind of guy the chicks go for. He would stroll naked on the beach. He had a very large penis.

One day I was getting ready to make my move on the barefoot hippie chick with the flower in her hair. Only Jim beat me to it. I watched as they strode off to his tent that night.

I was in a frenzy. I walked two miles to the nearest store, bought a bunch of beer and started drinking. It wasn't just that I had gotten rejected by this chick. It was *twenty years* of being rejected by the chicks. This was like a culmination.

So I'm sitting there later that night at my campsite, drowning my sorrows in a beer or twelve, and Jim shows up. He has whiskey. And marshmallows. We roasted the marshmallows on the campfire and took big pulls of whiskey. I'm incredibly jealous of this guy, envious. He's what I wish I was. The Cool Guy. The Guy Who Got the Chicks. But he's such a nice guy, I like him, too. Intelligent. Friendly. College Degree. Clean-cut. Good job in Oregon. Devoted girlfriend. "I'm on vacation," he said. He reminded me of the guys I used to play ball with and go to rock concerts with in high school. He told me about his life, and I told him about mine.

I'm drunk and weepy and in my *"the bitches-all-broke-my-heart"* mode. I needed someone to pour my heart out to, and he was a sympathetic listener.

"Sex ruined my life." I exclaimed in anguish.

"If you think sex ruined *your* life, sex *really* ruined my life," he said.

"Oh?"

Maybe it was because my own sex trip was so fucked up, and that I had worked for years in the porn business, and was generally sympathetic towards other people's weird sex trips, but it turned out he also needed someone to talk to, he needed to get some things off of his chest, too, and he sensed I was a sympathetic listener, too.

"Haven't you wondered what somebody like me is doing camped out here in the middle of nowhere?" he asked.

"No."

He confessed that he was wanted by the police in Oregon for having sex with a five-year-old girl. Second offense. He couldn't help it. He would never hurt a little girl. She was a friend of the family. She enjoyed it. They were just playing around. Now he couldn't decide whether to turn himself in, or hide out in the woods at Baker's Beach until the end of time. He was looking at twenty years in prison, at least. His girlfriend was wiring him money from Oregon to keep him afloat. But he was tired of running. But he was even more scared to turn himself in. He didn't know what to do.

We sat there around the campfire. Finished off the whiskey. Talked some more. The next morning, I hitchhiked back to Berkeley. On the streets, it's never what it seems on the surface.

Hate Man
Berkeley 2000

Hate Man is simply one of the most resourceful street people I've ever met. A lot of the practical skills I learned about surviving on the streets I picked up from Hate Man. If I wanted to show a new kid the ropes, I would recommend he spend a day following the Hate Man around on his street route and seeing how he operates.

Every town has their Town Character. And Hate Man is Berkeley's loveable (or should I say hateable?) town eccentric. Hate Man is a true legend of the streets.

In the '60s he was a reporter for the *New York Times*. As straight as can be. Married, with kids, in the suburbs. A "success." Except he was miserable. Then he got into acid and different therapy groups like Gestalt Therapy. He decided to drop out. Or "nut up" as he put it. He began wearing a skirt and living on the streets and developing his unique philosophy of negativity, "oppositionality," as he calls it. It's sort of a weird yin-yang number. Basically, he wants everyone to say they hate him, to "acknowledge negativity" and to not say anything positive around him.

*Chapter Twenty Two
Four Street People:
Profiles in Weirdness*

"Civilization has been miserable for 2,000 years because they're stressing the positive and repressing the negative, trying to have a nice day," he explains. So Hate Man took it upon himself as his personal crusade to restore the yin-yang balance of nature by saying, "FUCK YOU! I HATE YOUR FUCKING GUTS!" to the world-at-large on a regular basis.

"It's easy to relate to someone when you're getting along," explains Hate Man. "The trick is to still be able to care about the other when we're in opposition, when we hate each other."

Most evenings you can find Hate Man and his band of hate-cronies and street freaks hanging out on the campus late into the night. Ever the uncongenial host, Hate Man usually sets up his own makeshift "living room" with crates to sit on, a table with candles and flowers on it, and plenty of day-old coffee and whatever ground-scored refreshments were scrounged that day.

Hate Camp is sort of a floating men's smoking club: part Andy Warhol street theater of the bizarre, and part Primal Scream group therapy session. It has a surreal logic all its own. Stepping into Hate Man's late-night world is akin to stepping into the Mad Hatter's tea party, or the Bizarro Universe in Superman comics where everything is the opposite from how people normally operate.

"I tried Plan A: marriage, career, success. I climbed that mountain," explained Hate Man in an interview on the Dan Rather *CBS Evening News*. "Now I'm into Plan B, going down the other side of the mountain. B is for Bum."

If Hate Man is a bum, he is a veritable King of the Bums. Or should I say Queen, dress-wearing freak that he is?

He's a master of finding tweener spaces and claiming them for his own. Completely self-sufficient, Hate doesn't get welfare or eat at the free-meal places. He totally supports himself. He also not only cleans up after himself, but his whole crew. You can see him picking up cigarette butts, sweeping up the grounds, and urging the crew to piss in his piss jars instead of the bushes (you'd be surprised at how much heat street people heap on themselves simply by pissing where they shouldn't) which he personally cleans out.

He started a drum-circle scene ten years ago, creating the "drums" from discarded plastic buckets, sticks, and whatever metal objects he finds lying around. And he finds places to store all the stuff. Every night all the freaks get together on the campus for an hour-long bash session.

Followed by late-night Hate sessions — people screaming and yelling and getting their shit out in the open (and sometimes even dealing with it) — or just shooting the breeze in highly intellectual rap sessions. Often students will walk by and be flabbergasted at the level of discourse coming from these "bums." Or, just as often, they'll be horrified by all the screaming and cursing.

Hate Man definitely sees himself in the tradition of Aristotle and Socrates, offering up his philosophical system to young, inquiring minds. Personally, I think his philosophy is a bit whacked out, but I give him points for originality. And, in a scene of lost children, he's one of the few elder figures willing, and eager, to offer counsel and mentoring.

In a scene with very little stability, Hate Man offers some kind of stable core. Many a night when I've had nowhere else to go and nobody to talk to, I was happy to know that Hate Camp was going in full force, and I could drop by for some stimulating talk or hot coffee, or at the least, a couple of cigarettes. What can I say about the Hate Man? Is it any wonder I hate his fucking guts. FUCK YOU, HATE MAN! YOU DRESS-WEARING SHOULDER-PUSHING FREAK!

SKATE & SURF

Chapter Twenty Three
Getting Off The Streets

There's no easy formula for getting off the streets. If there was, there wouldn't be millions of people flopped out on the sidewalks. Basically, there are four ways to get off the streets:

1. **Get a job, motherfucker.**
2. **Get on welfare.**
3. **Have a rich old man.**
4. **All the weird little scams street people come up with to carve out a little personal space for themselves.**

I'm getting weary of laying out all these general principles. Each street person's situation is so unique, I have my doubts how much these general principles apply. So, let's take a look at the *specifics* of three of my different stints of homelessness, and how I got off the streets each time.

San Francisco 1978

Now the first thing you have to ask yourself if you want to get off the streets is, **Why did you end up on the streets in the first place?** I once made up a list of some of the main reasons people end up on the streets:

- mental problems,
- long-term drug and alcohol abuse,
- dysfunctional families,
- alienation from society and other people,
- childhood sexual abuse,
- Bohemian/countercultural leanings,
- lack of a marketable job skills,
- laziness,
- living in urban areas where the housing market is being swamped by millions of recently arrived immigrants.

And I realized I fit into just every category. So I guess it was inevitable that eventually I'd end up on the streets.

The *main* reason I ended up on the streets of San Francisco at the age of nineteen was that I was so fucked up in the head, I just couldn't relate to other people. The idea of dealing with people in a job setting was just beyond me. That's what drove me to the streets. That was my problem.

My first attempt to get off the streets didn't work. I figured: Maybe I could get a job as a professional underground cartoonist. That was my first plan. As an underground cartoonist I wouldn't have to deal with people directly, I could just mail off the work to the newspapers. I could deal with that.

So I spent two months sitting on my sleeping bag on that off-ramp at the foot of the Bay Bridge, working on a cartoon. I finally ended up selling it to the legendary *Berkeley Barb*. My first sale. I'll never forget the day it was published: July 7, 1977, or 7/7/77 for you numerology freaks. Then I sat back and waited for my paycheck for my two month's work, which turned out to be a whopping $30. So I realized I wasn't going to be getting off the streets any time soon as an underground cartoonist.

In a sense, your homeless tour doesn't really begin until the day when you realize that you really, really, really *want* to get off the streets: BUT YOU CAN'T. Before that, it's kind of a lark. But suddenly it gets very serious. I distinctly remember walking down 6th Street — Skid Row — thinking to myself over and over:

"THIS IS WHERE THEY PUT PEOPLE LIKE ME!"

The words were screaming in my head. I'm not sure who "they" were. All the unseen forces of society, I guess. And all the other people who were fucking with me — whoever the hell they were. And maybe even God Himself. Maybe God had put me here, as some kind of punishment.

Some Force had driven me to the streets. Maybe it was my destiny. I hadn't *planned* to be nineteen years old and living on Skid Row in the Tenderloin district. But here I was. I realized I was a trapped rat. A weirdo with nowhere else to go, except further down. Which frightened me. There was a line from a

Chapter Twenty Three
Getting Off The Streets

Bruce Springsteen song that used to play in my head — *Hiding on the backstreets* — as I skulked down the back alleyways of the city.

I spent a lot of time on Skid Row with the other street rats during this period. I spent a lot of time in the Tenderloin. The streets of the Tenderloin were a surrealistic cross between *Blade Runner*, *Mad Max*, and *A Clockwork Orange*, with a strong hit of Bukowski. It was futuristic *and* medieval at the same time. Like a neon fantasy with garbage. They were hard streets. Mean streets. Weird streets. And I was the classic skid row bum. And yet, somehow, I was proud to be there. For, as weird as it was, it was like walking onto the set of the most amazing movie. I probably would have enjoyed it even more if I was sitting in a nice, safe movie theater watching it happen to somebody else, instead of being stuck up to my fucking neck in it. And then people around me began dying, which gave a new sense of urgency to my desire to pull myself out of the skids. If I could.

Now sometimes, during these periods of personal floundering, you have to push it: take the bull by the horns and take bold, direct action. Other times you just have to sit back and wait: wait out the storm until it (hopefully) passes. There's a whole art to knowing which of these to do, and when. I had no answers. So I just waited.

Finally I figured: Maybe I should see if I can get a Real Job. This is the number one most recommended way to get off the streets. If you can, try it some time.

But one of the Catch 22s of the streets is: **You need a job to get off the streets. But it's almost impossible to get a job when you're on the streets.** It is difficult, for example, to wake up in the bushes, wipe the dirt out of your hair, and report to work at Bank of America. About the only job I was qualified for in my funky condition was bike messenger, which is the job I finally got hired for.

I spent the first two weeks on the job sleeping on an off ramp on 5th and Bryant, pulling myself out of the bushes and reporting to work, until I finally got my first paycheck, then I rented out a room in a flophouse for $17 a week.

That's all it took to get off the streets back then in 1978: $17. I rented out a little room in a flophouse on 2nd Street, the last remnant of the old Skid Row. And that's the heroic, and yet somewhat boring story of how I got off the streets the first time.

That shows you how much easier it was to get off the streets back then. Seventeen dollars a week. There were more of those cheap, residential hotels back then. Not just welfare hotels, but inexpensive hotels where working poor people and young people could live. Nowadays, you practically need $2,000 to rent a place — what with first, last and deposit. That is if you can even FIND a place.

Which makes me wonder, in yet another digression: Where did all those cheap residential hotels go? Again, I'm not a sociologist with an objective overview, but from my bum's-eye view it looked like this:

- Well, that flophouse on 2nd Street was sold to PacBell a few years after I moved out, and they turned it into an office building.

- The residential hotel my friend Duncan lived in got burned to the ground in an arson fire that a lot of people seriously suspected was started by the owner.

- And there used to be another flophouse right up the street from where I'm typing this book. A real junkie hotel. The hallways used to be filled with junkies laying around shooting up junk. Right there in the hallways. Finally, the junkies ended up setting the building on fire. And that was that. Today the

building has been renovated — gentrified if you will — and turned into an upscale apartment building for students, mostly clean-cut Asians. Maybe this is another example of brutal Darwinism in action.
- And then there was the residential hotel I lived in for thirteen years. Around 1990 the rents just started getting raised higher and higher — due to the squeeze from diminishing supply and increasing demand for housing — until the poorest people just got priced out of the market. But I digress…

Eureka and Arcata 1995

I managed to keep myself off the streets for the next sixteen years. Worked as a bike messenger. Published an underground tabloid for awhile. Finally began to eke out a living as a cartoonist. But in 1994 after about sixteen years of apartment living, it all began to fall apart for me again. I lost my apartment and hit the streets for my second major homeless tour.

There were several reasons I ended up homeless this time, not the least of which was my skyrocketing rent. I ended up five months behind when I finally bailed ship.

But the main reason was that my life was so unpleasant and unfulfilling that I just couldn't get it up to make the effort to keep it together any more. It's kind of that feeling where the deck of cards you've been dealt are so lousy, you just fling the cards in the air in the hope that they land in a better pattern.

My cartooning career had fizzled out. My relationships with women had fizzled out. My brains were fizzling out. Then, pushing 40, I got hit with a massive Mid-Life Crisis. Made the classic bonehead mistake of falling head-over-heels in love with this 17-year-old Deadhead street chick, and ended up belly-flopping pathetically into complete and total failure.

Also, too, after ten years of sitting behind a drawing board, I was itching for some action. And the streets seemed like a place to start. I started hanging out with musicians. I had some half-assed idea about becoming a professional musician or a Rock Star or something. Make records. And why not? My life had been so weird already, *nothing* would surprise me. Plus, I have this heart-felt belief that you can accomplish anything you set your heart on. Anything. You can be anything you want to be in this life. If you work at it, you'll get it. Either in this lifetime or the next. So be careful who you want to be.

Another odd thing about me was, I always moved towards what I loved. It's one of the few things that gave my chaotic and haphazard life any sense of direction. If I loved someone, or loved doing something, I would throw everything away to follow that muse. In fact, out of all the possibly worthless advice I've thrown at you in this book, one of the things I still feel pretty solid about is this tip: ***Find out what you love to do. And then go for it. Follow love's trail.***

So I grabbed my guitar and my four-track tape recorder — which I loved to play with — and hit the streets. It seemed incredibly cool at the time. Especially the 17- and 19-year-old Deadhead chicks I was suddenly hanging out with. For I was a fool. The classic mid-life fool. But it was incredibly exciting. Especially at the beginning. One more weird fantasy I was getting to live out.

So I started hanging out with musicians. Taking too many drugs (damn musicians). Recorded a compilation CD of local Berkeley street musicians. A minor classic, it'll probably be worth a fortune long after I'm dead. But a lot of good it did me while I was sitting there in the gutter.

So-o-o… I hit the road. Spent a year mostly camping in the Redwoods, smoking a lot of pot, and singing many horribly bad love songs while playing my guitar.

After about a year on the road, the romance definitely started to wear off. I realized I hadn't become a Rock Star. In fact, I had become a Fucked up Bum on the Streets. Plus I was going nuts again. I desperately needed a hole to crawl into. To lick my wounds. And plot my next move. If I even had one.

Chapter Twenty Three
Getting Off The Streets

For I had seriously shot my wad. I was now 40 years old with no job, no career, no family, no home, and no love. Holy shit. I had missed the boat big-time. Talk about Mid-Life Crisis. I wasn't even sure I *had* a life.

How I got off the streets this time was — no, not by becoming a Rock Star but — by getting on welfare. General assistance: $220 a month, plus $100 in food stamps. And I was damn grateful to get it.

Now here's an actual street tip for you, campers (I figured I should throw in a few of these every now and again, since that's ostensibly the purpose of this book): If you're new in town and applying for welfare, one thing you need to do is prove you're a resident of that county. One of the quickest ways to do that is to mail yourself a bogus letter, c/o "General Delivery" to the local post office. When you pick up the letter, it will be postmarked with the date and the county on the envelope. Within 30 days of that postmark you'll have established your residency. So there.

I wish I had a more gripping, heroic tale to tell here. Like I scratched and clawed my way out of the gutter and pulled myself off the streets by my own bootstraps. But that's how I did it. I got on welfare. And I was barely able to do that. For nothing in life is easy, not even getting on, and staying on, welfare. That can be very difficult to do.

(For example, in the East Bay, it's common knowledge that if you're white you shouldn't even bother applying for welfare in Oakland where reverse racial discrimination is rampant; you should instead apply in San Francisco. There's a similar, unwritten "Whites Need Not Apply" code of institutionalized racism at many of the black-only, federal housing projects. This government-instituted segregation is now being challenged by many poor Asian immigrants who are trying to get housing in some of those projects, with typically bloody turf wars erupting.)

Anyway, welfare seemed like a lot of money from my vantage point of having 12 cents in my pocket. With my $220 welfare check I was able to rent out a room in a welfare hotel in Eureka, the fabulous Greyhound Hotel, for $200 a month. That's how much it cost to get off the streets then: $200 a month. 1995. That's about as cheap a room as you were going to find. By this point, I was really going nuts. Hanging on by a thread. So I was grateful to have those four walls to crawl into.

After being on welfare for a year, President Clinton, that great liberal, enacted his sweeping "welfare reforms." What that meant, in practical effect, was: *Kick as many people off as possible.* It was the beginning of the end of the great gravy train that began with Lyndon Johnson's Great Society welfare program in the '60s.

How they kicked everybody off welfare was simply by increasing the red tape, increasing the hoops you had to jump through to get on and stay on. Stuff like requiring you to have copies of your birth certificate, etc. I saw the handwriting on the wall. And I was sick of the gig anyway. So I dropped off of welfare, and plunged back onto the streets, sinking gracefully like a stone, a big heavy stone, tied around my neck and dragging me down into a cesspool of madness. Yes, I was very fucked up at this point.

Berkeley 1997

I spent the next two years camping in the hills of Berkeley. Actually, they turned out to be two of the best years of my life. Now this might surprise some of you, but life on the streets can be a great way to live. It surprised the hell out of *me*. Hitting the streets this time was akin to falling off of a twenty story building. Only to land on a big, huge, comfortable pillow.

I don't wish to make light of the living hell that life on the streets can so easily become — Lord KNOWS I don't. But the fact is, if you can stay one step ahead of the physical discomfort — if you can

Surviving On The Streets

keep the bugs out of your hair, and the demons out of your soul — the streets can be a surprisingly great place to live. Especially if you don't feel like *doing* anything. The streets can be a great place to do nothing. Kick back and take a vacation for a year. You might need one.

The main reason I was on the streets this time was that I was utterly and completely burned out. To a crisp. My circuits had completely overloaded. There are a lot of people on the streets like that. They've simply run out of gas. So you sit there on a street corner for a year or six. With the boys.

Myself, I had completely lost my spiritual bearings. I needed to recharge my spiritual batteries. So I sat down in the Berkeley hills and meditated. For about two years. I just sat there. And for the first time in my adult life, I actually started feeling better. It was the first thing I had tried in this life that had actually worked. Imagine that.

How I got off the streets this time was: After two years of dropping out and doing nothing, I started to get the itch to do something again. Like write this damn book, for one thing. So I took some of the profits from the STREET CALENDAR we publish every year and rented out a little office in an office building for $115 a month. My office was just a little box, really, about the size of a big walk-in closet. But it was perfect for my needs. I set up my computer and started typing this book. And while I was at it, I brought up my sleeping bag and started sleeping in the office, too. (If the owner of the building happens to be reading this, I'm not technically *"living"* in my office, heh heh.)

And that's the incredibly exciting story of how I got off the streets that time.

I'll give you another example of the cool little scams street people come up with to get off the streets. One homeless friend of mine got a job working in my office building as a part-time janitor. It only paid $7 an hour. But, as a fringe benefit, he ended up sleeping for two years in a large, empty storeroom in the building. His room was probably twice the size of the dinky little apartments most people in Berkeley were paying $700 a month for. Plus, at night, when all the office workers went home, he had the entire run of the building to himself. FOR FREE.

This highlights two important points that I can't stress enough:

1. **GET INVOLVED IN THINGS!** You'd be surprised what unexpected bonanzas can arise from churning out a little honest effort. And,

2. **FIND WORK TO DO!** It's not just the job itself, but the different ways it can expand your opportunities. Especially if you're looking for them. A lot of street people would shrug off a little part-time janitorial gig. *"What good is $7 an hour going to do me?"* But you never know what fringe benefits might come along with the gig.

There are lots of other ways to get off the streets. Some of the homeless social agencies can help you make that transition from the streets to a more stable life. Other street people find the help they need at drug and alcohol detox programs. The welfare-to-work programs have also had some promising results getting street people back into the mainstream.

Some kids hit the streets for a year or two, go wild, have a lot of fun and adventures, and then put on clean clothes and get a good job working in a record store or a restaurant. A lot of people on the streets are like that. The streets are just a temporary phase they go through.

Other people get on SSI or get Section 8 Housing or get on some other HUD housing program and get off the streets that way.

Chapter Twenty Three
Getting Off The Streets

Others — some of the old-timers — adjust to being on the streets. They dig it. Or at least tolerate it. These types aren't even trying to get off the streets. They've accepted the streets as their natural milieu.

But there are a lot of other people who get stuck on the streets. They get stuck on the treadmill. They want to get off the streets, they want a better life, but they can't figure out how to do it. It can sometimes be a very, very difficult thing to do. Getting off the streets.

Whatever route you take with your life, I wish you luck, my friend.

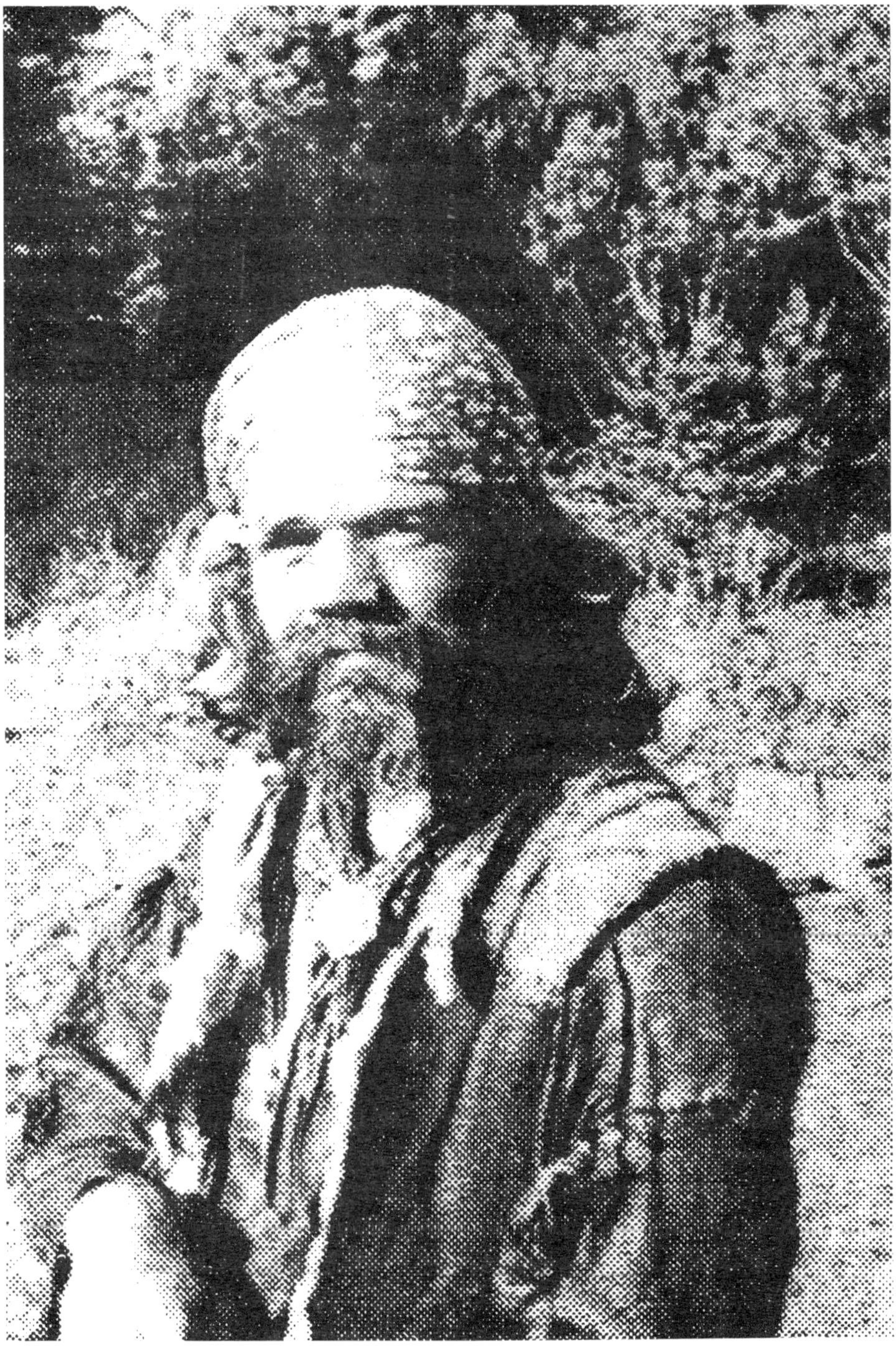

Chapter Twenty Four
Psychological Skid Rows

As I write this book, I keep coming back to one basic question: What exactly *is it* that you survive on the streets? There's the harshness of the street environment. The elements. The wind, the cold and the rain. The drugs. The violence.

But one thing that you most need to survive is your own mind. Your own nature. Your own psychological skid row.

When I look at the people who adjust to the streets, who glide through it easily with a minimum of damage, and then I look at the ones who got wiped out by the streets, the difference wasn't so much *what happened to them* — for we all get our weird tragedies thrown at us — but how their *minds reacted* to what happened to them.

If your head is in a good place, the streets can be Heaven on Earth. But if your head is fucked up, it can be Hell. Raw, cold Hell.

I suppose this is true in any walk of life. But on the streets perhaps it's more pronounced. Maybe because of the extreme conditions of the streets. When you go down, you can go *all* the way down, and then out and whooooops... there he goes.... and I've seen them go.

I've had friends commit suicide. I've seen 17-year-old kids O.D. on drugs. I've seen people driven to the nuthouses out of sheer madness. I've seen people flipping out in every way a human mind can flip out. You can overdose on the sheer tragedy of what you're forced to see. Seeing people flaming out before your eyes. Your mind will be tested. And if you have a propensity towards cracking, the streets can crack your head open like a walnut.

This chapter is very difficult for me to write. For my own mind regularly goes haywire on a periodic basis (if you've read the preceding chapters, that's probably not news to you). So I'm certainly no expert on offering advice when it comes to fighting these mental/spiritual battles. But I *do* know this: The most important battles you will fight are the battles you wage in your own mind. There is nothing more important than learning how to befriend your mind. For it can be your best friend. Or your worst enemy.

It was always the quirks of my mind that drove me to the streets. My seething rages that made it difficult to function. My sweeping depressions that dragged my spirit down, down, down into a bog of misery that I couldn't pull myself out of. And madness. Pure and simple madness. To have my own mind go berserk. Like a frothing, rabid dog. Like a runaway wild horse, a bucking bronco careening out of control.

To be a broken man. That's what drove me to the streets. Heartbreak. Not so much the purely romantic type. But the heartbreak of the soul. Heartbreak of the spirit. Heartbreak of the mind. It was as if the part of me that transmitted and received love was broken. For I was loveless. I kept making the same fundamental mistake: I kept seeking love from the world, from other people. I hadn't realized that the love was in my own heart. But I couldn't find it there, either. For that part of me was broken. I was a broken man. The streets were littered with such men.

I could blame society; I could blame the police; I could blame Reagan and Bush; I could blame the CIA. But it was my own inner mental quirks and spiritual deficiencies that kept dragging me to the streets. My neurosis, my psychosis, my insecurities, my dementia, my drugged-out lunacies, my damaged brain, my bitterness and rage, my incredible stupidities, my rages, my deep and profound unhappiness, my legendary depressions, my sexual frustrations, my sexual obsessions, my sexual stupidities, all my many other myriad stupidities, and all the other fucked-up shit stewing around in my brain (and all you shrinks can come up with big words like *"schizophrenia"* and *"bi-polar disorder"* to describe it, but I've never come up with a better definition: *"all the fucked up shit stewing around in my brain"*).

You can get overwhelmed by it. And believe me, I have been.

Being homeless, being on the streets, is a very difficult thing. A very restricted life. Your existence can get as narrow as the sidewalk you live on. It can be like playing a very difficult and demanding game — with severe penalties when you play it poorly. Which is why your mind must be sharp. You can't afford to be too sloppy. There are just too many ways to get wiped out in this game.

Bum Attitudes

Can I be more specific in terms of my own personal Psychological Skid Rows?

Let's start with my feelings that I'm a Cosmic Orphan who doesn't fit in anywhere. Who skulks and slinks through this world like a pariah in enemy territory. The streets are filled with many such types who feel they don't belong in this world.

Or how about my self-loathing? I hate myself. I'm a jerk. I'm no good. I'm guilty. Nobody wants me around. When you feel you're unwanted you often end up going where no one would want to be: the streets.

Chapter Twenty Four
Psychological Skid Rows

Or my barren spirituality. Without God this life is nothing. It means nothing. It adds up to nothing. It's just a lot of pleasant and unpleasant sensations and weird movies. Without God the nothingness of the streets is your natural milieu.

Or my lack of love. My lovelessness. This hideous state of unrequited love that I lived in. Even if somebody did love me, I didn't love myself, so how could I accept their love? And I had no love to give. Instead, at best, I beamed out sort of a feeble charm and charisma. But there was no warmth in me. I was freezing to death inside. Without love in my heart, is it surprising I ended up on the cold streets?

Or my dementia. After about the 200th acid trip, I realized: "Hey, I only get one brain and I'm scrambling the hell out of it; maybe I shudda' taken better care of it…" (uh duh). Crazy. Nuts. Bonkers. Do you know what it's like to sit in a $200-a-month flophouse hotel room, seething with rage, bouncing off the walls, screaming to nobody, screaming at the world, and silently screaming in my brain 24 hours a day? It made it very difficult to hold down a day job, for I couldn't hear anything except the hideous screaming in my brain. Considering the dark, macabre, Edgar Allen Poe world of my mind, is it any wonder I ended up walking in the twilight shadow world of the streets?

I was completely lost. What was life for anyway? I didn't have a clue. What was I *supposed* to be doing? I did not know. What should I *do?* Well, get up out of my sleeping bag and drink some coffee and then…

…from there it was touch and go. I went a lot of places. Walked through so many doors. Walked into many doors. But I was never sure if I was walking forwards or backwards. Or around in circles. I wasn't even sure what the *rules* of the game were. Or even if it *was* a game. Some people maintained it was a serious affair, this life of ours, grueling hard work and toil, with serious and potentially dire consequences.

It was a spiritual battle I was fighting. And losing. A battle I was seeing so many people around me lose.

Probably the biggest killer on the streets is the sheer pointlessness — the sheer purposelessness — of so much of it.

Blue

My friend Blue was extremely bright, intelligent, talented, funny, and good-looking, and from a good family. He had all sorts of things going for him. Except that his mind went haywire on him. For some reason, he suffered from a weird form of spiritual anorexia. He seemed to go out of his way to deny himself spiritual sustenance.

Eventually, Blue got worn down by the weight of his own mind, ended up on the streets, ended up committing suicide. The same day he killed himself, there was a story on the front page of the paper about a woman in Berkeley who was a quadriplegic in a wheelchair who had started her own successful business.

It's not *what* happens to you, it's how your mind *reacts* to what happens to you.

Dumpster Danny

Another friend of mine, Dumpster Danny, to walk past him as he sits there in the gutter reading his newspaper, you might think: There's another aging hippie bum with bad teeth. Except if you look closely you'll notice he's smiling all the time.

He once said to me: "God is everywhere. This world is nothing but the body of God. Which includes me and you and everyone else. This is Heaven on Earth."

I once lived in one of the richest suburbs in the country and I can assure you I met plenty of rich people living in Hell. And yet here was this guy living in the gutter, living in Heaven.

For some reason, the cops kept trying to run Dumpster Danny off the Ave. They kept giving him tickets for various criminal offenses, mostly involving sleeping and sitting and eating, things which Danny had a propensity to do on a regular basis. Once this cop threatened to give him a ticket for "slouching." If you're going to sit in the gutter, you have to have correct posture, apparently. Another time, this cop gave him a ticket for "littering" when he was feeding the pigeons. I guess he shouldn't have thrown those bread crumbs onto the ground. Danny just laughed about it and went on doing his thing. (Last time I saw him, he was still slouching.)

Rainbow Willie

Another street friend of mine, Rainbow Willie, is another guy who fought the spiritual battle in his mind and won.

Rainbow Willie was a black guy from Watts — one of the toughest ghettos in Los Angeles. Willie remembers going to school as a kid in the '60s with tear gas in his eyes from the Watts riots. But as he grew into a man, he got spiritual and transformed into sort of a black, peace-and-love hippie.

He lived in his car, this bomb of a '56 Chevy — the classic old boat with a brightly colored, psychedelic mural painted all over it, with a big Grateful Dead skull logo on the front hood. Just a classic car. You went tooling around in that baby, and it was like riding in the back seat of the funkiest old limousine. It was like being chauffeured by a psychedelic Lurch from the *Addam's Family*.

Anyway, one night, me and Rainbow Willie are kicking back at the International House of Pancakes, in this nice, quiet peaceful neighborhood. IHOP used to stay open 24 hours, and they used to have this deal "the bottomless pot of coffee," where, for a buck, you could get refills of coffee all night long. So we'd hang out in there all night, drinking and talking.

Suddenly, the peace of the evening was shattered when this young black man came storming into IHOP, carrying a big ghetto blaster, and blasting out this loud, angry rap music. You could see from the poor guy's face that he was seething with rage and anger and barely controlled violence. He was like a moveable storm. Finally, he stalked out of IHOP and down the street, leaving a trail of havoc in his wake. After he was out of range, Rainbow Willie turned to me and said:

"Some people carry the ghetto around with them, every step they take."

And some people carry Skid Row around with them in their minds, every step they take.

J. Paul Getty and Howard Hughes may have been billionaires, but in truth, they were nothing but Bums, because of the poverty of their minds. Whereas Dumpster Danny and Rainbow Willie may be bums, but in truth, they are Kings because of the riches of their minds.

Chapter Twenty Four
Psychological Skid Rows

Rainbow Willie was in the hospital recently for lung cancer. He's lived a harsh, outdoors life for years, and it can wear you down. For years he lived in a school bus in the middle of a cow pasture in Adin, California, population 240 (plus or minus one), up in the sticks of Modoc County. Gets well below freezing in the winter. Three feet of snow. Try sleeping in a school bus with nothing but a funky, wood-burning stove. He was trying to start a Rainbow Family hippie commune up there. It didn't work. But it was a noble try. Because he was a noble guy.

So anyway, I visited him in the hospital. Gave him a framed picture of the Star Trek crew, his idols, to bolster his spirits and facilitate the healing process.

"The doctors said I could have died," he told me matter-of-factly. No big deal. Not upset in the least, really. For what is death to someone who's already in heaven?

I mean, compare that with how I might have reacted. I'm the type, if I catch so much as a cold, it's a CRISIS! Yes, I am a whiner and a sniveler. Poor, poor pitiful me. Did I tell you how I SUFFER? And how about the very raw deal in life that I got? And — guess what? — I'm BITTER about it. And maybe I'll take it out on YOU! Yes, I'm fairly well acquainted with my asshole side. Christ, I have to live with myself and my mind 24 hours a day. At least you can get AWAY from me every now and then.

But my friend Rainbow Willie was at peace. Who can explain where that comes from? Except that some people have a spiritual wisdom to them. A peace of mind. Love. Whatever you want to call those good things of the spirit.

And if you truly want to survive on the streets, you might want to take out a little time and see if you can learn how to cultivate some of those good things.

It's not what happens to you, but how your mind reacts to what happens to you. Remember that, as you're walking about bitching about your shitty situation on the streets.

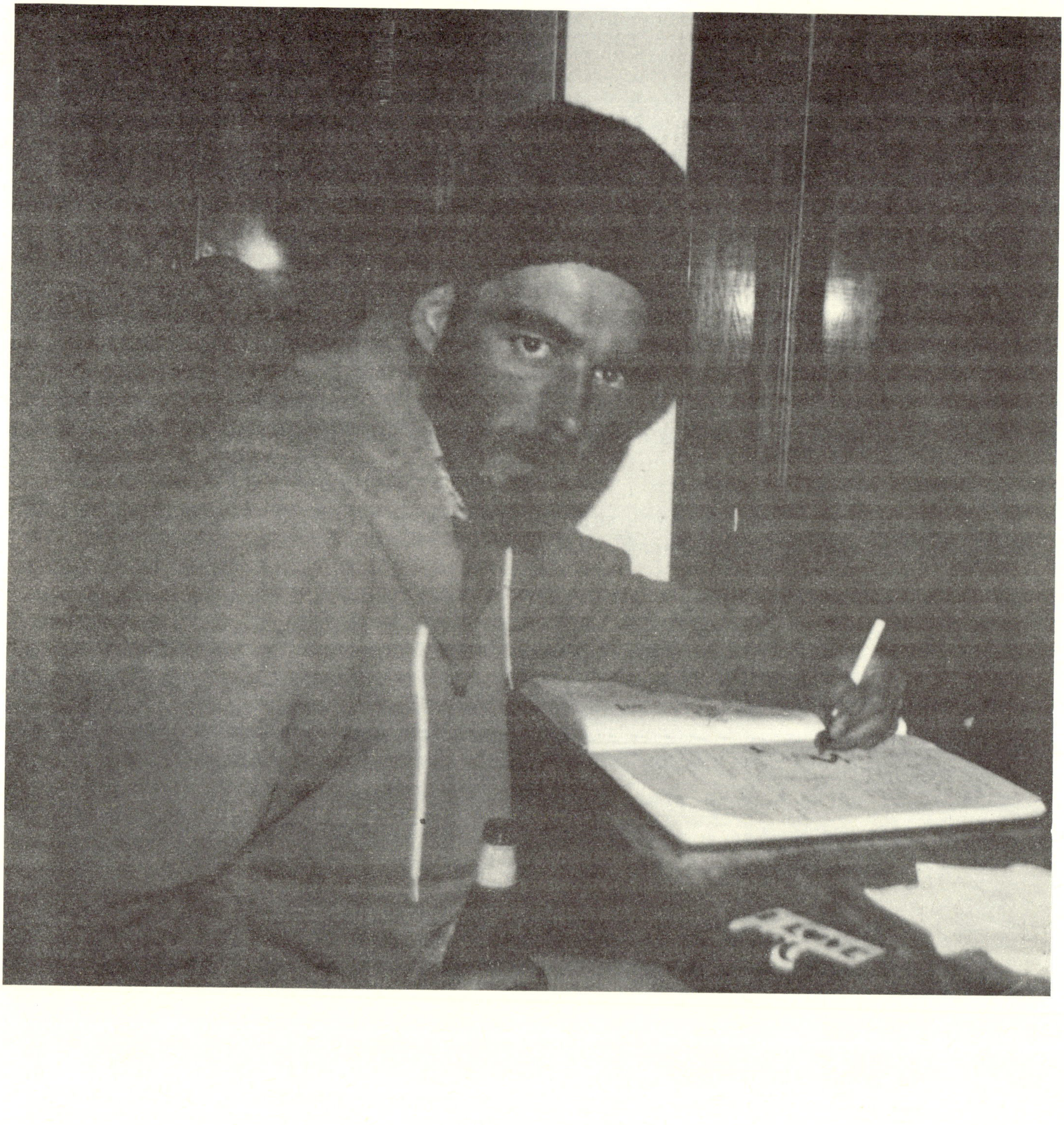

Chapter Twenty Five
Surviving on The Streets

To repeat the question I raised at the start of the previous chapter: *What exactly do you survive on the streets?*

You must survive the wear and tear of *living outdoors*. Sleeping in *the rain*. The *drugs*. The *poverty*. The *wingnuts*. The *cops*. The *violence*. The *weirdness*. The *tragedies*. You must survive all this. Coming at you one after another sometimes. But the thing you must survive, above all else, is **your own mind**.

For beyond all else, life is a spiritual battle at its core.

Many people hit the streets already deeply wounded. Then, the harshness of the street environment rips those wounds open even wider. It can be like stepping into a hurricane. A blizzard. You see people hit the streets spinning like a top. And they don't stop spinning until they've spun all the way off the face of the earth.

Each street person's situation is unique and individual. Probably the only thing I can offer in this book are a few general tips that worked for me (and quite a few that didn't, but maybe you can learn just as much from my monumental fuck ups):

Some General Street Survival Principles

- *Clean up your messes.*
- *Don't fuck with the cops (they might be better at it than you).*
- *Try to find some kind of work to do.*
- *Learn to spot the violent assholes before they spot you.*
- *Try to be as self-sufficient as possible.*
- *Avoid hard drugs (they don't call them "hard" for nothing).*
- *Avoid bad associations.*
- *Learn to read people: Trust nobody (until they've proven to be trustworthy).*
- *The more you give, the more you get back (but don't cast your pearls before bums).*
- *Don't just SIT there — get INVOLVED with something.*
- *Don't take any wooden nickels.*
- *Look both ways before crossing the street (and fight your jaywalking tickets in court).*
- *Feeding the pigeons can be considered a crime in a court of law.*
- *Never think of yourself as small (you're actually greater than you could possibly imagine).*

The streets can be like a banana peel you keep slipping on, a bog you sink deeper and deeper into. It took me five long years to write this book. One reason for that was because, halfway through writing it, I started to seriously wonder if I *had* survived the streets. For I was seriously damaged from my experiences. Which forced me to rethink the whole premise of this book. Maybe I wasn't any different than all the other *know-it-all* geniuses with their *do-as-I-say-not-as-I-do advice*.

But then I thought: Well, if I wipe out, then Loompanics could just publish it as **How NOT to Survive the Streets** and they'd only have to make minimal editing changes in the manuscript. And I felt better about the whole deal.

But that's the **schizo** thing about the streets. It can be **heaven or hell**. It's so precarious. It can go from heaven to hell in a blink of an eye. The streets are so fast-paced. Entire movies play out before your eyes within a week on the streets. One week, one day, on the streets can be a lifetime. Technicolor movies of mind-boggling depth and symbolism race across the screen of your mind. On the stage of the streets you witness the greatest Tragedies. The most passionate Love Stories. The weirdest Slapstick Comedies. The whole grand Search for Truth and Meaning!!! They all get acted out on the grand stage of the streets.

No movie can capture it. The closest I've seen to capturing the reality of the streets on film is Bukowski in *Barfly* and Ratso Rizzo in *Midnight Cowboy*. I've lived out scenes from those movies a hundred times.

*Chapter Twenty Five
Surviving on The Streets*

I love the scene where Ratso Rizzo is at the Andy Warhol Factory party, and he's at the buffet table, stuffing salamis and cold cuts into the pockets of his ratty-ass jacket. One of Warhol's superstars approaches him:

"You don't have to steal the food. It's free," she said.

"Well, if it's free, then I ain't stealing it," said Ratso.

And he stuffed some more chunks of cheese and hors d'ouvres into his pockets and made his exit with his dignity intact. That's the streets.

Some people adjust naturally to the rhythms of the streets. Others get worn down by it, every step they take. Drip by drip. I take all the statistics about the homeless with a big grain of salt, but I wouldn't be surprised if long-term stints of homelessness can take twenty years off your life expectancy.

There's no question that there is *something* you need to survive on the streets. I've mostly been giving you the **hard** stuff here in this book. The bad stuff you have to watch out for. The weird trips that can suddenly come barreling down at you at 90 miles an hour. But the other side of the schizo equation is ***how great the streets can be***.

That was a great surprise, the great irony, to me. I hit the streets totally fucked up, and the streets saved my ass. I can honestly say that landing up on the streets turned out to be one of the greatest things to ever happen to me.

That was the most odd and bizarre thing of all. Out of all the odd and bizarre things that happened to me, that was the oddest: After failing at everything I tried for 40 years, I finally just gave up and hit the streets in disgrace. A bum. A loser. A failure. And it was then that I had my first glimpses of True Success.

Like I said before: **Everybody knows that money, fame, and success don't necessarily bring happiness. But the other side of that equation is also true: poverty, obscurity, and failure don't necessarily bring *un*happiness.**

The streets can break your balls, or they can break your falls.

At its best, the streets give you the opportunity to retreat, to sit back, to regroup. To concoct *Plan B*. Followed by *Plan C*. Or, if you're a wingnut, *Plan $Q47^2\#AgggC$*.

The great saving grace of living on the streets is: If you can put up with the inconveniences of living outdoors, the great equalizer is that *you are suddenly freed from the tyranny of rent.*

Suddenly, I was freed from the pressure of having to pay the rent every month. Suddenly a big expanse of free time loomed in front of me. Free time: the great blessing (and curse) of street life. Ironically, not only was my home on the streets rent-free, but my "homeless home" in the hills was quite simply the most beautiful home I had ever had. Grazing deer. Wily raccoons. Soaring blue jays. Blood-sucking tics. Occasional demon from Hades. Fields of wild flowers. Gurgling creeks. The most beautiful home I'd ever had. AND IT WAS FREE. If anything fucked up my head more than anything, it was the sheer mind-boggling *irony* of the streets. Every story had some weird, ironic twist to it.

Freed from the constraints of job and family, the streets gave me the free time to *"Deal With My Shit."* It gave me the chance to drop out of society and focus inward on what was bothering me. It gave me the chance to "get spiritual," for lack of a better phrase. I hit the streets totally fucked up, and, two years later, got off the streets in a helluva lot better shape than when I went on. Again, the mind-boggling irony. Everything was backwards. I hit the streets and didn't go down — I went up! Maybe the title of this book should be *How to Be a Successful Failure*. The streets truly saved my ass.

And so, this book comes to an end. Writing a book is great fun. I highly recommend it. It's kind of like having an argument where you always get in the last word (well, at least until all the critics tear me a new asshole). I suppose I should make a boring little note about my use of the term *"street"* since I used it about five billion times in the course of this tome. The term *"on the streets"* (as in "Joe is on the streets") generally means the person is living outdoors or in his car. On the other hand, there are a lot of people who are part of *"the street scene"* who aren't "on" the streets. Then there are *"street musicians"* and *"street vendors"* which add even a different connotation to the word. And then there's somebody who has *"street smarts."* There's *"street cred."* There are *"streetwalkers."* And then, there are those damn *"streets"* themselves, those concrete things that we walk upon and drive upon, and occasionally sleep upon. *"The streets"* can mean almost anything. Was Jesus a *"street person?"* When I use the word *"street"* in this book, I reserve the right to have it mean any of the many different things it can mean.

Most of all, I see myself as an anthropologist studying this weird and bizarre street tribe or subculture. Or studying the weird patterns that the streets have imprinted on my brain.

But most of all, to my brothers and sisters on the streets, I wish you strength and courage and good fortune.

Some people complain that street people are a nuisance. But consider this: There are thousands of us out here on the streets of your city, with no place to sleep, or eat, or even sit, or go to the bathroom. Think how much of an inconvenience we *could* be, if the average street person didn't handle this difficult situation with incredible grace and style. And that's the truth of it. That's the heroic part of it. That so many street people make the best of a very difficult situation.

Like my friend said: "I've been on the streets for so long, everywhere I go is as much home as anywhere else."

For this world is your home, my friend. Your mind is your home. This whole world is your living room. Your playground. Your fantastic stage. To concoct the fantastic dramas of your fantastic life.

Gypsy Catano's Memorial Service

I'll end this sorta saga with a strange tale of life and death on the streets.

It was the funeral and memorial service for Gypsy Catano. Gypsy was a legendary rogue of the Berkeley streets. He died at age 47. (Or who knows how old he really was? Street people live lives far beyond the world of birth certificates, I.D. cards, and newspaper obituaries and statistics. We live mostly in the realm of legend and lore.)

Gypsy Catano's life suddenly came to an end one day when he choked on a chicken bone and had an epileptic seizure. Thus ended 47 years of spectacular wildness and excess. Gypsy was a drunk. A fuck up. A lunatic. An outlaw. A rogue. A wildman. A bum. Anything else you'd like to add. He was the quintessential street person.

And yet when he died, hundreds of people, from all walks of life, turned up for his memorial service at People's Park. True, half of them were there to make sure the bastard was really dead, as the saying goes. But we were *all* there to celebrate his wild and crazy life.

And I thought: There are normal, mainstream, law-abidin', tax-payin' citizens who die every day. And nobody mourns their loss. And yet here's this …this *bum* …who dies, and *hundreds* of people show up in the park to celebrate his amazing life.

Chapter Twenty Five
Surviving on The Streets

It was a candlelight memorial service. One by one, people stood in a circle near the legendary People's Park stage, and raised their candles in the air, and told their Gypsy Catano stories. Gleefully. For it was a happy occasion.

One person said: "The ironic thing is, Gypsy himself would have never gotten up this early in the morning to come to a memorial." That got a laugh.

I said: "I remember the first time I met Gypsy. He was wearing a brown-fringed leather jacket, and a necklace made out of bones. And he was wearing a stole around his neck. Only it wasn't a mink stole. It was made out of the fur of a dog that somebody had skinned and tanned. Gypsy did a quick puppet routine with the dog's head for my amusement. And then he went on his way. Gypsy Catano. Drunk off his ass. Off to get in a fight with somebody."

My great friend, B.N. Duncan — who is one of the great chroniclers of the Berkeley street tribe — held his candle up and read his handwritten eulogy to Gypsy:

"Gypsy Catano was a great man," read Duncan. "He was a unique individual. A wild, untamed spirit of the streets. A charming rogue. A charismatic, natural leader of the street community. Gypsy Catano had a yearning quality that was, uh, ...*AHHHHHH!*" Duncan screamed.

The eulogy Duncan was reading burst into flames when it accidentally caught fire from the candle he was holding in the other hand. Duncan threw the burning paper down on the stage, and stomped the flames out with his feet. Duncan picked up the charred, smoking eulogy, looked out at the audience, cleared his throat, and continued with his speech in honor of Gypsy.

And I had to laugh. Because it was such a perfect street moment. Street people are famous for stirring up the shit and causing a bit of a ruckus, whenever things get too staid or polite or civilized.

And I'm sure Gypsy Catano was sitting up there on a cloud, looking down on us, and just laughing his ass off at the whole spectacle.

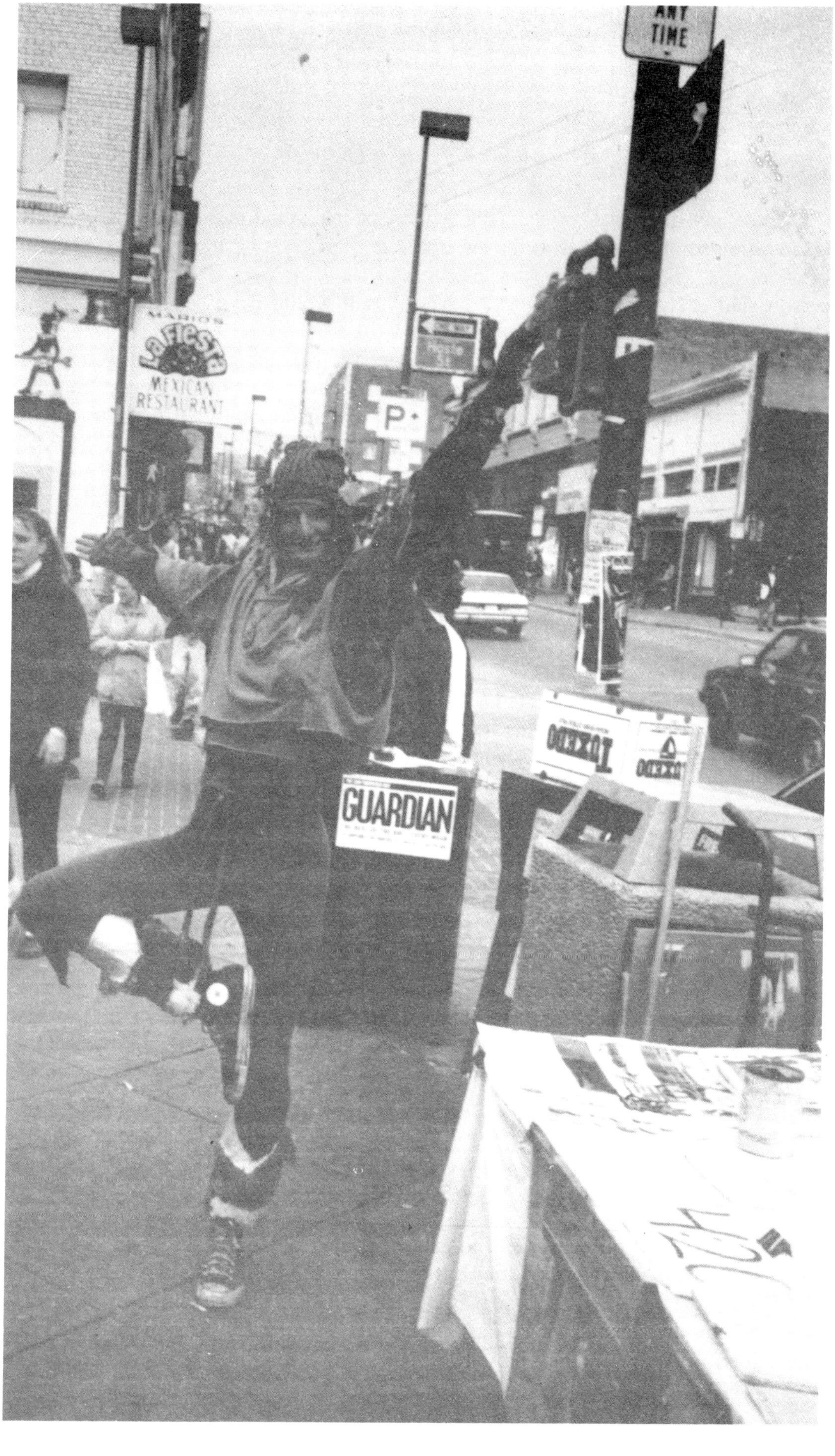
ANY TIME
MARIO'S
La Fiesta
MEXICAN RESTAURANT
P
GUARDIAN

Epilogue

It was another nothing day on the streets. Nothing much happening. I spent most of the day scrounging around, walking back and forth down every city street. I go back and forth in my mind: Sometimes I think I'm incredibly blessed to have the freedom to float along with the wind all day long. Other times I think I'm wasting my life walking around and around in pointless circles.

Elf was screaming into the phone: "I need money to get OUT of this town! I'm sleeping on the STREETS! This guy keeps trying to RAPE me!"

Elf had hit the streets at age seventeen. She was an adorable little waif. One of the most beautiful women I have ever seen. Now, two years later, she was completely crazed, driven completey berserk by what had happened to her. She had become a total loner. She didn't talk to any of the other street kids. She existed in a weird, psychotic dreamscape inhabited by spiders, trolls, wood nymphs, and demons. I had tried to help her get off the streets. But nothing I had done had helped. And maybe nothing in this book will help you either (sorry, no refunds).

I heard a mournful meowing sound coming from Elf's backpack. "Elf, is that a cat in your backpack?" I asked.

"Yes," said Elf. "I'm married to Peter Jennings. There was a war between animals and humans a million years ago. The humans lost. You're going to Hell! Do you understand me?"

Surviving On The Streets

Elf slung her pack over her shoulder, the cat meowing wildly from inside, and stormed off down the street.

I walked to the BART station. Sat on the bench smoking a cigarette. Sat there. I was in Hell all right. Lord knows I was. But I also lived in Heaven. For this world that we walk around in, it is the very body of God. It is awesome and mind-boggling, isn't it? This life of ours.

Another nothing day on the streets. About the only thing that happened all day was a fight that broke out earlier in the afternoon behind our vending table.

I hear this scuffle, turn around, and it looks like two guys are wrestling, horsing around. It always seems like guys are just playing around when I first see a fight break out. It's not until I hear the sounds of "THWACK! THWACK! THWACK!," the dull thud of one guy's fist colliding with the other guy's back, that I realize it's serious. I jump over and try to pull the one guy off of the other guy, but his arms are as strong as a bull and he gets a few more punches in.

"Break it up! Break it up! The cops are coming!" which is what I always say in these situations.

"I don't care! He's a child-molester and a woman-beater!"

Finally, I get them apart, and I'm surprised to find out the other guy is Stoner. He's got this wild-eyed look on his face, and now that he's up he's ready to go at the guy, so I've got to contend with that.

"This guy just attacked me for no reason!" screamed Stoner.

The cops were there by then sorting it out, so I disappeared. Five minutes later I run into Snake who's cooling his jets around the corner by Ann's Soup Kitchen. He's smiling gleefully, and fills me in on what the fight was all about.

"That kid is a new guy on the scene. He just got kicked out of Shattuck and now he's up here. We told him if he wanted to fit in with our scene he had to do what we said for two weeks as his initiation. He's our bitch-boy for two weeks. I told him: 'See that guy over there? He's a child-molester and a wife-beater. Go beat him up.' So he did!"

"You mean he didn't even know Stoner?"

"No."

I had to laugh as I walked down the street. A lot can happen even on a nothing day on the streets.

I walk up to Telegraph at around 8 p.m. Sheena, the latest reigning Queen of the hippie scene is holding court in front of Amoeba Records. She's surrounded by a gaggle of street guys, each one hoping that they'll be the lucky one tonight. Bald, young Pentagram, with satanic symbols tattooed on his forehead, is sitting on the sidewalk, prattling on with a bunch of black-clad, death-rocker types: "Vodka makes me go nuts, but 40s of malt liquor makes me happy." His voice has a manic happiness to it. Like he knows it's not going to last. Like it's going to be snatched away from him, soon. There is just something futile about it all, this artificial happiness that we try to get from some meager chemical buzz. And the unhappiness that seems to be everywhere in this world of ours.

Little Red was there, too, her face breaking out from shooting junk. She was with some new hippie boyfriend-of-the-moment. She's another tragic one. What happened to her? What happened to us? We all have our stories. Barely understood. Even by ourselves.

Back on the campus, that crazy black kid who's always sitting by himself on the steps talking to himself, is sitting there talking and singing and making weird noises to himself. Wailing out to nobody, out into the lonely night. Always alone. Dressed in rags. Where did he come from to end up so alone? Does he have family? Does anyone care that he sits there alone all day raving his nonsense to nobody for nothing? Only to walk a block-and-a-half up the street every night to curl up awkwardly in a doorway and sleep there all night without even a blanket. To walk back to the campus the next morning to do it all over again. For years at a stretch. What are these people for? Can somebody tell me? What strange karma are we all acting out?

I played drums for a while in the Hate Man's drum circle, pounding on buckets and metal objects with the other street freaks, chanting out my sacred mantra along with the rhythm (when we actually had one). Periodically, I would look up from my bucket at the faces in the circle with me. Some of them I have known for five, ten, even twenty years. The streets are indeed a family. A fucked up, dysfunctional family. But a family nonetheless.

Around 1 a.m., Hate Man came back from the Café German with jugs of hot, leftover coffee.

"Fuck you, Hate Man, I'm taking some coffee," I said.

"Fuck you, Splat, I hear you. There's also day-old pastries."

I poured some coffee and chocolate syrup into a bottle, and grabbed a couple of ham-and-cheese croissants, stuffed them into my pack. Tomorrow's breakfast. And some leftover burrito-and-rice for my birds and raccoons.

I walked through the dark, deserted campus, stopping only to plug my battery-recharger into an outdoor wall socket on the side of one of the buildings. Tomorrow I'll have fresh Double A's for my Walkman.

I headed up the street towards the Berkeley hills. As I walked higher and higher into the hills, I quietly chanted my mantra — *Om namah Shivaya* — under my breath. The streets were completely deserted and I was totally alone. I thought of what Elf used to always say: *"Alone but not lonely,"* and I only hoped she meant it.

After I passed the football stadium, I stopped and turned around. I looked down at the stadium below, the twinkling city lights of Berkeley, the Bay, San Francisco off in the distance, the Pacific Ocean beyond that, the dark, dramatic purple night sky above me. I yelled my mantra — "Om namah Shivaya!" — to the Heavens.

I continued walking up into the Berkeley hills. About a quarter mile up the main road, I darted off the road, climbed over the big tree branch that blocked the entrance of the trail that led up to my campsite, and plunged into the dark forest...

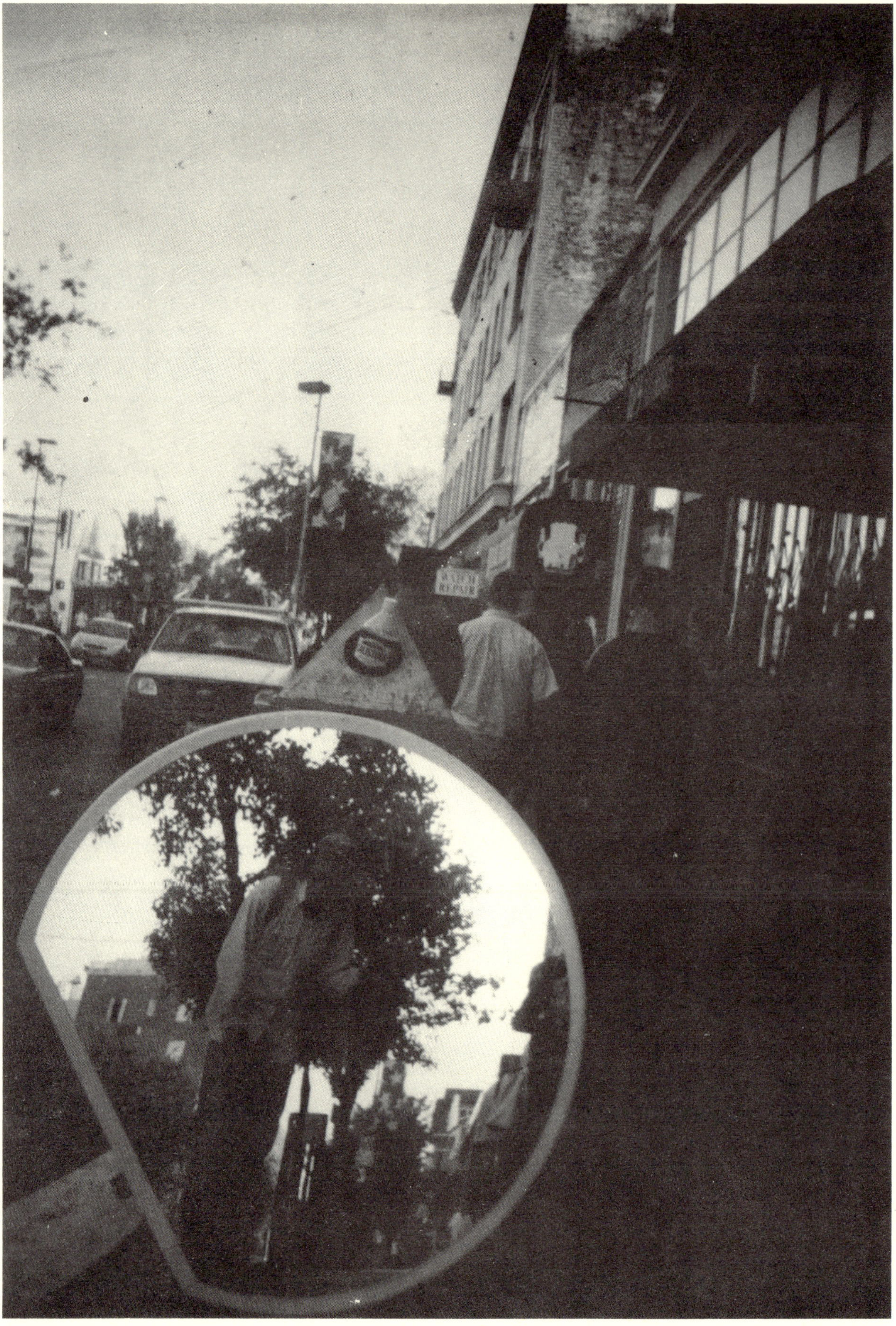

YOU WILL ALSO WANT TO READ:

- **14099 THE ART & SCIENCE OF DUMPSTER DIVING,** *by John Hoffman.* This book will show you how to get just about anything you want or need — food, clothing, furniture, building materials, entertainment, luxury goods, tools and toys — you name it — *ABSOLUTELY FREE!* Take a guided tour of America's back alleys where amazing wealth is carelessly discarded. Hoffman will show you where to find the good stuff, how to rescue it and how to use it. You'll find illustrated techniques, recipes for salvaged food, how to convert trash to cash, and how to handle run-ins with cops. It took the author a lifetime to learn this — all it takes for you is this book. *1993, 8½ x 11, 152 pp, illustrated, soft cover.* **$14.95**.

- **10065 HOW TO HIDE THINGS IN PUBLIC PLACES,** *by Dennis Fiery.* Did you ever want to hide something from prying eyes, yet were afraid to do so in your home? Now you can secrete your valuables away from home, by following the eye-opening instructions contained in this book, which identifies many of the public cubbyholes and niches that can be safely employed for this purpose. Absolutely the finest book ever written on the techniques involved in hiding your possessions in public hiding spots. Illustrated with numerous photographs, this book includes an index of hiding places and appendices of Simplex lock combinations. *1996, 5½ x 8½, 220 pp, illustrated, soft cover.* **$15.00**.

- **13063 SURVIVAL BARTERING,** *by Duncan Long.* What if you had no money? What if an entire society had no money due to the collapse of our banking system? Bartering will be the most important survival skill you can learn. People barter for different reasons — to avoid taxes, obtain a better lifestyle, or just for fun. This book foresees a time when barter is a necessity. You'll learn about; three forms of barter; getting good deals; stockpiling for future bartering; protecting yourself from rip-offs; and much more. Learning how to barter could be the best insurance you can find. *1986, 5½ x 8½, 56 pp, soft cover.* **$8.00**.

- **17075 THE HITCHHIKER'S HANDBOOK,** *by James MacLaren.* Hitchhiking is an American institution — and this book, written in the vernacular an style of the streets, explains how to do it correctly and efficiently! You'll learn little-known secrets of the road that will help you hitch free rides and get safely to your destination; how to dress, what to carry, where and how to position yourself and how to generate repeat rides. Plus tips on emergency sleeping resources, practical sign-making, avoiding trouble with the cops, and much more. Whether you're making an emergency commute to work or planning a trip across the country, this book serves as an invaluable guide. *1995, 5½ x 8½, 145 pp, soft cover.* **$12.95**.

- **88173 DON'T LET THEM PSYCH YOU OUT!,** *by George Zgourides, Psy.D.* This is a great book on "psychological self-defense." It gives you practical tools you can use to deal with the difficult people in your life: bosses, co-workers, relatives, spouses, bureaucrats, and salespeople — people who try to psych you out! Learn how to handle stressful situations: arguments, ambushes, and showdowns without losing your dignity or losing your cool. It won't make the conflicts go away, but it will give you the skills you need. *1993, 5½ x 8½, 198 pp, charts, glossary, soft cover.* **$15.95**.

☐ **40084 HOW TO SNEAK INTO THE MOVIES,** *by Dan Zamudio.* Why let Hollywood bigwigs, bad actors, and cowardly studio executives rip you off? The author has worked in several movie theaters and reveals all his tricks of sneaking into the movies, including the four basic ways to get into the movies free. Highlighted with true tales of sneaking into some of America's great movie palaces. If you are tired of being milked for box office duds, then lower your cost of movie-going and your risk of getting caught by learning exactly *How to Sneak Into the Movies! 1995, 5½ x 8½, 64 pp, soft cover.* **$8.00**.

☐ **40079 HOW TO STEAL FOOD FROM THE SUPERMARKET,** *by J. Andrew Anderson.* Written by a supermarket security guard, this book will give your budget a boost! Learn all the ins and outs of shoplifting success, including: do-it-yourself markdowns; scamming the scanner; how to dress for success; defeating store security; and much more, including the one mistake that trips up most shoplifters and the one item you must bring shoplifting with you. *This offer is not available in stores. Sold for informational use only. 1992, 5½ x 8½, 63 pp, soft cover.* **$10.00**.

☐ **94283 HARD CORE, Marginalized by Choice,** *by P.J. Nebergall. Hard Core, Marginalized by Choice* is a photojournalistic odyssey into the Punk world that permeates our current intercultural milieu. P.J. Nebergall has placed the modern punk phenomenon in its proper historical perspective by conducting hundreds of interviews and photo shoots with rebellious and disenchanted youngsters in both Great Britain and the United States. His text and photographs provide a penetrating glimpse into the philosophical musings and neotribal disfiguration fashion trends of today's disenfranchised youth. The author points out there is no reason to fear the unstructured nihilism from the Punks we encounter. *1997, 5½ x 8½, 112 pp, several photographs, soft cover.* **$8.95**.

☐ **17040 SHELTERS, SHACKS, AND SHANTIES,** *by D. C. Beard.* A fascinating book with more than 300 pen and ink illustrations and step-by-step instructions for building various types of shelters. The emphasis is on simplicity with easy-to-use tools such as hatchets and axes. Fallen tree shelters; Indian wicki-ups; sod houses; elevated shacks and shanties; tree houses; caches; railroad tie shacks; pole houses; log cabins; and many more. One of the great classics of outdoor lore. *1914, 5 x 7, 259 pp, illustrated, soft cover.* **$9.95**.

☐ **19205 KILL-AS-CATCH-CAN, Wrestling Skills for Streetfighting,** *by Ned Beaumont.* Sure, you know how to punch and kick, but how well can you fight at shorter range? When both you and your opponent are rolling around and wrestling on the barroom floor, are you confident you can win the fight? If you doubt your chances at close quarters, then you're not prepared for the reality of streetfighting. This no-nonsense primer offers an enhanced awareness of wrestling's methodology, and provides streetfighters with the winning edge it takes to come out on top. By reading this book and employing the methods it describes, you *can gain a superior edge in future altercations. 1998, 5½ x 8½, 208 pp, illustrated, soft cover.* **$16.95**.

☐ **64210 THE TEMP WORKER'S GUIDE TO SELF-FULFILLMENT, How to slack off, achieve your dreams, and get paid for it!,** *by Dennis Fiery.* Temporary employment, or "temp work," can be a treasure trove of opportunity for the dedicated practitioner. Rather than being a series of dead-end meaningless short-term jobs, temp work offers numerous advantages. This book explains how to effectively exploit and undermine the temp system. It contains all the information needed to successfully obtain steady, lucrative work as a temp, while satisfying the requirements of the employers who are seeking competent temp workers and fulfilling your own special needs. *1997, 5½ x 8½, 156 pp, illustrated, soft cover.* **$12.95**.

Please send me the books I have checked below:

- ❏ 14099, The Art & Science of Dumpster Diving, $14.95
- ❏ 10065, How to Hide Things In Public Places, $15.00
- ❏ 13063, Survival Bartering, $8.00
- ❏ 17075, The Hitchhiker's Handbook, $12.95
- ❏ 88173, Don't Let Them Psych You Out!, $15.95
- ❏ 40084, How to Sneak Into the Movies, $8.00
- ❏ 40079, How to Steal Food From the Supermarket, $10.00
- ❏ 94283, Hard Core, Marginalized by Choice, $8.95
- ❏ 17040, Shelters, Shacks, and Shanties, $9.95
- ❏ 19205, Kill-As-Catch-Can, $16.95
- ❏ 64210, The Temp Worker's Guide to Self-Fulfillment, $12.95
- ❏ 88888, Loompanics Unlimited 2001 Main Catalog, $5.00

*We offer the very finest in controversial and unusual books — A complete catalog is sent **FREE** with every book order. If you would like to order the catalog separately, please see our ad on the following page.*

LOOMPANICS UNLIMITED
PO BOX 1197
PORT TOWNSEND, WA 98368

SOS

I am enclosing $ _____ which includes $5.95 for shipping and handling of orders up to $25.00. Add $1.00 for each additional $25.00 ordered. *Washington residents please include 8.2% for sales tax.*

NAME _____

ADDRESS _____

CITY _____

STATE/ZIP _____

We accept Visa, Discover, and MasterCard. To place a credit card order *only,* call 1-800-380-2230, 24 hours a day, 7 days a week.
Check out our Web site: www.loompanics.com

"What can I say. Full admiration and respect for such an awesome range of really interesting books. It is so refreshing to see something that is not the norm and pushes out the boundaries a little." — William, United Kingdom

"Your web site is very user friendly and the order form a pleasure to deal with." — OEO

"As our liberty slowly disappears, your books hold a ray of light in our American Age of Media Misinformation and stupidity. My TV stays off and the pages from your unique books stay open!" — W.C., California

"I find your series of books quite interesting and informative... it's refreshing to find someone out there that can give me some useful information to protect myself and my family." — Mr. E., North Carolina

THE BEST BOOK CATALOG IN THE WORLD!!!

We offer hard-to-find books on the world's most unusual subjects. Here are a few of the topics covered IN-DEPTH in our exciting new catalog:

Hiding/Concealment of physical objects! A complete section of the best books ever written on hiding things.

Fake ID/Alternate Identities! The most comprehensive selection of books on this little-known subject ever offered for sale! You have to see it to believe it!

Investigative/Undercover methods and techniques! Professional secrets known only to a few, now revealed for you to use! Actual police manuals on shadowing and surveillance!

And much, much more, including Locks and Locksmithing, Self-Defense, Intelligence Increase, Life Extension, Money-Making Opportunities, Human Oddities, Exotic Weapons, Sex, Drugs, Anarchism, and more!

Our book catalog is over 250 pages, 8½ x 11, packed with over 800 of the most controversial and unusual books ever printed! You can order every book listed! Periodic supplements keep you posted on the LATEST titles available!!! Our catalog is **$5.00,** including shipping and handling.

Our book catalog is truly *THE BEST BOOK CATALOG IN THE WORLD! Order yours today. You will be very pleased, we know.*

**LOOMPANICS UNLIMITED
PO BOX 1197
PORT TOWNSEND, WA 98368
USA**

We accept Visa, Discover and MasterCard. Call 1-800-380-2230 for credit card orders *only,* 24 hours a day, 7 days a week.

**Or you can fax your order to 1-360-385-7785.
Check us out on the Web: www.loompanics.com**